# UNDERSTANDING THE VISUAL

# UNDERSTANDING THE VISUAL

Tony Schirato and Jen Webb

SAGE Publications
Los Angeles • London • New Delhi • Singapore

First published in 2004 by
Allen & Unwin
83 Alexander Street
CROWS NEST NSW 2065
Australia

Reprinted 2007



SAGE Publications Ltd
1 Oliver's Yard
55 City Road
London EC1Y 1SP

SAGE Publications Inc
2455 Teller Road
Thousand Oaks, California 91320

SAGE Publications India Pvt Ltd
B1/I 1 Mohan Cooperative Industrial Area
Mathura Road, New Delhi 110 044
India

SAGE Publications Asia-Pacific Pte Ltd
33 Pekin Street #02-01
Far East Square
Singapore 048763

**British Library Cataloguing in Publication Data**

A catalogue record for this book is available from the British Library

ISBN: 978-1-4129-0156-7 (hbk)
ISBN: 978-1-4129-0157-4 (pbk)

**Library of Congress catalog record available**

Typeset in 10/13 pt Hiroshige by Midland Typesetters, Maryborough, Victoria
Printed & bound in Great Britain by Athenaeum Press Ltd., Gateshead

# contents

# introduction

At the beginning of the twenty-first century, a plethora of books, journals, conferences and university courses suddenly appeared, all of them dealing with what appeared to be a new topic, a new area of study: visual culture. But what, we might ask, is new about it? After all, human beings have always looked at and seen the world around them, and made sense of themselves and others through their understanding of what they see. Writers, too, have always dealt with the visual world—from the ancient Greek philosophers, through the art writers of the Renaissance and the aestheticists of the early Enlightenment, to the art historians, film critics and media theorists of the nineteenth and twentieth centuries, people have studied visual forms and their meanings. So, given this, why write another book about it?

This book arises out of our own interest in bringing together some of the disparate threads of thinking and understanding across the many disciplines which have, in many cases, now been subsumed within the field of visual culture. Our central concern is to make sense of the importance of visuality to what people do and say, and how they act in their everyday lives. Very often, seeing is taken for granted, under a 'what you see is what you get' notion that relies on the naturalness of vision: 'Of course I know what happened,' says the eyewitness. 'I was there, wasn't I? I saw it with my own eyes.' We want to raise some questions about this attitude, and will argue that what we see is in fact what we make or are made to see: we see through the frameworks and filters produced by our culture and by our personal histories. Sight is, of course, a natural physiological process, but the perception and reception of visual elements is not; it depends instead on a number of factors which we explore in this book: our culture, our history, the context in which we are looking, what we already know about the world, what our own tastes, interests and habits predispose us to see, and so on. Looking and seeing, we argue, are neither straightforward nor natural—and they are far from universal. In this book we distinguish the tacit understandings people have of the visual domain from what we call visual literacies.

What do we mean by 'tacit' and 'literate' seeing? We can explain it most easily through Arthur Conan Doyle's example of the redoubtable Dr Watson, Sherlock Holmes' amanuensis, who is famous for his 'blindness'. Take him to a room in a great country house, and he will see only gross signs: carpets, paintings and windows. He is, of course, *looking* at the room—he can describe it and its contents, he can notice the way his friend Holmes moves about the space. But his looking is tacit because it does not allow him to make particular sense of—to read—the individual objects and traces in the room for any more than the most obvious functions. He can tell where he is and move about without falling over things, but he cannot engage analytically with what he is seeing, or what the 'signs' or clues might be telling him.

His friend Sherlock Holmes, presented with the same scene, will observe through what we call practices of visual literacy. In other words, he understands the rules and conditions of seeing a particular thing in a particular context; he takes an analytical and reflexive attitude to how and why he might be seeing it in a particular way; and consequently he will be able to extract a staggering amount of information from what is, to Watson, just a room. He will be able to observe that a crime has been committed by noticing the particular setting of a window frame, or a faint smudge on the sill. He will be able to distinguish the age, class and character of the criminal by the way a chair has been moved out of place, or a door left ajar. He will make an observation about the habits of the family whose home has been invaded—and all this on the basis of what is invisible to Watson, but what is to him both evident and clearly visible.

Of course, it is reasonable to suppose that when Watson is in his other identity—that of medical practitioner—his visual acuity is much sharper. When presented with a sick or damaged body, he would no doubt be able to see by his patient's posture, by the texture of their hair, or the colour of their gums the signs of illness which might well be invisible to Holmes. What this means is that neither man sees simply what his physiological—optical and neurological—functions permit; rather, each sees in terms of, and within the frames of, his interests, tastes, training and necessity. These are specific visual literacies which allow them to see in particular domains and for particular purposes. In short, as Bates Lowry notes: 'Looking and seeing are as different as babbling and speaking' (1967: 13). We intend, in this book, to provide ways of understanding the difference between looking and seeing by defamiliarising the physical act and by providing techniques for analysing what we see in its context, so that readers can move from the general familiarity that is tacit looking to the skilled understanding that is visual literacy.

Our second intention in writing this book is to add to the discussion about visual culture, thus helping to clarify the field. We can begin by explaining what we mean by the term 'visual culture'. The first, and simplest, definition comes from art historian Nicholas Mirzoeff, who writes that visual culture 'is not just a part of your everyday life, it is your everyday life' (1998: 3). So we can understand visual culture as incorporating everything we do, because everything we do includes navigating the things we see. We can list as part of this 'everyday life' a set of objects: furniture, cars, posters, postcards, paintings, sculptures, billboards, magazine covers, films, television, multimedia, fashion, kitchen utensils, architecture, shoes. And a host of ephemeral objects contribute to the visual culture that is our everyday life, including 'optical illusions, maps, diagrams, dreams, hallucinations, spectacles, projections, poems, patterns, memories, and even ideas' (Mitchell 1986: 9). These are all creations of human culture, patterned and crafted to fulfil a function (transport, cooking, clothing, entertainment) or to communicate something (selling a product, providing information, being in contact with others). Then there are all those things that also make up our everyday life, and that are certainly visual—in that we see them—but that don't, as far as we know, have a deliberate social function or intend any meaning. Here we include natural phenomena and vistas: mountains, skyscapes, rivers, plants. Often, of course, we treat these things as though they are messages—seeing in a red rose the idea of romantic love; reading a brilliant sunset as the promise of good weather to come; being conveyed by a desolate landscape into loneliness or despair. And finally, as part of the visuality that Mirzoeff insists is our everyday life, there are the metaphors we use to describe ordinary social interactions: telling a visitor that we'll keep an eye out for their arrival; promising a parent that you'll look after their child; warning an enemy to watch out; telling our friends that we'll see them later, and so on. So we include as valid objects of the study of visual culture everything from the earliest cave drawings, to the architecture and statuary of the ancients; medieval, Renaissance and modern art; the advertising flyers in our mailboxes; skywriting; football colours; billboards and posters; television shows; dreams; CD covers; movies; the shape of cars and bicycles; and of course all the visual aspects of digital communication technology. All these affect our ways of being in the social and physical world.

A further way of defining visual culture is as a field of study and a set of ways of understanding these physical and social phenomena. This is what is happening in the recent proliferation of publications and university programs titled 'visual culture'; it appears to be something new because, until the late 1990s, those things now called 'visual culture' were segregated off and studied across a number of quite distinct disciplines. These included philosophy, aesthetics, (Renaissance-era) astronomy, art, art history, other history, archival studies, film studies, media studies, what cultural historian Mark Poster calls the 'broader domain of the cultural study of information machines' (Poster 2002: 67)—in other words, new digital communication technology—and any number of studies into mass culture: advertising, the internet, document design, and so on (Elkins 2002: 94). What ties all these together and allows us to treat them as a single (if multiply organised) discipline is that they are all about looking at and making sense of the world, and this is a very ancient practice among scholars. Human beings are always making marks and looking at/reading others' marks, and western theorists have discussed these marks, and also used the idea of visuality as a metaphor for understanding and perception, for as long as they've been writing. (It should be noted that this is a peculiarly western approach—many Middle Eastern traditions, by contrast, focus on hearing as a privileged form on knowledge and understanding.)

The ancient Greek philosophers insisted on the importance of visuality for truth and knowledge: Heraclitus in 500 BC wrote: 'Those things of which there is sight, hearing, knowledge: these are what I honour most' (from Fragment #55). Plato, writing over a century later, argued that truth is embodied in what he called the Idea, which he understood as an actual form visible to the mind (or 'the mind's eye'). Nearly two millennia later, western philosophers were still committed to the visual field as a metaphor and a tool for knowledge: the sixteenth-century English philosopher Francis Bacon argued that objectivity can only be achieved through observation, while the seventeenth-century French philosopher Descartes insisted that: 'Sight is the noblest and most comprehensive of the senses' (Descartes 1998: 60). Indeed, even the word 'theory' comes from the ancient Greek word *teorin* (to see). Visual culture can therefore be defined not as things, but as a way of thinking, an intellectual discipline for making sense of the world.

This sort of approach has been hotly debated by scholars in the field of visual culture. In 1996 the art journal *October* published the results of a questionnaire about the interdisciplinary nature of visual culture which it had earlier distributed to its readers and subscribers. Theorists of visual culture have responded quite passionately to this questionnaire, many of them insisting that visual studies should be understood as media studies, because seeing is invariably accompanied by sound (especially in film and television), and sound is typically excluded from, say, art history approaches (Poster 2002: 67). Nicholas Mirzoeff argued something similar when he wrote, as part of a listserv discussion:

> I do think there's a considerable difference between art history and visual culture. Visual culture is, in my estimation, the study of the genealogy and practice of the visualization of modern culture. Its concentration is, then, on the interface between images and viewers rather than on artists and works. It is concerned with visual events in which information, meaning or pleasure is sought by the consumer in an interface with visual technology. Art history seems by contrast to be reasserting its role as the guardian of the aesthetic/high modernism. (Mirzoeff, 2000)

Our position is that visual culture is most profitably understood as all those visual artefacts, natural forms and ways of thinking that make up perception in our everyday life, as well as the interdisciplinary technologies of analysis that can be applied to make sense of them. Capital-A Art is one discipline that provides many useful techniques for anyone studying visual culture, and is one of the important fields of social understanding, history and culture; we therefore include it as a particular instance of the field, as something we can use to see and understand the world through seeing. Other approaches focus on the processes of spectatorship; the production of visual media, especially digital media; anthropology; how objects are designed; why some visual matter is considered beautiful or appealing; and the social and economic importance of media convergence in making sense of the world. One theorist may use analytical techniques drawn from the traditions of art history, another will use psychoanalytical perspectives, yet others draw on literary or philosophical analysis, or techniques from rhetoric or communication theory.

The approach we take to the study of visual culture comes from what is called *cultural theory*. Like visual studies, this is an interdisciplinary field that has close links with the humanities and social sciences—philosophy, sociology and literary studies in particular. It is, as the editorial statement of the journal *Cultural Studies* notes, committed to the theorising of politics and the politicising of theory, and hence is a discipline which is concerned with how to understand human and institutional relations and practices. Cultural theorists are always concerned to break with everyday notions about how the world works, and to understand the extent to which society is built on arbitrary divisions that serve particular interests. Cultural theory asks questions like: Why are things as they are? How could they be different? Cultural theorists engage in what sociologist Pierre Bourdieu calls 'an endless labour, endlessly recommenced' (2001: 110), by which the researchers strive to understand and demonstrate the social, historical, economic and political conditions that lead to the establishment of structures of power, and struggles for power, across society. This means that cultural theorists take a different approach to their research than do many of their colleagues in related disciplines. A literary scholar and a cultural theorist might both become experts in, for instance, the writings of Patrick White. Through close reading, the literary scholar might feel confident that he or she had come to know every possible meaning of his novels, and the context of his work. But for a cultural theorist, it is not enough to be an expert on the style and content of a novel or the inner world of a novelist; what we need to do is locate the novel and novelist in a context, and analyse that world, its values and its relations. So a cultural theorist would pay less attention to story and style, and more attention to the context in which White was writing, his own class and gender and educational background, who his publishers were and what they and the reviewers said about him, how and why his work came to be seen as so important that he won the Nobel Prize in Literature, and so on. This approach to research means that we treat visual culture and the processes of seeing as social practices that take place in particular contexts, which themselves have historical and cultural settings—including the specific moments in which individuals view them, and what each individual brings to their viewing of the object.

Cultural theory also comes with its own set of practices and its own vocabulary, which we will use throughout this book in developing our approach to the study, or 'reading', of visual culture. Firstly, we use the term 'reading' as a particular form of visual practice, and this is the topic of Chapter 1. Reading, we argue, is both an active and a creative process; and when reading the visual, we draw on our general and specific knowledges, our tastes and habits and our personal contexts (what Pierre Bourdieu calls the *habitus*) to make what we see, and to make sense of it. Each individual's habitus disposes them to frame the material that is in front of their eyes in particular ways, to value it differently and to negotiate it according to their own interests.

Imagine a child growing up at the foot of Table Mountain in Cape Town, South Africa. She is living between this internationally famous landmark and the very tip of Africa, where the Indian and Atlantic Oceans meet so dramatically. Visitors come from overseas to exclaim about the spectacular vistas that form the backdrop of her everyday life; they take photographs (thus literally framing aspects of the scene) and go on long complicated drives along the coastal cliff roads to the ancient forests, or inland to tribal villages; and they gaze hungrily at all they see, reading it in terms of their own background as beautiful, rare and exotic. The child, on the other hand, just feels carsick and would rather be at home with friends, or reading a book. For her, the scenery is practically invisible; for the visitors, it is overwhelmingly present. In the same way, for each individual looking at any aspect of visual culture, their own habitus—their personal history, their relation to their own culture, their own tastes and dispositions—will ensure that some visual phenomena are immediately visible and significant, while others (equally visible and significant to another person) are irrelevant and hence invisible. When studying visual culture, then, it is important that researchers understand their own habitus so that they can be reflexive about what they are seeing and what they might be overlooking, about how they frame what they see, and about why they might read and evaluate it in a particular way.

We also use the term 'reading' because one of the analytical tools we use to make sense of visual culture is *semiotics*. Semiotics is an analytical approach and a research methodology that examines the use of what are called *signs* in society. A sign is a basic unit of communication: most simply, it is just something that has some meaning for someone. In this book, we will focus on visual signs, but whatever form they take, it is important to remember that a sign means 'something', not 'one thing'. Signs take on meanings depending on the way they are arranged, and the contexts in which they are read. Our Holmes and Watson example can again demonstrate this: a tiny smudge on the floor is a sign which, for Watson, may mean 'careless housekeeping'; for Holmes, it may mean 'someone has passed this way'.

The name for a group of signs is *text*—a collection of signs which are organised in a particular way to make meaning. The meanings made will depend on which signs are brought together, and how they are arranged in relation to one another. Their arrangement may be deliberate: every element in a painting, for instance, will have been chosen and carefully placed by the artist. Other arrangements are quite arbitrary: the organisation of elements (or signs) that make up a natural vista, for instance, are all given and already present, but viewers will choose how they see and (mentally) arrange them to produce a satisfying effect. Two people standing side by side at a lookout at the same moment may well see the vista before them quite differently; one will say, 'Oh, how beautiful', and another, 'Oh, how desolate'. And two people at that lookout are unlikely to produce exactly the same photograph: one will include the eroded hillside and the marks of construction, while the other will place the frame of the image over to the side so that no erosion, no electricity pylons and no road are visible. And even if the signs are framed, fixed and apparently identical, different orientations or perspectives will produce different texts. The photograph of an eye which is reproduced in Figure i.1 is a text because it is made up of various signs: the component parts of the eye itself, the background, the location of the eye in

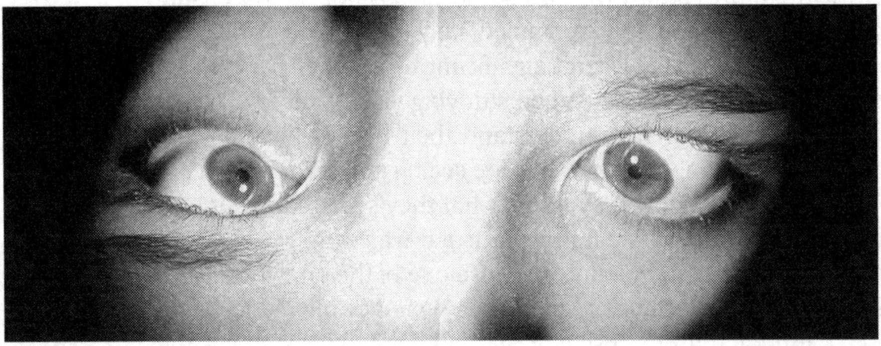

**Figure i.1 Light eye**

relation to the borders of the text, and the orientation of the text as a whole. But all we have to do is invert it and the arrangement of the signs changes, as do the meanings it makes. In the 'normal' orientation it means, perhaps, simply 'a photograph of an eye' or 'a direct stare'; turned upside down, it becomes 'an enigmatic look', or maybe just 'creepy'. The signs haven't changed, but their arrangement has changed because the whole thing is inverted; hence it becomes a second text.

In other words, a text comes to have meaning by virtue of the signs that make it up, the way those signs are arranged or organised in the text and also, importantly, because of its context. *Context* means the environment in which a text occurs and communication takes place. Contexts are extraordinarily dynamic and variable because they incorporate everything involved in that environment: the people, their history, current events, similar texts with which they are comparing this one, and so on. What this means is that signs and texts never have just one meaning, and never make meaning in a stable context. We develop this concept in Chapter 1, and describe how the fluidity of context affects the ways in which we read the visual world.

We do not, of course, see in a vacuum or make sense of signs and texts and contexts merely as abstract phenomena, and in Chapter 2 we move on to discuss the various principles of perception and technologies by which we see. These include human (sociocultural), physiological (optical/neurological) and machine (scientific/communicative) technologies which shape the way we perceive the visual world. There are also many ways of understanding this visual world, how it is put together and the extent to which visual texts can show us the 'real world': historically, people have posited various theories or stories about this, ranging from the idea that the world is God's book to the view that it is a host of elements whirling around according to the principles of quantum mechanics. In Chapter 3 we discuss some of these ideas, particularly those concerned with the social function of visual texts, and their role as pieces of communication; we also examine the degree to which linguistic models of communication can be applied to the analysis of visual texts.

One of the important ways of making sense of visual texts is through *narrative*, or stories that are organised visually. Writers on visual culture debate the extent to which visual texts, especially those that comprise a single frame, can tell a story in and of themselves. In Chapter 4 we outline what is meant by narrative, and examine how narratives emerge in visual texts. Some of the most important stories of our time are those told through visual art, social institutions that determine what can be said/seen and the economic market, and these are the subjects of Chapters 5, 6 and 7. Chapter 5 deals with the world of art, which is a privileged form within visual culture and has an often uneasy relationship with other, 'popular', visual media and forms. We discuss its character and identity, and explore the effect the idea of aesthetics has on readings of visual texts. In Chapter 6 we describe how systems of social organisation, including the government, normalise what we see and what we think, including what we understand by 'reality'. And in Chapter 7 we analyse the economic effects of a globalised market (including advertising and digital communication technologies like the Internet) on the visual field. All three of these major narratives of our time are worked out and disseminated through the mass media: from the promotion of 'important' artists and 'blockbuster' exhibitions, through the news articles and documentaries about who we are and what it means to be human, to the tsunami of advertising that sells us a way of looking and being and valuing. This is what we address in Chapter 8, with particular interest in how the media frames our world and our way of seeing it, and produces the world as a spectacle. Throughout, we illustrate our explanations and arguments with images and anecdotes that are highly eclectic, and for the most part have their bases in everyday life. We do this deliberately, rather than bringing in illustrations from specialist disciplines like design, art history, information technology or cartography, because our point is that seeing, as well as making sense of what is seen, is both an eclectic practice (emerging in various ways, and from various sources, using various skills and disciplines) and one that is part of everyday life.

One of the great strengths of this field of study, and of our approach, is that it too is eclectic—it brings together a smorgasbord of analytical approaches, methodological techniques and epistemological arguments. These include the careful observation of art historians, the attention to cultural specificities brought by anthropologists and cultural theorists, the reading of sign and text that comes from communication studies and of narrative that comes from literary studies, the precision of thought and argument that philosophy offers, and the understandings of the convergence of sound and image, form and content, dynamism and stasis offered by scholars of digital communication technologies. All these are grist to the mill when studying visual culture, and in developing the sorts of literacies that allow us to read and analyse the visual material that makes up our everyday worlds.

# 1 reading the visual

## introduction

I am driving along in a car in the country. As I drive, I am looking out the windows—straight ahead, to the right and left, through the rear-view mirror—at the sky, hills, bush, road and the other vehicles around me. I am moving along this road, and through this landscape, at speed—say, 80 kilometres an hour. Everything I see is seen at speed: I am moving past trees, meadows, cattle and slower vehicles; and faster vehicles are moving past me. Even though I am travelling at 80 kilometres an hour with my vision framed, and thus partially restricted, by the mirrors and windows of the car, I can still see and negotiate my environment (road, trees, road signs, other cars). I drive on the road, in the slower lane, seven car-lengths from the vehicle in front of me. I observe speed signs, and change lanes when I come across a slower car without causing any accidents.

Suddenly a kangaroo jumps out of the bush, and bounds across the road—a not unusual occurrence around here. I'm alarmed—I know from experience what damage a car can do to a kangaroo, and vice versa. I rapidly focus my attention on the kangaroo, taking in its speed, size, trajectory, distance from my vehicle, and the rate at which I am approaching it. In almost the same instant I break and swerve to the side (somehow I know there are no cars around me), and miss it. I drive on, more alert, occasionally scanning the bush ahead for more kangaroos. When I arrive at my destination (my parents' house in the mountains, a place I have driven to many times), I have almost no recollection of the drive, apart from the incident with the kangaroo.

I have arrived at my destination, and I am taking a photograph of part of the house and the front part of the property (see Figure 1.1). I am taking the shot from the same level as the house but 20 metres to

Figure 1.1 A Lake, a Tree

the side, and I am only framing part of the house (which includes the verandah, a typical rural feature) so I can include two sets of trees. The first set is located just in front of the house, and the trees are leafless; the second set is another 60 metres down the slope on which the house sits, and the trees are solid with foliage. The backdrop to the house and trees is a thick mist which has partly covered the lower trees, and seems to be moving towards the house.

I have a few things in mind which have led to this arrangement of the shot. I want to produce a sense of space (the house as one small part of a much larger property, which is one of the reasons I have included the second set of trees). I want to catch the property as it usually looks at this time of year. But I also want to emulate those landscape paintings and photographs which contextualise signs of human presence (the house) within the forces, power and rigours of nature (the trees and the enveloping mist). The leafless trees are situated at the centre, and take up almost half of the photograph, while the house is peripheral (and consequently relatively insignificant). My focus will be on the objects in the foreground (particularly the tree branches, and the way they tower over the house); the rest of the scene (the solid trees, the paddock, the mist) will be slightly blurred.

## the activities of seeing

Planning and taking a photograph is, like many human activities, an intensely visual experience; so is driving a car, where we are constantly visualising and making sense of the space through which we are moving. There is one big difference, of course: driving a car is a relatively unreflective activity and even below the level of consciousness, while taking a photograph is usually conscious, deliberate and self-reflective. In other words, we usually pay a great deal of attention to what we are doing when we are photographing a scene; but when we are driving a car we are often doing so on automatic pilot, and only pay close attention to what is around us when we need to (for instance, when a kangaroo jumps out of the bush or when we are looking for a place to stop and have lunch).

This difference between the two activities—a difference of levels of attentiveness, among other things—is one of degree rather than of kind because, whether we are aware of it or not, in both instances we are making (that is, actively 'bringing about') the (visual) world around us. When driving a car, or arranging a photograph, we are not simply seeing and taking in everything that is available to our range of vision. The space I photographed contained an extraordinary, almost infinite, amount of detail that I simply didn't see. There may have been rabbits, camouflaged and keeping still on the slope; birds blending into the branches of the trees; various plants and types of grass around the house; kangaroo dung by the lower trees; the front roof of the neighbour's house poking through between the bare trees and my parents' house; a small puddle created by a dripping tap, and many other details. Some of these things are more or less visible in the photograph, but the rest weren't seen and haven't been shown. Had I seen them, I might have changed the angle, distance, speed, frame and focus of my shot, and produced a different photograph ('puddle outside the house', 'rabbits in the paddock'). But every act of looking and seeing is also an act of not seeing, even when we are being attentive.

This is true to an even greater extent with the act of driving a vehicle. It seems strange to suggest that I can be more attentive and reflective when taking a photograph, which is a relatively trivial activity with no serious consequences (about the worst result would be that my parents dislike the way the house is shown, or maybe I could get the focus wrong) than when driving a car, where one wrong move could cost me my life. But a lot of our visual activity in driving is more or less automatic: we see where we're going and what is around us, but our attention is usually focused on only one or two spaces (the lane we're driving in, the car in front of us). And even here our attention is often more general than specific. We make sure we're driving within the lines that designate our lane, but we don't usually look to see whether the lines are all the same length, or partly worn away; or notice the texture, condition or colour of the surface of the road (oil stains, small cracks, small tufts of grass, squashed cigarette packets). And the car in front of us is often seen in a very indistinct way. We might be aware of the distance between the two vehicles, or the speed, size and colour of the other car, but we rarely look at it in a detailed way, and might be hard pressed to recall its make, year of production, condition of the tyres, number of people riding in it, or their gender, age and skin colour.

There are other reasons why we might not pay as much attention when driving as when taking a photograph. The trip might be over several hundred kilometres, and take hours. We simply can't look at things in a detailed and attentive way for that length of time, particularly when we're moving at speed. And moreover, while there is a link in photography between attention and enjoyment (we have chosen to look at things, frame them and capture them on film), a car trip is more often a means to an end rather than an end in itself (I drive to get to work, to visit my parents, to go to a shopping plaza). In other words, it is in my interest to be attentive when driving only insofar as my or somebody else's safety is concerned (watch to ensure that I'm not exceeding the speed limit, and that I'm travelling within my lane), for reasons of economy (I only have a limited amount of attention to give), practicality (I'm moving too quickly to take most things in), and in order to ensure that I achieve what I set out to do (get somewhere where I can see my parents, or take photographs, or go shopping).

## seeing as reading

We have covered three main points so far. Firstly, when we see things we are actively engaging with our environment rather than simply reproducing everything within our line of sight. Secondly, every act of looking and seeing is also an act of not seeing—some things must remain invisible if we are to pay attention to other things in view. Thirdly, the extent to which we see, focus on and pay attention to the world around us (the three actions are inextricably linked) depends upon the specific context in which we find ourselves.

While the process of making and negotiating the visual (whether driving a car or taking a photograph) is always informed by the notions of attentiveness, selection and omission, and context, there are other issues which we need to consider, such as when we do focus on, attend to and see something, and why do we see things differently over time, or from other people?

Consider the first paragraph in Stephen Crane's short story 'The Open Boat', which is about the experience of four men who take refuge in a rowboat after their steamer has sunk:

> None of them knew the color of the sky. Their eyes glanced level, and were fastened upon the waves that swept towards them. The waves were of the hue of slate, save for the tops, which were of foaming white, and all of the men knew the color of the sea. The horizon narrowed and widened, and dipped and rose, and at all

times its edge was jagged with waves that seemed thrust up in points like rocks. (Crane 1960: 140)

The men in the boat don't know or see the sky because their attention is focused on something of more immediate interest: the waves that threaten to overturn or smash their boat, and take their lives. They see the waves in great detail: they are 'the hue of slate', with foaming tops, and they seem sharp and threatening like rocks—that is, the waves are the same colour (and, by extension, hardness) of slate, and as the boat comes down upon the waves it appears to be landing on sharp, hard rocks.

Now we could say that the psychological state of the men in this extreme condition has produced an effect so that the waves have become, in their minds, like rocks. But, as we saw with our previous examples of driving and photography, every act of perception takes place within a context that orients, influences or transforms what we see. Observing a kangaroo from the balcony of a café at a nature park produces a very different sight from what we experienced when we swerved to avoid one on the road. Watching the approaching mists when we are deep in the bush with a broken ankle and unsure of our way home is a very different experience from that of treating the mist artistically, as an aspect of a photograph that depicts natural forces. And when watching a storm from the safety of a cliff we may see the slate-hued waves, and thrill to the drama and tension of the scene, but this does not equate with how the sea appears to Crane's men in that open boat.

Every perception and meaning is the product of psychological, physiological and, above all, cultural contexts (I'm stressed, I'm not wearing my glasses, I'm lost, I'm an artist). In other words, the things we see aren't simply 'out there' in any ideal or unmediated way; rather, we understand, evaluate and categorise—that is to say, see—things in terms of a set of resources that we take from our cultural contexts. It has long been accepted in what we call the human sciences and the humanities—particularly in disciplines such as sociology, anthropology, linguistics, philosophy, literature, psychoanalysis and cultural theory—that we make sense of our world through the different meanings, ideas and categories available to us. And it is this situation of a culture more or less seeing through and for us, combined with the inflection or influence of different psychological and physiological states, and of-the-moment contexts, that produces what we see.

We can carry this insight further by suggesting that when we see we are, in effect, engaged in an act of reading (the visual). When we read a book we try to follow, consider and understand the material at hand (the words, the sentences, the story), and we end up making both meanings and connections between different meanings. In Jules Verne's *20,000 Leagues Under the Sea*, for instance, we come to understand that Captain Nemo is keeping Professor Aronnax and his companions prisoners aboard the *Nautilus*, and that he is obsessive about not returning to land; we infer that Nemo has suffered some great psychological hurt or loss, and that he will never let them leave the giant submarine alive. We could say that the story of the book is about the relationship between two different sets of wills, and how this is played out (will the *Nautilus* destroy other ships? Will Aronnax and his friends thwart Nemo or escape?). But no two people will read the book in exactly the same way: some readers will see Nemo as a heartless murderer, while others will see him as rightfully enacting revenge on a world that robbed him of his wife and children, who were killed in a naval battle. The point is that the same book will be subject to different readings and interpretations precisely because people approach it from different backgrounds and perspectives.

There is another reason why the book will be subject to different readings: readers will want different things from it. A person with two hours to devote to a rollicking adventure will read it differently from someone studying the book for a school or university exam. Roland Barthes writes in *The Pleasure of the Text* that, when he has a story in front of him, 'I read on, I skip, I look up, I dip in again' (Barthes 1975: 12). And he refers to 'two systems of reading: one goes straight to the articulation of the anecdote, it considers the extent of the text, ignores the play of language'—if I read Jules Verne, I go fast—while the other reading 'weighs, it sticks to the text . . . [and] grasps at every point' (Barthes 1975: 12).

These descriptions of different ways of reading a book could just as easily be applied to practices and ways of seeing. Barthes' reference to his 'skipping and dipping' style of reading, for instance, pretty much sums up the orientation of the car driver who takes in the (visual) bare minimum, while the reader who 'weighs things' and closely examines the text is like the photographer carefully attending to and considering everything within the photographic frame.

When we read a book there is always a context to that act of reading; we might, for instance, try a book because we are familiar with the author's other works or critical reputation, or simply because we wanted to pass the time with a 'quick read'. But even if we had never heard of the book or the author, we have access to other signs, such as the title, which would help us categorise—and thus prepare for—what we were about to read. We would probably expect *20,000 Leagues Under the Sea* to be an adventure story rather than a scientific study of deep-sea life simply because we know that adventure stories have titles that refer to exotic, dangerous and far-away activities and places, while scientific works are much more specific about their subject, and the language used is usually less accessible (for instance, 'Protandry and the Evolution of Environmentally-Mediated Sex Change: A Study of the Mollusc' is clearly not an adventure story). Similarly, everything we look at and make sense of, whether it is a photograph or a set of objects within our purview, comes with a history of commentaries, meanings and annotations which disposes us to read it in a particular way.

## the habitus and cultural literacies

The relationship between those forces which dispose us to categorise and see the world in certain ways, and the kinds of visual texts that subjects make, can be usefully explained through reference to two contexts—one taken directly, and the other extrapolated, from the work of Pierre Bourdieu. The first is the habitus, and the second is cultural literacy. Bourdieu famously defines the habitus as 'the durably installed generative principle of regulated improvisations . . . [which produce] practices' (Bourdieu 1991: 78). In other words:

> Habitus can be understood as a set of values and dispositions gained from our cultural history that stay with us across contexts (they are durable and transposable). These values and dispositions allow us to respond to cultural rules and contexts in a variety of ways (they allow for improvisations), but these responses are always determined—regulated—by where we have been in a culture. (Webb et al. 2002: 36–7)

Our cultural history and trajectories naturalise certain values and ideas, and effectively determine our worldview—that is, they predispose us to see and evaluate the world in certain ways. Central to this is what Bourdieu terms *distinction*: this is tied up with the notion of taste, which generally means having a refined, educated, sophisticated and aesthetic worldview, rather than simply seeing, evaluating and categorising things 'naively' (say, in terms of their use value). A good example of distinction as it manifests itself in everyday life is this story about the philosopher Ludwig Wittgenstein, who was taking a walk in his garden. His gardener was surprised to see him, and said

'Professor, what are you doing here?' to which Wittgenstein is supposed to have replied, 'What are any of us doing here?'

In order to see how distinction, and habitus, influence the way people see, let's consider Figure 1.2, a photograph of a pile of dishes and utensils, presumably left sitting in the kitchen. According to Bourdieu, a sophisticated habitus would be perfectly capable of seeing—in fact, might be disposed to see—what was within the frame as something other than a simple reproduction of a domestic scene. A so-called sophisticated eye might see carefully arranged patterns and motifs (note how the utensils are all pointing one way), references to other texts (the wobbly pile of dishes as a Tower of Babel) and social commentary (the dishes as an index of the chaotic state of modern life). People who did not share this habitus might dismiss such readings as boring or pretentious. They could respond that everybody knows what the kitchen is like in a shared house, and what an unwashed pile of dishes looks like—and they are neither beautiful, nor capable of saying anything meaningful.

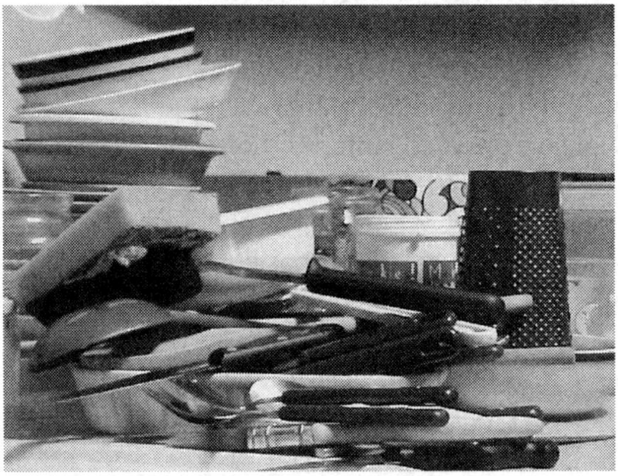

**Figure 1.2 Everything but the . . .**

Distinction would not only dispose people to see this photograph as meaningful or beautiful, however; it would also supply them with the knowledge and ability that would make such a perspective possible, and provide it with legitimacy. The name we give to this combination of knowledge and skill is *cultural literacy*. When we think of the notion of literacy, we usually associate it with reading and writing skills but in this case the term refers to a general familiarity with, and an ability to use, the official and unofficial rules, values, genres, knowledge and discourses that characterise cultural fields. Cultural literacy in this sense is not just familiarity with a body of knowledge; it also presupposes an understanding of how to think and see in a manner that is appropriate to the imperatives and contexts of the moment.

One way to demonstrate what we mean by this is to give an example of a lack of literacy. In the Marx Brothers' film *Animal Crackers*, Groucho Marx is playing a famous explorer, the guest of a woman (played by Margaret Dumont) who is a member of high society. Another guest is a rich art collector who is showing his most recent acquisition, the famous painting 'After the Hunt' by the French artist Beauregard (a painting which shows a hunter and his hounds). The painting has been stolen and replaced by a copy. When it is unveiled, the owner laments that this is not the original. When asked how he can be sure that it is a fake, his reply is that anyone can see that it is a poor imitation. He is about to explain what he means, presumably by referring to the poorly drawn details and inferior brushwork, but before he can do so Groucho adjusts his glasses, focuses on the painting and says, 'My God he's right. One of the dogs is missing.' The owner was showing his art literacy by being able to distinguish, at the level of technique and detail, between a masterpiece and a forgery. Groucho shows his lack of literacy by introducing a naïve, content-related issue ('There's one less dog!'). Of course, Groucho's illiteracy has a point to it: it demonstrates that while a 'high art' habitus allows people to see particularities like texture or subtleties of light, it also blinds them to what is in front of their noses. The owner presumes that a forger will at least get the details right (only one man on a horse, precisely five hounds). But Groucho, who has a more practical way of looking at things, sees what is obvious to him but hidden from the supposedly sophisticated eye.

This very peculiar and seemingly naïve (to the owner and the rest of the party) way of looking at and making sense of art is not in any sense idiosyncratic or accidental. Put simply, the cultural contexts, fields and institutions that Groucho inhabits and moves through (what we call his 'cultural trajectory') now effectively 'inhabit' him, influencing and determining what and how he sees. If Groucho were to become part of this more 'sophisticated' circle, their way of seeing would become more natural to him, and eventually influence, even determine, what he sees.

## seeing in context

Our situation is pretty much the same as Groucho's, in that what we see is inextricably linked to, and is a product of, our cultural trajectories, literacies and contexts. This applies even when we see something for the first time. Given that we know, think and see within our cultural frames, a truly 'new visual experience' is almost impossible to imagine. Even if we were subjected to something literally 'out of this world', like being abducted by aliens and taken to another planet, we would still see by using the categories and forms of evaluation that characterise our habitus. This would happen partly because we set up and make use of distinctions such as human/alien, even though we've never seen a 'real' alien. Of course, we have seen representations of aliens, which are normally distinguished from humans by their colour or size ('little green men'), body parts (Zaphod Beeblebrox, in *The Hitchhiker's Guide to the Galaxy*, had two heads which were always arguing) or supernatural abilities (Superman can leap tall buildings in a single bound).

The process through which we might see an alien—real or imagined—is more or less the same as what is involved when we categorise 'real people' or groups within our culture. We start off with a binary concept (human/alien) which is 'filled out' by various signs (humans walk upright and have one head), and when we come across something or someone which doesn't fit into one part of the binary because of an excess (an extra head) or lack (no head at all), we simply categorise, evaluate and see them (remember, this all happens more or less simultaneously) as the other part of the binary (the alien).

There is another interesting aspect to this question of what happens when we see something 'for the first time', and the answer is that often . . . we don't see it the first time we look at it. The musician Tom Verlaine, formerly of the New York 1980s punk band Television, sang in his song 'Postcard from Waterloo' that 'I recall the actor's advice/That nothing happens til it happens twice'. The point he is making is that the first time something appears which doesn't obviously correspond to categories with which we are familiar, or which we don't expect to see, we are likely to miss it. Using a similar logic, science historian Thomas Kuhn writes that the physicist Roentgen's 'discovery' of X-rays was at first:

> greeted not only with surprise but with shock. Lord Kelvin at first pronounced them an elaborate hoax. Others, though they could not doubt the evidence, were clearly staggered by it. Though X-rays were not prohibited by established theory, they violated deeply entrenched expectations . . . By the 1890s cathode ray equipment was widely deployed in numerous European laboratories. If Roentgen's apparatus had produced X-rays, then a number of other experimentalists must for some time have been producing those rays without knowing it. (Kuhn 1970: 59)

How do we come to see what we have been overlooking? Kuhn writes that, in the scientific field: 'Discovery commences with the awareness of anomaly . . . with the recognition that nature has somehow violated the paradigm-induced expectations that govern normal science' (1970: 52–3). In other words, our habitus disposes us to see certain things, but occasionally there is a misfit—or an anomaly—regarding what we expect to see and what we visually 'register'. Once this anomaly is repeated, we might start to reconsider what it is we are seeing—or overlooking.

We can exemplify this by returning to Verlaine's reference to the 'actor's advice' about things needing to happen twice. What this means is that we sometimes fail to see the significance of something until we are aware of what we could call a pattern. So, in Peter Jackson's film *The Fellowship of the Ring*, the hobbit Bilbo Baggins is represented as an inoffensive, generous and altogether nice type who seems untouched by desire, passion or greed. But he has a secret: he owns a ring that has cast an evil spell on him. We see signs of this when the wizard Gandalf asks him to hand over the ring, although the first few manifestations (a slight hesitation in responding to Gandalf's request, a strange look on his face as he ponders what to do next) could easily be overlooked. It is only when his determination to keep the ring leads him to act 'out of character' (he becomes suddenly violent and irrational), and when his face is completely transformed by the power of the ring (his features become contorted with rage), that we notice the pattern and understand the secret—he is possessed by the power of the ring. If we are familiar with Tolkien's story before viewing the film we will expect this to happen, and see what is happening 'the first time'; if we aren't, however, then Bilbo's hesitation and odd looks will just be part of a Kuhnian anomaly—until we perceive them as part of a pattern.

## techniques of seeing as reading

Up to this point we have concentrated on explaining how and why people see in particular ways, and we have referred to habitus, cultural trajectory and cultural literacy as the most important factors in determining what we see. But we also suggested that, whether our seeing is conscious or unconscious, the process of reading the visual relies on the same techniques. The techniques we will consider include selection, omission and frame; signification and evaluation; arrangement; differentiation and connection; focus; and context. It is important to keep in mind that there is no necessary temporal distinction between these techniques: they are part of the same process of making the visual, and one cannot be conceived without regard to the others.

The first and most important techniques of reading the visual are *selection and omission*; as we pointed out earlier, every act of looking and seeing is also an act of *not* seeing. Consider the text shown in Figure 1.3, a photograph of a woman sitting on the steps of a house with a dog. The photographer probably had a considerable amount of material to play with; there is a house, perhaps extensive gardens, a lawn, other people and animals, a street, other houses and maybe some cars. The photograph only shows us a selection of these: it includes a woman, a dog, the steps, some flowers or bushes, the lower part of the door and a shuttered window. We could consider a number of other aspects of the selection/omission process, such as the fact that we can see the woman's boots, but not her eyes.

**Figure 1.3 Lassie, *c.* 1920**

The selection of these details (and the omission of the others) helps to constitute and make the visual. It doesn't matter whether we are looking at a photograph, painting or a street scene: by paying attention to and focusing on the woman and her dog in this space, the viewer effectively constructs a *frame* around the scene. This is productive in two ways. Firstly, it suggests a set of relationships between, and stories about, the various parts—perhaps the woman is playing with her dog at her house; perhaps she is simply relaxing on her steps. Secondly, it establishes a (usually temporary) hierarchy with regard to the potentially visible; that is to say, whoever took this photograph or observed this scene decided (at a conscious or unconscious level) that this content within this space at this time was interesting or worthy of attention. In other words, they made an *evaluative* decision. This may have been careful and deliberate (they set the scene, posed the woman, took the shot) or spontaneous (they were wandering by, the scene appealed to them, they took a photograph). Either way, these acts of selection, omission, framing and evaluation produce a visual *text*.

What do we mean by the term 'text'? Usually we think of a text as something like a book—that is, it is an object that consists of words on pages, sometimes accompanied by photographs, divided into chapters, authored by someone, with a title and a cover. Sometimes we extend this to cover other mediums, such as film and television. The defining characteristic of a text is that it is (or is treated as if it were) a unit: we think of a book or a film as a text because the various parts are both related and bound together. This occurs through an arrangement of what we call signs, which can be defined, very generally, as something (say, a word or a photo) that is read as meaningful by someone (a reader or photographer). A group of signs is being read or treated as a text when someone considers all the signs as a unit. For example, we usually treat a book as a text which is made up of signs that possibly include the name of the author, the colour of the cover, the title and the publisher's name. In other words, a text is made up of signs that are considered to exist in relation to other signs, the sum of which is denoted by a frame of some kind.

The most important point to keep in mind about this definition is that texts are not simply objects which always retain the status of 'text'. Rather, texts are produced or created; this process of production is an ongoing one; and the status of signs and texts is always relational and contingent. In other words, there are no natural units of signs within cultures—or anywhere in nature, for that matter. Every time we treat something as if it were a text, we create a unit out of an infinite number of potential signs. So the person who took the photograph of the woman sitting on the steps took a number of potential signs (the woman, the dog, the steps, the house, the door, the garden) and included them within the frame of the camera's lens, and subsequently the frame of the finished photograph. Exactly the same kind of process occurs when someone walks up to a scene and notices certain details within the frame of focused, attentive vision.

There is (at least) one major difference between these two visual activities. When we look at a photograph, television, film screen or painting, we normally apprehend something that is in front, distanced and detached from us, whereas the texts we create as we see the world are all around us, like the visual equivalent of surround sound or virtual reality; we are located within them and they in us. So there are several technical tasks we have to perform, consciously or otherwise, in order to stitch together (what Jacques Derrida in *The Truth in Painting* calls 'suturing') all these elements so that they appear to be a single, continuous visual world.

Two important factors here are *attention* and *focus*. If we are attending closely or carefully to an event, person, thing or scene, we will create a text that is made up of what we can call *contiguous elements*. So if we were staring out of a window we might see tree branches waving in the wind directly in front of us and a cloudy sky above, but we would also be likely to include the window and curtains or blinds, the computer that is partly between us and the window, a section of the desk on which the computer is sitting, the telephone and the pile of books slightly to the side. We might be more peripherally aware of other objects within our purview, such as the walls of the room, bookshelves, papers, carpet or the ceiling. Our eyes may be caught by the colour or movement of things—the deep purple of the walls, the brightly coloured, whirling images of the screen saver on the computer. But the decision about what is included within the main frame and what is left to the periphery is very much of the moment. In other words, if I watch the computer screen or look out the window, the function or context of my looking and seeing (whether to do something specific like check email, or just to look dreamily away from my work) will determine what is included in the visual texts I produce.

## seeing in time and motion

A number of elements contribute to or facilitate the process of suturing the world to make a text. Colours help us to differentiate elements within our purview (the green of the trees and the blue of the sky); so do shape and movement (the still, rectangular window, as opposed to the relatively amorphous, waving tree branches). The use of colour, shape, movement and other elements (such as texture, distance and light) does not occur in an unmediated way, however; rather, the extent to which, and the how, we recognise, know and use them are tied up with our immersion in, and relationship with, our cultural world and its categories. We need to bear in mind that notions such as colour, shape and texture are culturally specific; we naturalise the world, give it stability and coherence, and are able to understand and explain it through our ability to maintain the (optical) illusion that what and how we see, and the texts we create, are real.

Of course these visual texts are ephemeral. In a sense they are never stable or really 'themselves'; after all, as I watch the trees, time is passing. I am changing and so are the trees. This is even more pronounced, and the texts that are produced are far more impressionistic, when we or the world are moving at speed. Even if I am keeping still, the slightest movement of my eyes or head automatically changes what is available to me to be processed, combined, textualised and read. If I look slightly to the left, I might notice a bird on the window ledge, a poster on the wall, a brightly coloured paperweight—and so I make a new text. Moreover, the dreamy state that induced me to look out the window might be replaced by a more focused mood, set off by some detail: I notice the paperweight keeping down a pile of papers I have to read, so I suddenly focus on them.

We suggested that this process of production is an ongoing and transformational one, and the status of signs and texts is always relational. Let's consider the first of those points, using the example of the photograph of the woman and dog to which we referred earlier. The photographer who took that shot could have taken a second photograph from 10 metres further away, this time including the whole of the house, more of the garden, and fourteen other dogs standing in the doorway. This would have produced a different text because the potential relationship between the various signs (and therefore the meanings available to anyone making sense of the text) would have been considerably altered; in the first shot, for instance, the woman dominates space, but she would be only one small part of the second shot. But the same principle (that remaking a text always transforms the text) would apply even if the photographer stood on the same spot and took another shot from the same angle, with the same frame. Why? Because time will have intervened in some way. In the most obvious case, some additional detail will have moved into the space of the frame—for instance, the fourteen dogs originally standing just outside the frame could all have run down and jumped on top of the woman. This would produce a different set of relationships between the signs, a different set of meanings and a very different text (say, to being potentially comic). But even when there are no new signs, the original signs within the frame will have changed in some way (the woman may have noticed the photographer and smiled, for instance).

Gilles Deleuze draws attention to this issue in his discussion of Henri Bergson's theorising of the relation between movement and instant (that is, time). Bergson puts forward the proposition (a paradox of sorts that he takes from the Greek philosopher Zeno) that movement and instant are both inextricably linked to, and inexplicable without regard to, one another. At the same time, neither is real in any sense—they are artifices or illusions of perception. As Deleuze writes:

> You cannot reconstitute movement with positions in space or instants in time . . . You can only achieve this reconstitution by adding to the positions, or to the instants, the abstract idea of a succession . . . And thus you miss the movement in two ways. On the one hand, you can bring two instants or two positions together to infinity; but movement will always occur in the interval between the two, in other words behind your back. On the other hand, however much you divide and subdivide time, movement will always occur in concrete durations . . . thus each movement will have its own qualitative duration. (Deleuze 1986: 1)

In other words, no matter how quickly we look at the same scene of the woman and the dog again and again, and no matter how much we are given to believe that things are the same (because it seems to be the same text), things have changed in the intervals of perception. But we can't capture the movement of time (the changes that differentiate one text from its successors, such as the woman beginning to smile, or the dog looking up) because the text is only available to us as a frozen instant, a text in time.

The second point we made is that the relationship between, and the status of, signs and texts are always relational and contingent. What do we mean by this? We suggested that a text is made up of different signs considered and framed as a unit—a woman, a dog, some steps together forming a photograph. But what if the photographer, or someone watching the scene, ignored everything except for the woman, so that she alone was in the frame? We could now say that, whereas before the woman was a sign in a text, now the woman had become the text, and the various details regarding her body and clothes (her boots, trousers, jumper, face, hair, hands) constituted the signs that made up the text. This process could continue almost ad infinitum. If we focused on the woman's face, it would become the text, and her eyes, nose and mouth would be the signs.

## text and intertext

Figure 1.4 provides a good example of the relational character of signs and texts. There are five photographs arranged on a single page. They were not originally taken as a series, intended to be placed together, or considered for public consumption; rather, they were private family photographs which we have put together, not entirely arbitrarily, to make a text.

1.4a

1.4c

1.4b

**Figure 1.4 Five found photographs, Wellington, New Zealand, 2000**

1.4d

1.4e

We can say that the combining of these particular photographs was not arbitrary because they are clearly connected through content (members of a family appear and reappear in them) and social function (they are all identifiable as being family portraits or photographs).

Each of the photographs can be read as a sign within the larger text. We could focus on one of the people (the woman in Figures 1.4a, 1.4b, 1.4c, 1.4e; the man in Figures 1.4b, 1.4d) and read between and across these signs, relate the content of each to that of the others, and produce a narrative or account of their lives (from youth to middle age, say). We might take this text as being about the family and its history, which would involve identifying the different generations and their relationship to one another, through reference to features such as clothes and physical characteristics. Each of these photographs-as-signs would have meaning in relation to the way they were read and contextualised with regard to the other signs—that is, their meanings and status would be determined by their textual place. But there is nothing to stop us from considering each of these photographs individually as collections of signs—that is, as texts. So the largest of the photographs (figure 1.4e) has a plethora of potential signs (the two women, their facial expressions and poses, the space between them, the rural setting) which can be collected together and read in relation to one another as a text without referring to any of the other photographs.

A sign, we have suggested, is anything that is treated as a meaningful part of the unit that is the text. We identify signs and group them together as if they were a unit by a process of relating available material to the other texts and text-types with which we are familiar from our memories and cultural histories. The use of other texts to create new texts is called *intertextuality*, and the term for text-types is *genre*. In order to consider these two concepts and how they inform or influence visual activity, let's look again at the series of photographs in Figure 1.4.

We made the point that every photograph in the collection is made up of potential signs (the people, their clothes, their facial expressions and poses, the space between them, the setting) that could be treated as individual texts—without needing to refer to any of the other photographs. But when we consider that text with regard to one or all of the other photographs, we are making use of intertextuality—which means the process of making sense of texts by reference to other texts, or to meanings that have already been made in other texts. Let's look at Figure 1.4e. We can identify two obvious signs—the two women in the foreground sitting side by side, smiling. We don't know anything about their relationship or their histories, so how do we make sense of or read those two signs? We can do so intertextually—by looking at some of the other photographs. The woman on the right of Figure 1.4e appears also in Figures 1.4b, 1.4c and 1.4d—or at least we presume that is the case because of the physical similarities between the various women in the shots. In Figure 1.4b, the woman is sitting very close to a man about her own age who probably has his arm around her waist or back. In Figure 1.4c she is much younger—perhaps in her mid-teens—and is posing with two adults and a boy, perhaps her parents and brother. In Figure 1.4d she looks slightly older than the woman in Figure 1.4e; she is at some kind of social function, and is the only person in the shot.

Taking these photos as a collection, we can 'read' a kind of narrative of the woman in Figure 1.4e. We have the woman-as-girl, growing up in what looks to be a middle- or upper-middle-class family in the first part of the twentieth century (which we identify from the hairstyles and clothing). She had a relationship with, and perhaps was married to, the man in Figure 1.4b. She was fair-skinned and probably lived in a sunny country (in three of the four shots she is wearing head covering of some kind, although this may be explicable in terms of the clothing fashions and conventions of the time). She probably grew up and lived in the country, rather than the suburbs or city. The young man we take to be her brother in Figure 1.4b is carrying rifles, and the houses and physical environments in Figures 1.4b, 1.4d and 1.4e all have rural characteristics (the rough stone material of the house in Figure 1.4b; the water tank in Figure 1.4d; the forest and sparsely housed scene in Figure 1.4e).

We might search these photographs for signs that would enable us to generalise about her history and life (she grew up and lived her life in the country in the mid-twentieth century), her nationality (Australian, New Zealander or South African), her predilections (in all the photographs she is wearing white shoes) and many other things. Some of these generalisations might be relatively obvious (for instance, the relationship between her clothes, her age and the approximate period in which she lived), while others are little more than conjecture (were the couple in Figure 1.4b married? Does the presence of headwear mean she was sensitive to the effects of sunlight?).

We could go on like this indefinitely, bringing in new intertexts that change the way we read the photograph we originally considered (Figure 1.4e). The important points, however, are that we can and do read texts such as Figure 1.4e intertextually and, even when we don't know specific details about those intertexts, we are disposed and able to make sense of and read them (we presume, without knowing for certain, that Figure 1.4c is a family shot showing parents and children). We are able to do this because every reading of a text is informed and influenced by our intertextual reference to and knowledge of the text-types that characterise our culture—what we call genres.

## texts and genres

Genres—which we discuss in more detail in Chapter 4—can be defined as 'text types which structure meanings in certain ways, through their association with a particular social purpose and social context' (Schirato and Yell 2000: 189). We normally think of genres in terms of cultural fields and mediums such as fiction or film—for instance, detective, science fiction or romance novels; and action, horror or erotic films. Each of these genres is identifiable in terms of its content, narrative, characterisation, discourses, values and worldviews. A detective film will usually have a certain kind of content as a constant (a crime, or an act of violence), which will require the intervention of a detective who will investigate the scene, question suspects and take testimonies from witnesses; hunt for, find and analyse clues; and eventually uncover secrets, overcome the criminals and solve the crime.

There will, of course, be variations across these texts. A film of one of Conan Doyle's detective stories will represent Sherlock Holmes as detached, observant, attentive, analytical, incorruptible, well-mannered and supremely self-confident—all of which is shown in the way Holmes moves, speaks, looks and acts. The values and worldviews represented in the film (if they are faithful to Conan Doyle's original fictions) will usually be socially conservative, and pretty much in keeping with the dominant social values of the time and place (so servants will be treated as if they are naturally less valuable, interesting and intelligent than members of the middle or upper classes). Finally, the descriptions of places and events will be strongly informed by what we could call scientific orientation: rooms, furniture, spaces and people will be described and shown in careful, precise detail.

Not all detective films—or plays, cartoons or video games, for that matter—reproduce or partake of all of these conventions. The so-called 'hard-boiled' detective films made from novels written by American writers such as Dashiel Hammett and Raymond Chandler will vary or even repudiate some of these characteristics (most obviously, the detective might be a drinker and gambler who may become sexually involved with suspects, and may work outside the law). But, by and large, there are enough constants and carry-overs from Holmes to the hard-boiled detective stories (and later on, to the forensic, feminist and historical detective forms) for us to categorise them as belonging to the same genre.

Who decides to which genre a book or film—or any other text—belongs? Michel Foucault's work alerts us to the ways in which ideas, worldviews and categories (of people, thought or texts) are institutionally produced. That is to say, different fields and the institutions within them produce (authorised) knowledge and statements through which we see, categorise and make sense of the world. With regard to films, for instance, a variety of fields (academe, the media, government) and experts (film studies academics, film critics, politicians) will analyse, and make pronouncements about, a film's value and genre; and this will effectively determine where a film is shown (mainstream, art house or 'adult' cinema), what rating it receives, and therefore who is allowed to see it. Moreover, these comments, classifications and ratings will also orient the way audiences understand and evaluate a film.

The films around which these questions and issues are often played are those which have explicit sexual content—which usually means they will be categorised as pornography. But sexually explicit films are sometimes given a rating which allows them to escape this classification. For example, two French films with explicit sexual content were shown in Australia over a period of three years—*Romance* (directed by Catherine Breillat, released in 1999) and *Baise Moi* (Coralie Trin Thi, 2002). *Romance* was not finally classified as pornography, despite the fact that there were scenes showing actual sexual activity and implied depictions of sexual violence. The main reason the film received a restricted classification was because it was considered an art film: the director was known to be interested in, and had dealt with, philosophical, political and social issues (the nature of desire, masculine violence, the dehumanised state of modern society), and these same 'serious' issues were talked about and represented in the film. If we go back to our definition of genre, we see that it refers the 'particular social purpose and context' of text types. *Romance*, presumably because of the status of its director, was considered to be showing sexual content in order to explore contemporary social issues. In other words, unlike pornography, the sex scenes (as far as the national censorship board was concerned) had an artistic, social and educational function, rather than being intended simply to produce sexual arousal.

*Baise Moi* was released in Australia three years later. Again, the film seemed to be oriented towards—or at least to be informed by—social criticism and artistic features, and it was being shown as an art house film. But after originally giving the film a restricted classification, the censorship board reversed its decision, which meant that the film had to be withdrawn from cinemas. On the face of it, there was very little to differentiate the film from *Romance*, but in three years the social and political climate had changed sufficiently for the two films to be given entirely different classifications and categorised as separate genres—*Romance* was effectively categorised as an art film, *Baise Moi* as pornography.

These kinds of official classifications—and effectively generic categorisations—of texts influence and orient audiences with regard to the way they see and read a film. Let's return to *Romance* as an example. There is a scene in the film where the female protagonist has had an argument with her boyfriend, and has decided to pick up and have sex with a stranger she has met in a bar. The two characters are naked and lying in bed, and are clearly about to have intercourse. As the man moves his penis towards her vagina, the woman comes out with a monologue about the ways in which men take sexual advantage of women. The man stops, pulls back his penis and looks (vaguely) thoughtful. The woman then produces a second monologue, this time about how it isn't that simple—that sex is not simply an issue of domination. The man listens to what she has said and, taking her words as a positive signal, moves his penis towards her vagina a second time. Once again, however, she produces a monologue that seems to contradict her previous utterance ('And yet'). The man again withdraws his penis and goes back to looking thoughtful.

Now there are a couple of ways in which this scene (and, because this scene is reasonably representative, the entire film) can be read or responded to. The first response is in terms of sexual excitement. The sight of naked bodies about to engage in sexual intercourse is content normally associated with pornography—and, of course, one of the more obvious social functions of the pornography genre is to engender sexual excitement and pleasure. The second response, more or less diametrically opposite to the first, is to laugh—to treat this scene (and the film as a whole) as ludicrous, pretentious and (unintentionally) comic. After all, the very mechanical back-and-forward movement of the penis, and the incongruous combination of sexual activity and philosophical clichés, means that pathos is in danger of being supplanted by bathos. But the fact that this film was shown in art cinemas, received very positive reviews from critics and was the work of a 'serious' director probably meant that those two responses were foreclosed—at least for many people in the audiences which saw it.

Genres then, like intertexts, do not provide us with special access to visual reality; rather, they are frames and references that we use to negotiate, edit, evaluate and in a sense read the visual as a series of texts. And the way in which socio-cultural fields and institutions categorise people, places, events and texts in terms of certain genres (often based on or associated with evaluative binaries such as normal/perverted, civilised/barbaric, good/evil, art/pornography) orients and disposes us to see and read the visual world in particular ways.

## conclusion

What is important, in any consideration of how we read the visual, is that as 'readers' we are also 'writers', selecting, editing and framing all that we see. Most of the time this work is unconscious, but even when our seeing is conscious and attentive, we will still make what we see by using the same kinds of techniques (such as selection and omission), and be limited in what we see by factors such as context, habitus and cultural literacy. In our next chapter we extend this inquiry to take into account what we could call the 'prosthetics of seeing'—that is, we consider the relationship between visual apparatuses and technologies, and the types of 'visions' they produce.

# 2 visual technologies

## introduction

In the previous chapter, we outlined some of the central mechanisms and techniques by which people make sense of what they see. In this chapter we take up the mechanics of visual perception more specifically. This includes the physiology and neurology of seeing—how do our bodies and brains engage with the world around us?—and also the visual apparatuses and technologies people have developed over the centuries as aids for seeing. We address the relationship between mechanisms of perception and the types of 'visions' they produce. We also look at cultural frames such as photography, film and 3-D or interactive devices, and discuss their effect on seeing and perceiving. Central to the question of perception is how space and objects, and movements in space, are arranged and 'mapped' in the two-dimensional format that constitutes much of visual culture. We also examine the ways in which post-Renaissance notions of 'seeing' and mapping space have contributed to our understanding of the contemporary world. And finally, we discuss some of the technologies of reproducing line and image—particularly the digital technologies involved in seeing—and discuss their effect on our perspective of the world.

## physiology and seeing

Modern neurophysiology has determined that something like half the brain is dedicated to visual recognition, and that how and what we see is tied up with our physiological structure. Our optic nerve comprises some 800 000 fibres, over 120 million rods and over seven million cones. This means that an enormous amount of information can be transmitted swiftly and accurately to the brain (Jay 1993: 6). The eye focuses the image on the retina, just as the camera focuses an image on film. The retina then organises the material which has been focused on it by using its photoreceptors (light-sensitive cells). This is where the rods and cones come into play, the rods processing dim light, and the cones processing colour and bright light. The photoreceptors transform what we have 'captured' visually into recognisable objects, and it is not until this work is completed that the image goes to the brain via the optic nerve, to be processed further there (Hoffman 1998: 66).

Obviously the process of visual perception is very physical—eyes are focusing on objects; rods and cones are processing matter; and optic nerves are transporting the images they have recorded. The history of theories of perception shows that the writers and thinkers of the past two and a half millennia have experienced a surprising degree of agreement about the physicality, and the tangible quality, of the process of perception. They have, of course, differed on how this process works: the ancient Greek philosopher Plato proposed the notion of vision by 'extramission'—that we see as the effect of a stream of light that flows out from the eye and strikes objects outside the body (Plato, *Timaeus*). His student, Aristotle, had a different explanation: he argued that the water in the eye transmits an image through to the soul. Although those who followed Plato and Aristotle took various perspectives on vision, we can trace the focus on the tactile aspect of seeing to the eighteenth-century philosopher René Descartes, who wrote that images are 'received by the external sense organs and transmitted by the nerves to the brain' (1998: 61), so that the process of sight is like that of a blind person feeling their environment by the use of a stick (Descartes 1998: 64). Even as late as the early twentieth century, the psychiatrist Sigmund Freud wrote that seeing is 'an activity that is ultimately derived from touching' (Freud 1905: 156).

But seeing is more than touching: Descartes may have used the analogy of feeling one's way through the world, but he did not assume that seeing depended only on a sensory experience. Instead he insisted (as do contemporary physiologists) that our senses are inadequate for perception—we need to make sense of what we see using rational thought (Jay 1993: 72–3). So, though sight might appear to be a perfectly natural physical action, neurologists insist that both the ease with which we see and the apparent truth of what we see are deceptive. Seeing, they tell us, involves a huge amount of practice, and the application of an enormous portion of the brain (Hoffman 1998: xi); and the brain sees not just 'what is out there', but what it constructs from the matter it collects in seeing. Think of colour, for example. As early as the eighteenth century, scientist Isaac Newton wrote: 'Rays to speak properly are not coloured. In them there is nothing else than a certain Power and Disposition to stir up a Sensation of this or that Colour' (Newton 1730/1952: 124). We identify colour not by itself, but by its context—by the relation of light to colour, by other colours around it, and by what we already know. A stop sign, for instance, looks red at any time of day, though if we were to measure it with a spectroscope, its shade would vary remarkably with the light (Finkel 1992: 402).

Not only does the brain make up, or construct, what it sees, but it is also liable to be fooled by what is seen. We perceive topographical maps and contour lines (see Figure 2.1a), for instance, as three-dimensional and varied in depth, even though they are only lines on a flat page or screen. And, despite the incredible receptive facility of the eye, it is (we are) fooled by light, distance and intensity. Figure 2.1b is a common puzzle: we are asked to determine, without measuring, which line is longer. And though we are likely to know, from previous experience, that they are precisely the same length, virtually everyone will see the upper line as longer. Similarly, we see the centre of the star image in Figure 2.1c as being much whiter and brighter than the paper outside the lines, although in fact there is no difference at all. Cognitive scientist Donald Hoffman calls this predilection to produce what we see an 'elaborate fabrication', and writes that we don't see what is there, but only 'how things appear to me' (Hoffman 1998: 6). That is to say, we see *relationally*—when we observe something that really exists in the material world and relate with our view of it to bring it into our meaning world. We also see in a *phenomenal* sense—when we see visions, mirages or other 'imagined' things, for instance, and also when we construct what we see gestaltically (Hoffman 1998: 6). This means that we do not see, even in neurophysiological terms, simply what is there; instead, we are confronted with an incredible variety of possibilities.

This is partly to do with the construction of the eye and the physiology of seeing. The eye is constantly in motion, so we can't really fix our gaze in any prolonged manner or produce an arrested image, as is possible through technological imaging. Instead, our brains must make up an image out of constantly changing, and often scanty, clues (lines, signs). Nor do we see in a neat frame, but are always reframing as we move our eyes across a scene or object, and as we move our heads or bodies within the viewing field. Further, we have binocular vision: we have two eyes but see only one image (or, rather, the brain decodes the image seen by each eye into a single impression). Binocular vision means that we are always seeing the world from two perspectives, triangulated; this means we have a large field vision,

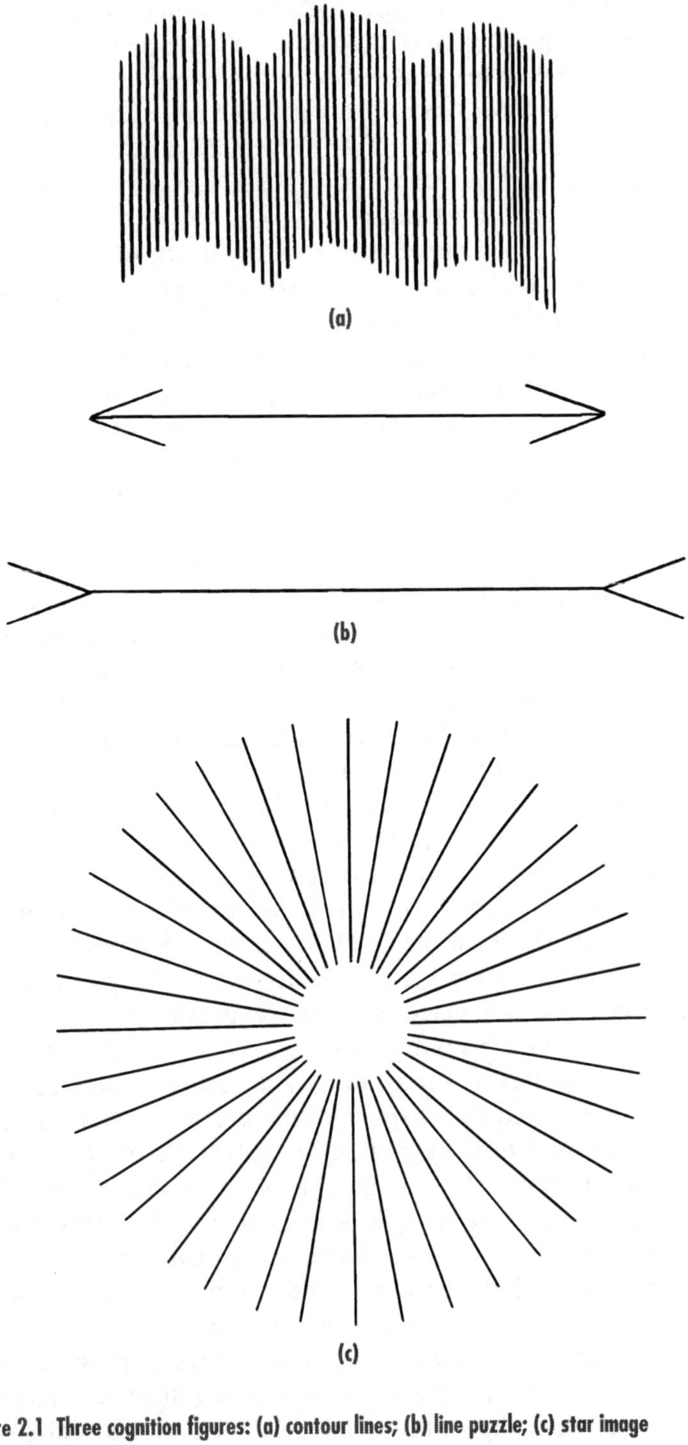


Figure 2.1 Three cognition figures: (a) contour lines; (b) line puzzle; (c) star image

better peripheral vision than we would have if we were monocular, and the ability to perceive distance, depth and three-dimensionality. We also have a 'blind spot', the macula, which prevents our taking in a whole visual field without constant scanning and comparison of what we see (Gombrich 1982: 50). And the structure of the eye means we only see an image sharply at its centre, unlike a camera where, if the lens aperture is set to allow great depth of field, the photo will show everything in the frame with equal clarity and focus (Snyder 1980: 505).

Given the problems inherent in receiving an image of what is actually out there, what is there to prevent us from making up everything we see idiosyncratically? Why is it that virtually everyone would see the top line in Figure 2.2 as longer than the lower line? According to Hoffman, it is because perception is governed by a kind of grammar: 'We see the same things because we construct the same things. And we construct the same things because we use the same rules of construction' (Hoffman 1998: 74). These rules, for Hoffman, are physiological—to do with brain function.

## seeing in the world

But in fact we don't consistently see the same things in the same way. For instance, we went to an art gallery a few years ago to see an exhibition of the works of hyperrealist artist Jeffrey Smart (see thumbnails of his work at www.philipbacon.com.au/artist/smart/smart-p1.html). After spending an hour or so looking at his various cityscapes, with their blocks of colour and fine attention to detail, we sat in the gallery's café, looking out across the inner cityscape, and saw it not in terms of itself (a collection of office buildings and apartment blocks, the loop of roads around the harbour, the harbour bridge) but as framed, with each window of each apartment building seeming to have been placed there according to the rules of hyperrealist perspective. We saw not with our own eyes and in accordance with everyday scanning of a familiar scene, but as though we were looking at a flat representation of the city, artificially heightened and alive, perfect and yet somehow slightly awry.

The point of this story is not simply to compound what we have been discussing about the tendency of eye and brain to conduct 'elaborate fabrications'; rather, it is an example of how cultural frameworks interlace with the physiological when we read our surroundings. John Berger writes that seeing is more than just the work of the eye and brain; it is also, importantly, relational. We see what we look at, and we see it not just in and of itself, but in relation to ourselves: how close it is to us; how it makes us feel; how it fits into our current state of mind and social framework. 'Our vision,' Berger writes, 'is continually active, continually moving, continually holding things in a circle around itself, constituting what is present to us as we are' (1972: 9). This is pretty much what was happening when we looked out and saw not a living city, but a Jeffrey Smart image. We had not seen it that way before, and perhaps will never see it that way again; but for that moment, because of the way in which our eyes had been 'set' by a cultural influence, we couldn't see it in any other way.

What is happening in this sort of experience? We can identify here another component to the physiology of vision—something which is not just the function of the nervous system, but isn't just a personal quirk of vision either. Rather, it is a blend of the personal, the physiological and the cultural. French theorists like Blaise Pascal, Maurice Merleau-Ponty and Pierre Bourdieu describe and analyse ways of understanding the world that help us to make sense of our experience because their work insists that we aren't just the sum of the electrical impulses in our brains; and we aren't just the sum of everything our culture says people ought to be. Rather, we are beings who live in bodies and who have emotional lives which affect our sense of the world—what we see, how we see it and what it means to us. If you're myopic, for instance, you see the world in soft focus—you see a different world from that seen by your friends with 20/20 vision, and your sense of the world is different because of your body and its abilities, compared with theirs. And this happens all the time, in all sorts of ways: when you're ill, the very air may appear faintly yellow; when you're inebriated, objects in front of you seem to weave and sway; when you're deep in thought, the world becomes fuzzy and indistinct; and when you're elated it may well appear bright and clean, regardless of how it actually is. As Pierre Bourdieu writes: 'The relation to the world is a relation of presence in the world, of being in the world, in the sense of belonging to the world' (Bourdieu 2000: 114). So we see and perceive not because we are looking at the world from the outside, as it were, but because we are part of everything within our gaze.

## tacit seeing

This 'everything' includes our habitus (our background, tastes, tendencies and dispositions) as well as our physical aptitude and status. What we can take from this is that the ability to see, and the ways in which we make sense of what we see, are firstly neurophysiological—we need the ability to capture and process images, and transfer them to the brain. But what we choose to look at and see, and where our focus lies, have a different point of origin, which is dependent on the body but influenced by individual tastes and dispositions, and the cultural framework in which our ideas, values and habits are laid down. We see, in short, under the principle of constancy: 'past experiences of the viewer will influence what is perceived' (Wallschlaeger and Busic-Snyder 1992: 307). As an example, in the 1980s the BBC produced a film based on a research project conducted by a group of British sociologists (screened in 1987). Part of their experiment was a kind of play staged on the public transport system, where a pair of young white men entered a carriage and 'mugged' a black man. The members of the public sitting in the carriage were interviewed about what they had seen, and an embarrassingly high proportion of the white respondents reported that the black man had been the mugger. What they saw and how they processed it was framed not just by neurological processes, but by the cultural environment and its values and rules (which valued white people over people of colour, and attributed criminal tendencies to the latter), and by their own habitus (which clearly generated racist attitudes). In short, they saw what they expected to see—or, as Bates Lowry (1967: 13) might have put it, their visual perception was to seeing as babbling is to speaking: they looked without really seeing.

At times, we all look without seeing; this is often necessary to allow us to get through each day. Think of the act of walking, for instance. If I focus on the individual movements and moments of balance, I'll probably fall over, but if I simply walk along, I will be able to cross a road without any major disasters or embarrassments. Similarly, if I had to pay careful attention to every aspect of everything in my visual field, I wouldn't be able to make sense of anything: I'd be overwhelmed with visual stimuli. So, instead of carefully thinking about each movement of foot and leg while walking, or focusing analytically on each thing before my eyes while seeing, I tend to function according to a conscious–unconsciousness: what Michael Polanyi terms 'tacit knowing' (Polanyi and Prosch 1975: 34), which means having just enough awareness of walking, or seeing, to achieve an aim (to cross the road, to read a novel). Tacit knowing, or tacit seeing, allows us to function despite the fact that we are constantly being distracted—our eyes are always being captured by something new across the way; our attention is easily diverted by noises and other sensations; our moods and prejudices colour what we see.

## seeing as literacy

Tacit seeing is fine if we simply want to get through the day's responsibilities and activities, but it is insufficient if we want or need to make sense of what we are seeing. As an analogy, consider the processes of communicating in language. The school system trains children to develop sophisticated literacies in the various components of written language—we learn the shapes of letters, we learn the look of words, we learn grammar and syntax—and, with these literacies (and discipline-specific training), we can write or read anything from abstract philosophy to shopping lists. If we are to develop similar skills in the manipulation and interpretation of visual texts, then we must again learn a number of skills and knowledges—or literacies. Just as we needed to learn how individual letters were shaped, we need to learn how to produce and read the basic components of visual texts—point, line and plane. Point is the simplest visual element: it has location, but no dimension. Line is a point in motion, and is one-dimensional—only able to extend along one direction. Plane is two-dimensional, having both length and width. Together with the effects of light, hue and colour saturation, tonal value, texture and scale, dimension and motion, these three elements make up the visual field we observe, and convey the impression of density, movement and dimension. By knowing these elements, and how they are combined, we have the basic skills to read visual texts.

Look, for example, at the image reproduced in Figure 2.2, Enzo Plazzato's 'Jeté'. We can identify line, plane, light and texture in the outline of the shape, the sweep of limbs and fabric, the texture of material, the varying density of light across the curves—particularly the hair, muscles and ribs. We can also identify dimension by comparing one part of the object with another. Motion is implied by the arrangement of the whole—most viewers would read it as an arrested moment in mid-leap. Its title, 'Jeté' (a ballet step), tells us what is happening, but even without the caption there is no doubt that this is someone in full flight. An utterly still statue, reproduced here in an utterly still photograph, calls up movement because of the combination of line, texture and bodily organisation.

But knowledge of lines, planes and other elements is not enough on its own. One of the technologies of visuality is depth, which is in fact physiologically unattainable. The eye sees only two dimensions, and has to manufacture depth on the basis of the clues before it (Hoffman 1998: 23). We make the assumption, with our two-dimensional eyes and from this two-dimensional reproduction, that this is a statue in three dimensions because of the way light falls on

**Figure 2.2 'Jeté' by Enzo Plazzato (Italy, London, 1921–1981). The statue is on Millbank, near the Tate Gallery, in London. It is one of 9 cast in bronze, and the model for the sculpture was dancer David Wall. The original clay model was made in 1975.**

the curves, and because of the density of the colour against the lightness of the sky/background. A second very important technology of seeing, related to depth, is dimensionality, which is practically impossible to read in an image without additional cues. We can't, for example, tell by looking at the photo of 'Jeté', how large the statue is, how high it is elevated, or what the distance actually is between the viewer and the statue. Insufficient clues have been incorporated to allow us to guess this aspect reliably. By adding in other literacies, we might be able to clarify some of these. We can assume it is probably elevated (because it seems to have been shot from below), and we can assume it is relatively large, firstly because it must be quite high to have so much clear sky above it in the middle of a city, and secondly because we can assume that the building against which it is photographed is a major city edifice.

If we do not know how the visual elements are combined, we will not be able to read a visual text: contemporary researchers, for instance, can only make educated guesses about the meanings of cave paintings, particularly those that are non-representational (comprising lines and dots rather than figures). People are always subjective mark-makers, and subjective readers of marks. But what of a more objective viewing machine, the camera? This is a form of visual technology with which most people are very familiar, and which seemed at first to offer the promise of a rational vision, one uncoloured by the vagaries of neurological perception, the limits of eye function, and the personal distractions and tacit seeing that affect human beings. With photography, none of these obtain because the camera simply focuses on the image and records it, freezing time in what ought, logically, to be a true and pure account of the space in front of the lens.

Of course, it does not fulfil this promise. For the most part we treat photographs as though they produce 'a perfectly realistic and objective recording of the visible world' (Bourdieu et al. 1990: 74), but the more skilled we become in taking, processing and reading photographs, the more aware we are that a photo is just another image that shows us what we want—or have chosen—to see. We only photograph the things we want to keep as memories: weddings, the stages of our children's development, the kitchen before and after the renovations. As we discussed in the previous chapter, we carefully select what will be in our photographs, and edit out those elements we don't want to recall. And by using the appropriate computer program, we can digitally manipulate pictures—lift elements out, drop elements in, sharpen up the image, change the colour. Photography has not shown us a pure image uninflected by taste, habitus, neurological distortions or other distractions, but has instead given us another way of

**Figure 2.3 Onoe Matsusuke I (1770); Ippitsusai Bunchô (Japan, 1725–96)**

representing the things about us that must still be rendered sensible, or readable: it produces a visual text which is more or less true to the object depending on how we look, what we know and what we expect to see.

Still, an image does not need to replicate its subject to be a good likeness, or to be read as such. Look, for example, at the *ukiyo-e* woodblock print reproduced in Figure 2.3. None of us has ever seen a man who looked precisely like this man, and yet he is immediately recognisable as a person—and as a person with specific features of gender and age. Although this print obeys none of the Western rules of visual culture in that period (it was first published in a book dated 1770), and although it is very flat and stylised compared with the narrative realism that characterised European eighteenth-century works or with contemporary photographs, we can identify its content (and this without being trained in eighteenth-century Japanese culture, the oeuvre of the artist or the mannered cultivated world reflected in the *ukiyo-e* art). We can see, for instance, that the man represented here is in motion—less dramatically than the young man in 'Jeté', but he is pictured in the moment of turning to look over his shoulder at something. And if asked what is going on, we might say that 'a man in courtly dress is turning around'. In fact, of course, there is no movement at all; this is what Gombrich calls an 'arrested image' (1982: 248).

## arresting reality

The arrested image is most often associated with the field of photography because photographs perfectly freeze time and motion in a way that no other art form really achieves. Paul Virilio (1994: 2) cites the sculptor Rodin to the effect that paintings and sculptures (any non-photographic art) effectively convey the sense of movement because they don't freeze time, as does a photo. Rather, paintings or sculptures—or woodblock prints—rely on the eye movements of the viewer to convey the appearance of movement. We read the statue of Jeté, running our eyes across the sweep of limb to capture a sense of the leap. We run our eyes over the *ukiyo-e* print, looking back to see what has caught the man's attention. Because time doesn't really ever stand still, so Virilio's argument goes, a photograph—which freezes time and motion—is 'false' in this respect. Martin Jay takes a similar line, writing that photographs rob 'life's flowing temporality by introducing a kind of visual rigor mortis' (Jay 1993: 134). Our eyes, as we noted above, are always moving; time too is always moving, and with it the material objects on which we gaze. Because the camera freezes a moment, it reminds us that time is constantly passing, yet we treat the arrested motion as a falsehood, and behave as though the movement in a painting is 'true'.

This is curious, because in other respects we typically behave as though photographs show 'exactly what happened'—what Barthes called 'the reality effect'. We look to the photo finish shot to confirm an uncertain end to a race, for instance, and to candid shots to show the moment 'as it was'. But photographs are not, in fact, necessarily true to how we think something should or does look. Think of the numbers of passport photographs that do not look anything like the person whose identity they confirm; or how subjects will often shriek with horror or mirth at how they appear in snapshots. This is partly a matter of the subject's vanity, no doubt, but there is a degree to which this response is valid: the instantaneous, unstaged photograph cannot show us what we think we saw, because it freezes time while we see in time. This is why movie stills photographers will stage shots from scenes, rather than just run the camera and select a single frame. Whenever time and motion are frozen, things are shown out of place—someone may be in motion, but the freeze effect means they are shown with a leg hanging in mid-air; someone else may be speaking, but the freeze effect means their mouth appears to gape vacantly; and there is always someone whose eyes are closed. In real time, the viewer would not notice this; it would be part of the whole moment, in motion. But in a photograph, it can be horribly evident.

The unreality of so many photographs is also based on proximity and perspective—as we discussed in Chapter 1—which can show us the world in an unfamiliar way, and from unexpected angles. Such work disturbs viewers partly because it jolts us out of our complacency about our lived environment and its spatial dimensions; such photos trouble us because they show us the world in a way that we don't (think we) actually see it. Just the tilting of a lens can render a building oddly foreshortened, and moving in very close to an object changes its appearance. In Figure 2.4 we see an ordinary fork, foreshortened and massified. The close-up photo means the fine scratches on the tines are rendered here into a kind of cross-hatching, which catches the viewer's attention and produces the effect of texture. The tone—or the degree of darkness or lightness caused by light reflecting off the surface of the tines—communicates a pattern of depth and intensity. The lighter and brighter parts seem closer, the darker parts recede, the shadow at the top left conveys an impression of depth, and the intensity of the black-and-white tines against the grainy grey background creates an effect of the solidity and volume of metal against air. The proximity means the shape of the fork as a fork is lost, so that it becomes first an object of the gaze, and only subsequently decoded to be seen as an everyday object. Together, the angle and play of light, and the limited depth of field, focusing attention on the light curves of the tines, mean that the fork is presented in a heroic guise, with a sweep of metal and balance of light and dark that makes it appear to be like no other fork we have seen.

**Figure 2.4 Topography of the fork**

This may seem a surprisingly 'ordinary' example, but it demonstrates how easy it is to defamiliarise the familiar. American poet Charles Simic remembers sending off a series of poems to a literary magazine and receiving the reply, 'Dear Mr Simic . . . you're obviously a sensible young man, so why do you waste your time by writing about knives, spoons and forks?' One of Simic's poems describes a fork as:

> This strange thing must have crept
> Right out of hell.
> It resembles a bird's foot
> Worn around the cannibal's neck.
>
> As you hold it in your hand,
> As you stab with it into a piece of meat,
> It is possible to imagine the rest of the bird:
> Its head which like your fist
> Is large, bald, beakless and blind.

## space and perspective

All the same, there is a truth to reality presented by photography, and it is the truth based on what Gombrich calls 'the eye-witness principle' (1982: 253). As Gombrich explains it, the eye-witness principle was developed by the ancient Greeks (to whom we owe so much of what we know about vision), and it means simply that everything in shot or frame is what a viewer would have seen if standing in the same place, and at the same time, as the camera recorded the image. It is a reality that is not a reality, because no one can stand perfectly still and gaze undistractedly at one spot. Our eyes don't allow it because they are always in motion and because we are binocular. Test this by looking at something close to you, and then alternately opening and closing each eye: the object will seem to shift across your field of vision, you will have much less depth of vision, and less will be visible. Monocular vision has only one perspective and hence flattens out the field of vision to one dimension. So for the eye-witness principle really to work, the viewer would have had to stand still, look directly at—and only at—the object in shot and, unless the object were distant, close one eye (Gombrich 1982: 258). Despite this, the eye-witness principle is the foundation for the whole study of perspective which was realised in the Renaissance and dominated visual art until the nineteenth century.

Perspective in visual images means that the arrangement and relative size of objects is true to the eye-witness principle, so that the whole image is dependent upon the point of view of the potential beholder. John Berger describes it in wonderfully simple terms, writing that the gaze of the viewer 'is like a beam from a lighthouse—only instead of the light travelling outward, appearances travel in . . . Perspective makes the single eye the center of the visible world. Everything converges on to the eye as to the vanishing point of infinity' (Berger 1972: 16). Linear perspective as we now understand it begins with the Renaissance artists' development of proportional systems, and their attempt to create a simulation of the actual vista and thus achieve beauty and order in art works.

Of course, perspective had been understood much earlier than the Renaissance: the artists of this period, many historians insist, rediscovered it from the writings and art works of antiquity (Veltman 1998). They cite as evidence the writings of the ancients (especially Euclid) on various mathematical principles known in the ancient world, on shapes like the cone and the pyramid, and on the design of Greek temples, urns, statues and other works (Wallschlaeger and Busic-Snyder 1992: 220). The approach to perspective used in the ancient world is not precisely the same as the linear perspective pioneered by Renaissance artists, however. Ancient Roman and Greek artists tended just to use techniques like foreshortening and the diminution of objects within pictorial space to designate their position and proximity. Renaissance artists, in contrast, used geometrical plotting in their attempt to show the world 'as it really is', and to replicate depth in two dimensions. Central to their approach was the intersection of lines at a specific vanishing point on the horizon, which created the effect of depth and dimension—the effect of looking through a frame, or a window, on to the real world.

The 'reality' of this effect, though, is a fantasy: we do not in fact see in perspective because, as we noted in reference to the eye-witness principle, this would demand a monocular view—we would have to stand in one spot and close one eye to see the world in linear perspective. So, despite the apparent naturalness, or 'truth to referent', that perspectival images present, Gombrich insists that perspective 'does violence to the way we see the world' (1982: 258). And it is in fact not 'natural': it is first a mathematical and technical system, and only then an artistic system, and it makes use of geometric ratios and specialised perspectival instruments to produce internal balance, harmony of elements and the effect of photographic realism. It works extremely well. Look, for example, at the photograph of the train in Figure 2.5, which shows linear perspective in the way the railway lines, the lines of the train and its carriage and the horizon lines of the tops of the shrubbery all implicitly converge at the vanishing point. The relative size of the various objects in the shot also heightens the perspectival effect, with the size of the stones in the foreground compared with the miniaturised train in the background indicating both the distance between the two, and their relative proximity to the implicit viewing position. Together the elements and their organisation within the frame convey an impression of the world laid out before us, and an impression of spatiality.

**Figure 2.5 Maryborough train**

Linear perspective is, then, a powerful reality effect, because it mimics the way in which we seem to see in normal vision. It is also a political gesture: European linear perspective developed and was used to privilege order and a particular ideal of beauty. In doing so, it obeyed and supported the important stories and values—especially

Christian stories and values—that were dominant at the time. The spatial harmony of linear perspective, for instance, reflected the symbolic harmony of the world in God's order. The regular pattern of lines disappearing to the vanishing point on the horizon alludes to a point beyond which we cannot see—the horizon where objects disappear—and thus offers the promise of a reality beyond what we can see. Also, much of the art created in the late Medieval and Renaissance period comprised representations of Bible stories; more 'realistic' representations made the stories seem more true, supporting the principles of Christian faith. Ernst Gombrich writes, in *Means and Ends*, of 'the increasing demand for what I have called dramatic evocation, the return to the desire not to be told only what happened according to the Scriptures but how it happened, what events must have looked like to an eyewitness' (Gombrich 1976: 32). Linear perspective, by putting the viewer of a Bible painting into the position of eye-witness, 'proved' the truth of the story ('it must be true: I saw it with my own eyes').

## beyond linearity

We should avoid the temptation to collapse all forms of linear perspective under a single logic, however. Just because something looks as though it is obeying similar rules of internal order doesn't mean that it is attempting to do the same sorts of things. Other cultures may use elements of linear perspective, but with a different set of imperatives. Japanese *ukiyo-e* ('floating world') woodprints, an example of which was reproduced in Figure 2.3, are generally considered by art historians to have been developed out of Chinese woodblock prints which incorporated a Western (linear) perspective. It would be common sense, one might argue, to say that the *ukiyo-e* works are therefore not really Japanese, but are inherently 'like' both their Chinese and Western antecedents. But this really can't be supported if we look at the works. As we can see in the print by Bunchô in Figure 2.3, it is not 'realistic' in Western terms—remember that this was produced at about the same time when Western artists like the Spaniard Francisco Goya were producing 'realistic' images that incorporated the vanishing point and geometrical arrangement associated with linear perspective (see thumbnails of Goya's etchings at www.artgalleryone.com/Goya/LosDesastres.htm). Nor does it convey the volumetric quality (depth and three-dimensionality) sought by so many Western artists. Moreover, to argue that the meanings and logic are the same because a similar technique is being used would be to do a violence to what Japanese writers at the time considered these *ukiyo-e* prints were representing, and how they were representing it. The point and the context of the *ukiyo-e* works were to represent the 'floating world' of the Japanese court in the seventeenth century, to capture the life and values and aspirations of the people. Ryoi, writing in 1661, described the world which is pictured by the *ukiyo-e* artists:

> Living only for the moment, turning our full attention to the pleasures of the moon, the snow, the cherry blossoms and the maple leaves; singing songs, drinking wine diverting ourselves in just floating, floating; caring not a whit for the pauperism staring us in the face, refusing to be disenheartened, like a guard floating with the river current: this is what we call the floating world. (cited in Veltman 1998)

This story of the *ukiyo-e* does not, then, bear a resemblance to contemporary works in Europe or, arguably, in Africa or Oceania.

Still, every work has perspective of some sort, according to Panofsky (1991: 41)—it need not necessarily be the vanishing point perspective associated with the Western tradition, but it must deal with space and relation. Maps are one of the several important visual technologies that render space, and permit a knowledge of place to viewers with appropriate literacies. Although a map looks nothing like the landscape or cityscape it represents, the symbols (the post office sign, the one-way arrows on appropriate roads, the blue squiggle of a river) and scale tell us how to navigate its space. Michel de Certeau writes about these various perspectives, in his work on spatial practices. He begins his chapter by looking down on Manhattan from a skyscraper high above the city, and writes of 'this pleasure of "seeing the whole", of looking down on, totalising the most immoderate of human texts' (1984: 92). In fact, by looking down on to the city, much as cartography insists we look down from a very high point, the city is reduced from living world into semi-static text. Those at ground level, though, see a very different 'text': 'they are walkers . . . whose bodies follow the thicks and thins of an urban "text" without being able to read it' (Certeau 1984: 93). Urban walkers pick their way blindly with regard to the whole text/map of the city; map readers in a sense are blind with regard to the everydayness of moving about on the streets, but maps give them considerable literacies about the abstract shape of the space, and relation of road and bridge and building.

Other kinds of perspective are found in many video games, especially those which make use of high-quality graphics to convey the

**Figure 2.6 Screenshot from *The Age of Emperors*, showing the multi-dimensional topography players have to master.**

player through the story and action of the game. *The Age of Emperors* series, for example, manages several types of perspective, and demands sophisticated visual ability of its readers/users. Much of the matter on screen has a simple two-dimensional perspective: it is just iconography or text, printed on the screen as it might have been printed on paper—the player's score in the bottom right corner; the portrait and name of the protagonist at bottom left; the 'life' and energy icons at the top; the simple story of the game, or sometimes instructions on the rules of the game, crawling along the very bottom of the screen. Off to centre right is a simple map of the fantasy world, showing where the protagonist is in relation to topographical features—another two-dimensional rendering of space, representing the folds, dimensions and curves of the world on a flat screen, as a flat object. This two-dimensional perspective lays out information which is there not for focused attention, but for quick scanning before and while the player gets on with the real object: playing the game. For this, the graphic resorts to three-dimensional effect, because the point of it is to secure the player's attention, and draw the player into the world of the game—a world that satisfies the demands of reality effect. It does this by unfolding the action of the game across the whole screen (overlapped in places by the basic two-dimensional information) as a movie-like image, with characters running, leaping and fighting in a picture plane that makes use of linear perspective to render depth and space. At heightened moments, the perspective is distorted for dramatic effect: a sword sweeping through the air trails its shadow behind it, more like a still cartoon than a moving image—a technique that attributes great power to the swordsman, because it appears that the very air has been shattered by the stroke. The spatial dimensions of the game/story world are heightened by the use of atmospheric perspective—the further away objects or people should be, the fuzzier their focus becomes. At times the game graphics makes use of forced perspective—a moment of great rage, or powerful gesture or great speed on the part of a character is rendered by bending the objects about them, and distorting their 'real' spatial relation to the character form; all attention is centred on the character, and the viewer feels physically hauled into the scene. These various uses of perspective are combined to provide the whole world of the game: an all-involving experience that means the player can become entirely absorbed by the act first of seeing/watching and, allied with that, of causing the objects in the field of vision to move in predictable ways.

## new technologies of seeing

Added to the questions of perception that stem from the multiplicity of perspective and attitude, the uncertainty about neurological processing of the visual field, and the impact of our habitus on what and how we see are the effects of the many mechanical aids to vision that have been developed over the centuries. Arguably, it was the invention of technological viewing devices that put the lid on the notion that what we see is what is really there. Martin Jay cites the film critic, Jean-Louis Comolli, in this regard:

> At the very same time that it is thus fascinated and gratified by the multiplicity of scopic instruments which lay a thousand views beneath its gaze, the human eye loses its immemorial privilege; the mechanical eye of the photographic machine now sees in its place, and in certain aspects with more sureness. The photograph stands as at once the triumph and the grave of the eye . . . Decentered, in panic, thrown into confusion by all this new magic of the visible, the human eye finds itself affected with a series of limits and doubts. (Jay 1995: 350)

Technology is defined variously, of course. We understand it to be a range of objects (tools, and other instruments and devices) and we understand it as a sort of knowledge—'know-how' and skill. Technology can also be understood as an organising principle and a process—the way in which a society constitutes itself and its formations, and then brings people and machines together to produce goods and services. The current era is marked by an incredible range of visual technologies, using all the senses of the term presented above. It includes the older forms of film, video and television; the newer ones of computers, the internet and virtual reality; and the 'scientific' mechanisms of microscope, telescope and digital imaging.

But technology is not a twentieth-century phenomenon. Optical technologies dating from the Renaissance and earlier laid the ground for contemporary visual technologies which allow us not only to see better, further and closer, but also to store images and hence retrieve visual memories. Many of the technologies developed centuries ago are still in use now. The perspective window, for example, is literally a window—a pane of glass—through which the artist can observe the subject, and on which the image in the picture field can be traced. This instrument, written about by Leonardo da Vinci in the fifteenth century, still has applications: some contemporary computer drawing programs use the same principle, showing objects in a scene from the virtual camera's point of view and ensuring that those objects closest to the viewer are largest, and that the vanishing point is always in the centre of the picture field. Another very ancient device still in use today (in a developed form) is the camera obscura (literally, 'dark room'). Effectively, it involved allowing a pinhole of light to enter a darkened space and reflect on the opposite wall, where the image reflected will be upside-down. This instrument was described by the fifth-century BCE Chinese philosopher Mo-Ti and the fourth-century BCE Greek philosopher Aristotle, and later described by Leonardo da Vinci, though it wasn't developed into a portable device until the seventeenth century, when it was widely used by artists as a drawing tool. With a few amendments—notably the addition of light-sensitive paper on the reflective wall—the camera obscura became the photographic camera still used today.

Just as technology is not new, it is not something divorced from people, or just a tool to be picked up and discarded at will. Technology is irreducibly social, because people and technological objects together produce our everyday life world. Sigmund Freud insisted that technology is an extension of human being, making us 'prosthetic gods'—a notion taken up by the nineteenth-century philosopher of technology, Ernst Kapp, who saw the new communication technologies (railways, telegraphs) as externalising, or extending, the human body's circulatory and nervous systems (Ebersole 1995).

It is important, though, to avoid notions of technological determinism: as Žižek writes, the effect of technology on our lives 'does not depend directly on technology, it results from the way the impact of new technology is refracted by the social relations' (Žižek 1996: 198). Like all the things we do that are social, cultural and economic, cultural politics and dominant ways of organising the world will shape our possibilities. Still, artists have long picked up on the possibilities offered by technology to do what they do: produce images. Even as early as the Renaissance, people like Leonardo da Vinci moved freely between explorations of technology and art (Rybczynski 1983: 12).

An example of this interface between the human and the machine, and of art's ability to overlap the two, is shown in Figure 2.7. Here we see the torso of a man overlaid with what might be neon lighting tubes, or computer components. The human is rendered part of the machine—a cybernetic being. And (in a sort of Freudian joke) a carrot is laid upon the genital region of the man, and labelled 'this is not a carrot'. Here we have an obvious visual gag (when is a carrot not a carrot? When it's a penis) with several intertextual references: Freud's discussion of slips of the tongue and jokes (he uses as an example the joke 'When is a door not a door? When it's ajar'); and Magritte's famous painting 'This is Not a Pipe' (thumbnail at www.uwrf.edu/history/prints/magritte-pipe.html) both in the title and in the construction of the carrot image. What is interesting about this work is that the human disappears, effectively, as human; there is no face, there are no eyes, so there is no way of making a contact or identification. Instead, there is simply the body and its wiring, presented as a kind of sexual object, but rather more as a technological object—a machine that lacks hands, feet and face (and penis) and therefore is operable only through its technological interface.

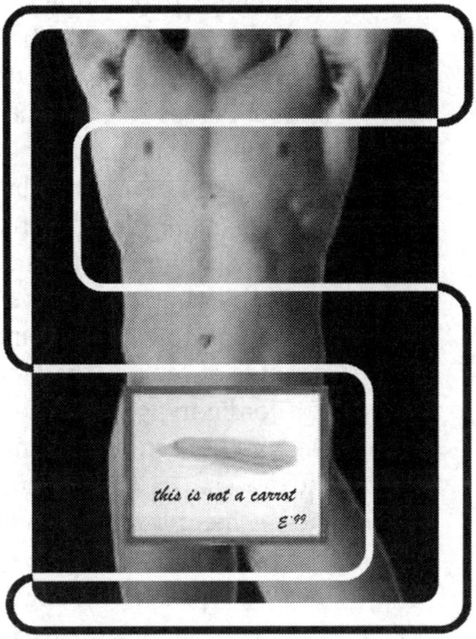

**Figure 2.7 Wear art**

What we can take from this is that technology is not just know-how, or designed devices; it is also a verb, a principle of action. Movies provide perhaps the best—because they are the most familiar—example of this. A movie, Vivian Sobchack insists, 'is an act of seeing that makes itself seen, an act of hearing that makes itself heard, an act of physical and reflective movement that makes itself reflexively felt and understood' (Sobchack 1995: 37). But it doesn't simply act on us; rather, it acts *in* us, interfacing with us in the production of a visual/visceral experience. When we watch a horror film, for instance, our eyes are functioning to perceive the matter on the screen, and our brain is decoding what we see; but at the same time our emotions are brought into play, our heart is racing, our stomach is twisting, our whole self is involved in what is no more than the play of light and sound.

## conclusion

The technologies of vision range from the viewer's neurological system through our embodied dispositions, the effect of the world upon us, the effect of our own habitus, the perspective from which we view an image, the lines, textures and colour of an image to the use of optical instruments which render the world in a particular way. These latter devices—visual technologies which have continued to be developed from the ancient world right through to the twenty-first century—have changed the way we see, and the way we perceive ourselves and/in the world, by providing frames, focus and both monocular and linear perspectives. Now the digital manipulation of images extends the whole argument further, contributing to a growing crisis not just of vision, but of meaning and being. Dinosaurs lumber across screens, moving precisely like living creatures; and in texts like *Tomb Raider*, confections of pixels—v-actors (virtual actors)—are becoming almost indistinguishable from human actors. No visual image can be trusted, because all are potentially able to be digitally enhanced or manipulated.

In this chapter we have ranged across these many technologies of perception to explain something of the physical and cultural determinants of seeing. The fact that we see at all coherently seems quite extraordinary, given the multitude of aspects possible and technologies that inflect our visual field. But we do, for the most part, and for the most part we make sense of—render 'real'—the things we see. The bio-engineer Leif Finkel writes of the perplexities of vision:

> We grope our way, largely in the dark, about our respective caves. The world, to a large extent, is a vision of our own creation. We inhabit a mixed world of sensation and interpretation, and the boundary between them is never openly revealed to us. And amid this tenuous situation, our cortex makes up little stories about the world, and softly hums them to us to keep us from getting scared at night. (Finkel 1992: 404)

The 'groping in the dark' which Finkel writes about has attracted the attention of philosophers, psychologists, medical practitioners and other 'experts' over the last century; they are all fascinated by how it is that we see, and make sense of ourselves and of the world through this mixture of 'sensation and interpretation'. In the next chapter we trace some of the main arguments about visual culture, and how in different periods people have made sense of the processes of sight and perception.

# 3 communication and the visual

## introduction

We have argued that seeing is a kind of reading, one which makes use of particular technologies and various skills in framing, selecting, editing and decoding the visual material that surrounds us. Perhaps no one really needs finely honed skills to function in the ordinary sense as a visual being—indeed, most of the time people get along just by relying on habitual ways of seeing and making sense of what they see. Visual literacy, in contrast, is a very complex practice which demands more than just everyday practices: it requires specific skills in the processes of seeing and reading, the relationship between representation and reality, and the ways in which visual experiences are also moments of communication.

Because of this complexity, the principles and processes of perception have engaged the attention of scholars across the history of Western culture. In this chapter, we trace some of the central ideas of why we decode texts in particular ways, and how the 'truth' effect (or reality effect) of visual experience works to communicate ideas and ideologies within cultures. Underpinning our approach is the argument that if we wish to observe in a more analytical and self-reflexive way—and understand why we see things the way we do—then we need to learn how to defamiliarise the process of seeing. We can do so by developing the literacies that allow us to recognise the extent to which we see through the frames of our cultural location, and by developing skills in analysing how visual culture acts as a medium of communication.

## the 'seeing subject'

Seeing is on the one hand an automatic, physiological function we perform without thinking and, on the other, a complex and absorbing process. Eyes in particular fascinate us. They are the 'windows to the soul'; parents tell their children to 'look me in the eye' as proof that they aren't lying; lovers and flirters use eye contact to seize, hold and caress the object of their desire. And writers, philosophers and social scientists have long wrestled with what it means to be 'seeing subjects': human beings whose feature characteristics are that they access the physical and intellectual world through vision.

Seeing, and making sense of what we see, are thus neither simple nor natural. Indeed, the art historian Bates Lowry notes that our ability to see is similar to our ability to speak: 'We are not born with a knowledge of how to see, any more than we are born with a knowledge of how to speak English. We are born only with the ability to learn how' (1967: 13). W.T.J. Mitchell extends this sense of the complexity of seeing, by drawing a distinction between reading ('decipherment, decoding, interpretation') and spectatorship, or 'just looking' (Mitchell 1994: 16). Provided we have the physiological ability, we can all look; however, our ability to 'read' or 'see' (that is, to interpret) is contingent: what we see is not what we get—rather, it is what our eyes have been socialised to see, and our minds to interpret.

So what we make of what we see is determined by our cultural context, our own habitus, what we know about how meanings are made in our culture and the particular field in which we are 'seeing'. Victor Burgin explains this in writing about the act of looking at a photograph of a set of stones: 'If I go on to remark that the photograph depicts a temple, that the temple is ruined, and that it is Greek, then I am relying upon knowledge that is no longer "natural", "purely visual"; I am relying upon knowledge that is cultural, verbally transmitted and, in the final analysis, ideological' (Burgin 1999: 45). We are not just living creatures who notice what is around us, but subjects—individuals in society—who learn to see in particular ways, and for particular purposes.

The twentieth century produced a number of critics and theorists, from several fields and disciplines, whose work deals extensively with how we see, what we make of what we see and what it means to be a 'seeing subject'. Whether they were concerned with individual identity or with how societies more generally are organised, each turns to an idea about visuality to explain what it means to be human. So, as W.T.J. Mitchell writes:

> mental imagery belongs to psychology and epistemology; optical imagery to physics; graphic, sculptural, and architectural imagery

> to the art historian; verbal imagery to the literary critic; perceptual images occupy a kind of border region where physiologists, neurologists, psychologists, art historians, and students of optics find themselves collaborating with philosophers and literary critics. (Mitchéll 1986: 10–11)

We can, for example, read the works of American psychologist and philosopher William James for examples of how neurological/physiological information makes sense of how people see and what this means about how they understand themselves and their world. Or we can read psychiatrists like Sigmund Freud and psychoanalysts like Jacques Lacan for examples of how, in their disciplines, images are considered central to an individual's personality and behaviour. Freud made much of the deviance he called 'scopophilia', or the desiring gaze we bend upon the world—'I am what I desire; and I desire what I gaze upon' (1905)—while Lacan, who followed and developed Freud's theories, argued that identity emerges at what he calls the 'mirror stage' (Lacan 1977), the point at which a small child can recognise itself as an individual, separate from its mother and from all the other matter of the world.

Other writers have explored visual culture to explain broader issues of society and culture. Anthropologists such as Claude Lévi-Strauss, for example, make sense of the life, values and organisation of traditional cultures by analysing the sorts of clothes they wear, the shape of the dwellings they build, and the colours, lines and textures of their decorative art. Cultural theorists like Stuart Hall take a similar approach in analysing contemporary cultures: they argue that the way in which visual objects are produced and displayed, and what counts as beautiful or as valuable tell us a great deal about what that society's values are, what sort of meanings (or stories) are dominant, and who has power in the community. And theorists of spatiality, such as Henri Lefebvre, analyse visual culture as data that can be used to explain everyday life. The interior design and the scale of a home or public building, for example, give clues to the value of the individuals who occupy those spaces; the design of a map can show how a society understands space and dimensions. During the second half of the twentieth century, writers like Fredric Jameson and Jean Baudrillard analysed visual culture as instances of what is called postmodernism: a set of theories and practices which describe the contemporary world as a kind of MTV clip, a plethora of images whirling in promiscuous uncertainty (or, as Moe from the television cartoon 'The Simpsons' defines it, postmodernism is 'Weird for the sake of weird'). Yet others, like Paul Virilio, have turned their attention to digital communication technologies as providing ways of understanding questions of reality and virtuality. Throughout the literature, it seems, our universe—from the widest sweep of space and history to the most secret inner self—is understood as something we grasp through vision and the metaphors of seeing.

## seeing and sense

But despite this theoretical emphasis on visuality and/as identity, there is considerable anxiety about what it means to access the world visually rather than through literary means. The media routinely run scare stories about declining literacy levels, and lard these with complaints that, though young people might be very competent in dealing with video games, movies, television and graphic novels, they don't read novels, poems and newspapers, and therefore they (and by extension, society) have lost a precious skill. It's not just tabloid editors, educators or frustrated parents who sense that society is becoming increasingly visual; many theorists have weighed into this argument too. Nicholas Mirzoeff, for example, expresses a widely held view when he writes that 'modern life takes place onscreen . . . Human experience is now more visual and visualized than ever before' (Mirzoeff 1999: 1).

Of course, this is not in fact saying very much, because Mirzoeff does not point out precisely what he means by 'visualising' or 'visualised' experience, and how it might be different from the visualising and visual experiences of people in other times and cultures. After all, human beings have always lived in a world that is packed with visual objects and phenomena, and have always looked at and made sense of the things about them. The early cave paintings are testament to the importance, from the beginnings of (textual) human history, of seeing and reflecting on what we see. Mirzoeff does argue, though, that the material we now view is far more complex than the sorts of objects and phenomena that characterised the visual domain of earlier centuries. Common sense and basic observation would suggest that this is a reasonable argument, and a number of writers agree with Mirzoeff. Donald Hoffman, for instance, points to the complexity of material incorporated in an MTV show, any video game or visual reality experiences (Hoffman 1998: xii). Even a television advertisement may include a startling combination of shapes and colours, rapid movements and jumps from scene to scene (and of focus within scenes), morphing and animation, song and story, and all the multiple associations of sound and movement with purely visual phenomena which film and digital technologies enable. Urban landscapes, too, are packed with visual images—building designs, advertising billboards, the many shapes and colours of vehicles, store windows, mailboxes, cashpoints, traffic lights and so on.

## visual saturation

Look at the image presented in Figure 3.1a. It is an ordinary noticeboard located in an ordinary city street. It makes use of no digital technology, has no cunning printing devices, sound or movement, and makes no specialised use of linear perspective. Hence we could say it is a less complex text than, say, a video game. But the multiple shapes, textures and sizes of the papers attached to the board, the complex layering of individual parts, the range of fonts, styles and layout—and of course the various colours not reproduced here—all render it a text that is not easily accessed. The process of reading it is terribly complex too, because it is loaded with distractions. Where do you begin to read this text: at the top left? At the centre? At the 'noisiest' or the largest sheet? And how do you read it sensibly when you are being bombarded by a baffling array of distractions—the sounds and movements of people passing by; cars and buses on the road just

Figure 3.1a

Figure 3.1b

**This suburban notice board and Hong Kong electronic streetscape both demonstrate the visual 'clamour' that assaults us daily.**

behind you; the click of the traffic lights signalling pedestrians to cross the road; the hiss of automatic doors opening and closing; the texture, shape and colour of the wall and pavement that frame the noticeboard. The clamour of colour and sound that interfere with the reading of the simplest visual text, and the range of signs within any text, mean that there seems no end to the variety and complexity of the visual matter before our eyes.

But the number of signs we see (and process) in any given day, the volume of individual signs in a text, the array of colours, the degree of movement and even the degree of distraction involved in its reading do not necessarily constitute the level of its visual complexity. The art historian James Elkins argues that we are in fact less visually complex now than in earlier periods. Genuine complexity, he writes, emerges at the Renaissance (because of the many new visual technologies and systems of perception developed then) and ends at the late nineteenth century. By the beginning of the twentieth century, he suggests, Western principles of thought and perception had moved away from visual to written forms, producing what he calls 'generations of speed-readers who can only read simple [visual] sentences' (Elkins 2002: 97). Certainly digital communication technologies—some video games, MTV, web browsers—encourage a fleeting, flickering glance rather than the concentrated gaze associated with art. And even art receives less and less attention; Jeannette Winterson in *Art Objects* (1995: 8) suggests that her readers try spending an hour looking at a single work in an art gallery and promises great return on this investment, but curators of art museums have told me that the viewing standard is more like fifteen seconds per work. What this suggests is that the apparent complexity of contemporary visual texts is not substantiated by how people use the texts, because the design of texts made and disseminated through digital communication technologies lends them to the easy reading—or 'looking'—of habituation.

## images as signs

The notion that, despite all the intuitive evidence, we are no longer as visually complex as people in earlier periods is developed by the US historian Martin Jay (1993, 1995). His central argument is that we are living in a deeply non-visual period, not because there are now fewer visual texts or because the texts are simpler in design, but because we make sense of the world by using non-visual analytic devices. Jay's point is supported by fairly recent philosophical writings: the nineteenth-century philosopher Friedrich Nietzsche, for example, wrote of his own visual scepticism: 'I do not myself believe that anyone has looked into the world with an equally profound degree of suspicion.' (Nietzsche, 1986: preface). The early twentieth-century philosopher Martin Heidegger, deeply influenced by Nietzsche's work, was likewise sceptical about the extent to which we can rely on visual skills, and famously opposed to the centrality of the seeing subject in Western thought. He argued that aural perception was more reliable than visual (Jay 1993: 268).

Twentieth-century scholarship continued in this strain, because it was marked by what is called the 'linguistic turn'—a move within the Humanities to focus almost exclusively on literary texts, and to use the analytical devices associated with literary texts to make sense of society, visual images, individual psychology and so on. All social practices, in other words, were understood as meaning-making practices, or semiotic events (Evans and Hall 1999: 2). Under this analytical principle, visual texts are considered to communicate according to linguistic rather than iconographical rules, and scholars who subscribe to this view argue that we can approach them just as we might approach a novel or other written text.

Semiotics is certainly an effective tool for analysis because, as we indicated in the introduction, it deals with signs—anything which stands for something—and, in general, even obscure visual images can easily be imbued with some meaning. Look at the image in Figure 3.2,

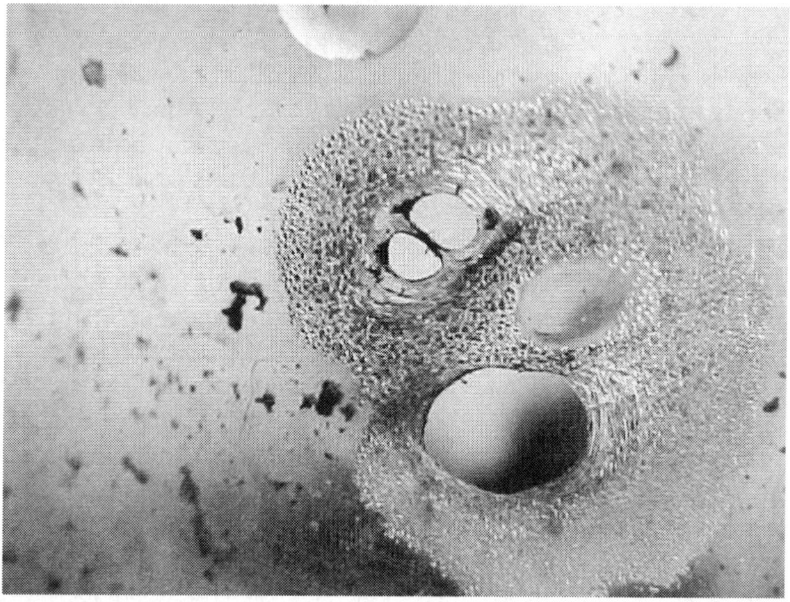

**Figure 3.2 Landscape**

for instance. A rough survey (of friends and colleagues) brought up a range of interpretations: it was a photo of rotten eggs, and hence communicated the idea of decay; it was a planetary image, and hence conveyed the idea of unthinkable vastness; it was of the bubbling volcanic mud pools at Rotorua, New Zealand, and hence a representation of the exotic; or it was a piece of abstract art, and hence was all about the inarticulable. Although they couldn't be certain what it actually represented, everyone was confident that it meant something—that it was a sign, and not just patterns on the page.

## images and meaning

The semiotic principle of analysing signs is attractive because it makes good sense in terms of how people approach texts, and it has been thoroughly tested over a considerable period of time. Though it is usually associated with the French linguist Ferdinand de Saussure and his *Course in General Linguistics* (1907), the idea of language as a series of signs is found as early as Aristotle, who defined the human voice as *semantikos psophos*, 'significant sound', or sounds that make meanings (cited in Agamben 1993: 125).

But semiotics is about more than just meaning. Its basic principle is that language is not simply a naming device, but rather a differentiated symbolic system. Each word (or sign) applied to an object or idea can be understood and identified because it is distinguishable from every other word (or sign) that might have been used (Mitchell 1986: 67–8). It would be unthinkable to exist in a world where a hammer could also, and simultaneously, be called a toothbrush. And because of familiarity, the thing we call 'hammer' comes to take on what appears to be a quality of 'hammerness', and may be treated as though there is something inevitable about its identity and its name—something that seems to be entirely natural.

However, this principle of difference, and hence the technique of (linguistic) semiotics, can't easily be applied directly to visual culture. Look at the photograph of Trafalgar Square in London in Figure 3.3 to make sense of this. The signs in this photograph don't take on meanings because of difference, in the strict (semiotic) sense. We don't identify the images of buildings as buildings because they are not people or pigeons; rather, we identify them as buildings in relation to the people and pigeons. We see the buildings, the people, the pigeons and even the paving as a totality that makes up the image of an urban space, and thus the whole works together to construct the image we see. We can say, then, that visual signs work analogically, producing a story that we identify not in terms of difference—the digital on–off/same–difference of the linguistic model—but through the combination of internal elements, and because of intertextual literacies that confirm for us, on the basis of experience, what they mean.

The linguistic model also fails as a technique for reading the visual because, as Roland Barthes points out (1977), images both do and don't have a relationship to linguistic texts; imagery may be a language, but it doesn't work like linguistic language, or possess the sense of grammatical organisation and structure (in terms of verbs, subjects, connectors and so on) that we expect from words. Images don't have a tense—for instance, if we look again at the photograph of Trafalgar Square in Figure 3.3 we might say 'that's Trafalgar Square', or we might—with equal confidence—say 'that was the Square in 2000'. Past and present coexist in a still image. As James Elkins argues, pictures (visual images) are not like language because they are not made of semiotic marks, or signs that relate to each other on the basis of a structured relation of difference. And so, he writes: 'Pictures are difficult objects: they resist interpretation because they resist words' (Elkins n.d.).

Figure 3.3 Trafalgar Square

## the pictorial turn

So, despite the apparent convenience of the semiotic/linguistic approach for the analysis of visual texts, most theorists—even those who read visual texts in terms of semiotic principles—consider that they are substantially different from linguistic texts. How, then, can we make sense of images as communication? We could take up what is called the 'pictorial turn'. The logic here is the need to understand pictures as things in themselves rather than simply matter that must be reduced to words. British cultural theorist Stuart Hall describes this approach as meaning 'realized in use. Their realization requires, at the other end of the meaning chain, the cultural practices of looking and interpretation, the subjective capacities of the viewer to make images signify' (Hall 1999: 310).

This sounds very much like the linguistic approach—that their meanings are realised because they are translated into language—but Hall's point is that the image works not just discursively, or linguistically, but at the level of the subconscious; it is as concerned with feelings as with sentences and stories, and involves our whole being, not just our abstract intellectual identity. In the previous chapter we described the physiology of seeing, and this is involved here, because seeing/reading the visual is, as the phenomenologist Maurice Merleau-Ponty writes, a very physical activity (Merleau-Ponty 1962: 407). Even at the most basic level of understanding, we usually have to move our bodies to see a visual text: we walk around a sculpture or through a park; we move closer to and then further away from a painting or building. So visual culture incorporates texts, the reading of which involves the body and the emotions, and which therefore are a sensate rather than a purely intellectual means of communication.

The pictorial turn is, obviously, an analytical approach that is semiotic at some levels: it involves identifying signs, and analysing how they come together to make up a text within its contexts. But it is not simply semiotic analysis in Saussure's sense of it being a 'science of signs' because this approach to visual culture demands that the analyst take into account considerably more than the arrangement of signs. Using this approach means accounting for cultural and personal acts of looking and interpreting, with all the subjective, emotional and even unconscious responses each of us brings to this work. Analysing visual culture under this perspective is thus not simply an intellectual or abstract task, but one that involves the physical aspects of the material world, and the material being of the analyst: 'seeing as being'.

This approach to the work of the analyst isn't confined to those of us who analyse visual texts; the logic of the pictorial turn is central to any number of highly intellectual and scientific pursuits. Michael Polanyi writes that research scientists are able to practise their 'art' because their whole body—using 'the trained delicacy of eye, ear and touch'—is put to work to test scientific knowledge against observed events (Polanyi and Prosch 1975: 31). Doctors and scientists rely on their eyes (and ears, and senses of smell and touch) at least as much as on conscious reason. So visual culture, as Mirzoeff writes, 'is not simply the medium of communication and mass culture. It offers a sensual immediacy that cannot be rivaled by print media: the very element that makes visual imagery of all kinds distinct from texts' (1998: 9).

## communicating and cultural fields

Whether we remain committed to the linguistic turn, or take up the analytical attitude associated with the pictorial turn, we are acknowledging that visual texts are not just wallpaper, but are always the stuff of communication. However, they do not communicate objectively or in a vacuum, and any instance of visual (or linguistic) communication is invested in what Pierre Bourdieu calls the 'cultural field' in which the communication is made, and in which it is analysed. To consider the aspect of cultural field, we must take into account the socio-cultural status of the fields, groups and individuals producing visual texts, and the ways in which different fields, different individuals within fields and different ways of negotiating the fields affect the degree to which the meanings made are seen to be authoritative, or 'true'. Mark Poster develops this issue, arguing that we do not see simply 'what is there', but that what he terms 'different visual regimes' (Poster 2002: 68)—or different economies of looking and seeing—obtain at different historical moments and in different contexts.

Let's consider this by looking at the reproduction of a drawing titled 'The Straight Parts of Your Body' (see Figure 3.4). If we circulated this text across various fields and contexts, the response we would most likely receive was that it is 'sweet' or 'quaint'—in other words, that it is naïve, childish and not in any way representative of the real world. The reasons for this are obvious. Firstly, it looks like a child's drawing, and children are usually understood, within Western culture, as having at best a tenuous relation to reality. Children aren't educated, and lack access to the kinds of knowledge (say, science or art) normally understood to have a special status when it comes to accessing or reproducing the real. This is mirrored in the terms used by the child-artist to categorise the various parts of the drawing: 'straight parts', 'finger', 'toe'. They belong to an everyday discourse, rather than a scientific or an aesthetic one. Secondly, the

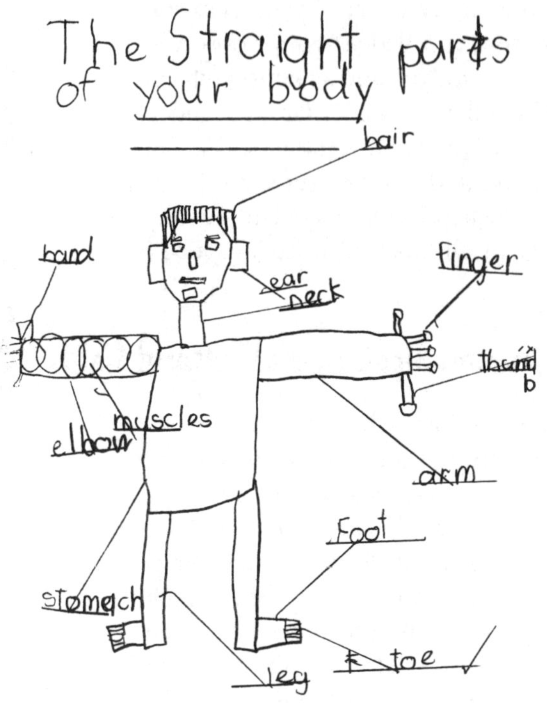


**Figure 3.4 The Straight Parts of Your Body**

very irregular drafting—the use of circles to represent muscles; the size of the thumbs in relation to the hand—disqualifies it as emanating from the field of science because it doesn't truthfully represent either a human body or its 'straight parts'.

The binary adult/child is one of many distinctions that help to determine whether visual texts have any authority to represent reality (adults' may, children's don't). But, as we pointed out above, the extent to which texts can communicate the 'real world' is partly determined by the field from which they—or the people evaluating them—emerge. If we asked a group of children in a preschool about the drawing, for instance, they might accept it as realistic. And there are fields where scientific representations are given the status normally reserved—outside the playground, at least—for a child's drawing. We were once involved in a project with academic staff from a university engineering faculty. Staff from the communication studies department explained the project and the rationale behind it a number of times without getting their message across to the Professor of Engineering, who didn't seem capable of grasping what to us were straightforward concepts. Eventually the professor picked up a whiteboard marker and started drawing diagrams, while being corrected and advised by the communication staff. He drew a series of circles, each with a label, with lines and arrows indicating the relation between each component. In short, he produced a predominantly visual description to sum up, for himself, what the project was about, and what was required to be done, by whom, when and where. The professor explained that he and his staff nearly always drew up these kinds of diagrams whenever they needed to explain, understand or communicate anything of a complex nature. Later some of the communication staff characterised what had happened as an example of how engineers 'can't think', but what it actually evinced was the status of the visual within different fields—or what Mark Poster calls 'different visual regimes'. Within engineering, communicating by means of the visual is perfectly legitimate, while the communication staff saw it as childish, or socially incompetent.

## visuality and reality

The visual regime that is relevant at a particular moment will determine the extent to which something will make meanings, and the extent to which those meanings will be taken seriously in society. But the actual truth value of the meanings is never fully reliable. The general visual regime which has dominated in the twentieth and early twenty-first centuries has been one marked by technological sophistication, which means that images may well be less 'truthful' or reliable than in earlier periods (regimes) because they can now be altered quite seamlessly, and visual hoaxes are easily perpetrated.

A very famous hoax is the case of the Cottlingley 'fairies', where two children produced (trick) photographs of fairies, and apparently fooled many adults who we might think should have known better. This story sparked a number of novels and films, including two movies produced in 1997: Charles Sturridge's *Fairy Tale: A True Story* and Nick Willing's *Photographing Fairies* (also titled *Apparition*). This hoax took place nearly a century ago, when viewers were perhaps less alert to trick photography, but even now, when our

**Figures 3.5a and 3.5b To a twenty-first-century viewer these Cottingley fairy photographs from 1917 are clumsily manipulated, but they fooled viewers as astute as Sir Arthur Conan Doyle, creator of Sherlock Holmes.**

culture is so thoroughly saturated with digitally altered images, we seem no more critical or sceptical about visual texts. The airbrushed photographs of celebrities which keep them young, slender and beautiful across the decades; the magic of digital remastering which means dead movie stars like Humphrey Bogart can appear in contemporary advertisements; the hologram of an apple in the Vancouver Science Museum; the transformation of a pool of metal into a muscled man in the film *Terminator 2*: all these are familiar images, and we know something of the technology that produces them. Yet we will still duck as an arrow flies out of a 3-D screen towards us, or gasp at the sight of an alien space ship hanging over a cityscape. They are obvious illusions yet, despite the many evidences of visual hoaxes, tricks and misrepresentations, and despite the fact that we know what we see is not necessarily what we get, we still tend to believe what we see.

This belief is based in part on common sense and familiarity. If we look again at the photograph of Trafalgar Square in Figure 3.3, for example, we can be reassured that we know what is going on, that the camera has reproduced only 'what was there'. The familiarity of the scene, and the everyday quality of the actions and objects and persons represented there, confirm the authority of the eye to see what is really there, and thus confirm our sense of the order of the world. But we don't have to resort to visual hoaxes to undermine this confidence—almost any 'art' photograph is likely to do so, and to call into question this certainty about what the world looks like. The photograph 'Landscape' reproduced in Figure 3.2 does precisely this. Here, as is the case with the Trafalgar Square photograph, the lens has seen something and reproduced it faithfully; however, because a technological device sees in a different way from the human eye, what it reproduces doesn't necessarily make sense. This is in fact a very close-up photograph of the bowl of a hookah (a water-cooled smoking pipe), but the everyday eye cannot easily get this close to the object, or frame it in such a way. Because of this, it looks unfamiliar to us, and less like a household object than like a watery scene—a murky pond, perhaps, or a bubbling mud pool. The shape of the whole object, the framing of its surroundings and the context of other signs in which it is found and 'read' are missing in this perspective and cannot be recalled. What this suggests is that the eye in fact has little authority, and familiar ways of seeing cannot be relied upon to deliver up to us the truth of what we see, or the likeness of what we see to an established reality.

Of course, not every visual image is designed—or even expected—to be involved with the retrieval of the real, and what is meant by reality changes across time, culture and contexts. Religious institutions and fields, for instance, usually insist upon the transcendental nature of reality—the everyday phenomenal world is considered either a stage on a journey to a more profound reality (say, heaven) or simply an illusion, a kind of false consciousness that has to be overcome in order to achieve enlightenment. Science, on the other hand, tends to understand what is real as that which can be observed, demonstrated and proven, while the media use terms like 'reality' in a rather nebulous manner, equating reality with what is happening in the 'real world', with what 'everyone thinks' or with the 'voice of the people'.

When it comes to visual culture, the term 'reality' is usually a shorthand way of saying that some representation is 'true to life'. What is meant by 'true to life' itself depends itself on culture and context; it might be possible to argue that both fourteenth-century BCE Egyptian art and paintings by Dutch artist Johannes Vermeer (see www.cacr.caltech.edu/rroy/vermeer/thumb.html) or American artist Norman Rockwell (see www.artcyclopedia.com/artists/rockwell_norman.html) are 'realistic', but the works hardly resemble one another. They do, though, resemble something, and in this we can identify an idea about reality and visual culture that has been central to theories of visuality and culture across Western history. Its basis is the ancient Greek notion of *mimesis*, or the imitation (the reproduction) of reality, which in effect posits that the objects we see are only imitations of an ideal form. This does not mean that the objects we see are just dreams, or reflections of the perfection found in the transcendent world. Everyday objects do, of course, have material integrity, but their role is to recall to us the ethical ideal of which they are the mimesis (or imitation), and to relay that ideal into the everyday world. In the twentieth-century example of the 'fairy photographs' hoax, the point was to trick people into seeing something that wasn't there, but under the principle of mimesis the point is not to trick the eye into thinking it sees reality, but to persuade viewers that there are ideals to which we can aspire (Melville and Readings 1995: 8). A beautifully crafted bowl, for instance, might remind us of the ideals of balance and harmony, and persuade us that this is a good—or the best—way to be.

Western visual culture comes out of this ancient Greek tradition, with its emphasis on Form, and also out of the Christian tradition with its emphasis on the centrality of faith: 'the evidence of things not

**Figure 3.6 Detail from 'The Garden of Earthy Delights' (*c.* 1504), one of Hieronymus Bosch's most visually challenging religious allegories.**

seen'. Consequently, it is concerned to reflect (somewhat) faithfully the world as being made up of signs of a greater truth—the heavenly realm. This was especially evident in visual works and in visual interpretation during the medieval and Renaissance periods because, in each period, visual culture—both natural and of human production—was considered to be there to reflect, or tell, something about God. The historian Johan Huizinga wrote: 'The Middle Ages never forgot that all things would be absurd . . . if by their essence they did not reach into a world beyond them' (cited in Eco 1986a: 52), and Michel Foucault refers to the Renaissance as the 'age of resemblances' because everything was assumed to resemble (to echo or imitate) something else.

What this picks up on is the mimetic idea that objects point to a transcendent world. In the Christian era, the important issue was how to decipher visual objects—and the everyday world—in terms of God's code. Everything was there not just to be looked at, not just for its beauty or pleasure, and not just for its utility or everyday function, but as a reflection of some aspect of God and God's story—in fact, as semiotician Umberto Eco writes: 'The Medievals inhabited a world filled with references, reminders and overtones of Divinity, manifestations of God in things' (Eco 1986a: 53). White was not just a tone, but a symbol of light and goodness, as black was a symbol of evil. Unicorns, pelicans, lambs, fish, doves, rams and a number of other things had not only their literal meaning, but also symbolised Christ in the right context. Everything one could look at had its obvious meaning and function (a candle is a means of illumination) but also had its allegorical meaning and function (a burning candle could symbolise eternity or divine salvation; a guttering candle could remind us of the transitory nature of life).

## reading the real

The medievals were not alone in their tendency to read visual objects as having meanings, or seeing in them something more than their obvious or functional identity. Aristotle had prefigured something of this, writing in his *Poetics* (350 BCE) that:

> the reason why men enjoy seeing a likeness is, that in contemplating it they find themselves learning or inferring, and saying perhaps, 'Ah, that is he.' For if you happen not to have seen the original, the pleasure will be due not to the imitation as such, but to the execution, the coloring, or some such other cause.

Let's put these ideas to work now by 'reading' the photograph shown in Figure 3.7. This is a very familiar image in our culture and provides many examples of what Aristotle called 'learning', 'inferring' and

**Figure 3.7 Wedding group**

'identifying'; it also has a kind of mimetic role, reflecting something of an ideal, and it can be read as a kind of allegory.

How can we bring these ideas together? Firstly, a wedding photograph is a point of enjoyment, as Aristotle would term it, because it provides pleasure for those involved and their friends and relations: the pleasure of 'Ah, that is he (or she)' because it memorialises the couple and the day. For us, who 'happen not to have seen the original' (since this is a photograph found in a second-hand shop), it also offers a pleasure: observing the clothes, the bodily arrangement within the party, the looks on their faces—even the pleasure of guessing who is related to whom and in what context. It therefore produces a satisfying story.

It is certainly a realist image, because it represents an actual historical moment and (we assume, based on what we know of the genre) the people reflected in it would easily be recognised by those who know them—it actually looks like the original that is the couple, their family and the moment of their wedding. But it is also unreal, or hyperreal, because even highly realistic works—mimetic works—are still not the thing itself, but only resemble the thing. Besides, few people look in everyday life as they do in their wedding photograph; the image is an ideal representation of them at their best and most polished. The combination of real and not-real shows how the photograph works mimetically, or rhetorically, by drawing attention away from the actual humdrum, everyday identity of the people shown there, and instead reflecting an ideal—marriage, fidelity and love.

Aristotle insisted that the pleasure of realist works is in 'learning', 'inferring' and 'identifying', and we can interpret the work, following Erwin Panofsky's model, by deciphering it across three interpretative strata: its material structure; the factual meanings of the text and its signs; and specifics of its context. In the case of this wedding photograph, the first stratum is easily deciphered: we can perceive an arrangement of lines and light in differently shaded and shaped blocks, and in particular configurations and spatial orientations. The second stratum is simply a reading of the conventional subject matter, in terms of recognising the pure forms as particular objects with a social meaning (Panofsky 1955: 54). In this instance, we can identify the bride and her bridesmaids, the groom and his groomsmen, the drapes, the carpet and so on. We can also read the motifs—flowers, lace, bodily postures—and identify in them something of the genres and narratives they convey. This is also a relatively simple process of deciphering, because it doesn't require any literacies beyond everyday knowledge. We can easily define the blobs and lines as people, furniture and flowers because we are familiar with people, furniture and flowers; and we can define the motifs and gestures because weddings and wedding photographs are very familiar genres in Western culture and convey a very familiar story—being in love, making a commitment, gathering with friends and family, wearing your best clothes, and so on.

The first two strata, then, are interpreted through the things we already know. Neither requires any literacy beyond the everyday knowledge that comes from the viewer's own history (habitus). But this does not complete the interpretation of a visual image, either from Aristotle's point of view (that we must learn), from the allegorical Christian view (that we must decipher the divine code in all things), or from a contemporary cultural perspective which insists that what we see is not necessarily what we get, and therefore we need to analyse, and not just identify, what we see. Panofsky writes: 'To understand this . . . I must not only be familiar with the practical world of objects and events, but also with the more-than-practical world of customs and cultural traditions peculiar to a certain civilization' (1955: 52). He goes on to explain it more particularly as an interpretative attitude determined 'by ascertaining those underlying principles which reveal the basic attitude of a nation, a period, a class, a religious or philosophical persuasion—qualified by one personality and condensed into one work' (Panofsky 1955: 55). The nineteenth-century French poet Baudelaire had already articulated this, in writing about the mimetic function of fashion plates from the 1790s:

> What I am glad to find in all or nearly all of them, is the moral attitude and the aesthetic value of the time. The idea of beauty that man creates for himself affects his whole attire, ruffles or stiffens his coat, gives curves or straight lines to his gestures and even, in process of time, visibly penetrates the very features of his face. Man comes in the end to look like his ideal image of himself. (1972: 391)

But unless Baudelaire had a knowledge of the ethos and aesthetics of the 1790s, he could have read these fashion plates only as a quaint reference from the past.

To apply this notion to our wedding photograph, we might, for instance, identify the apparent age gap between bride and groom, the formality of the arrangement of the whole party, and what appears to be the discomfort expressed by the groomsmen. Then we could analyse this further in terms of its socio-historical location (mid-twentieth century) and make some statement about the gender politics that obtained then (women might be lovely but remained in many ways the possessions of their husbands) or the class politics (marked by the apparent discomfort of the young men, particularly compared with other images we might know of contemporary young professional men). In this way, we can move from an interpretation based on familiarity with forms, genres and narratives to the application of literacies which allow us to understand and critique the reality of what we are shown, and what it is communicating.

## the reality function

Photographs and other communication technologies may give us very recognisable images but, as we have argued, they are no more reliable at retrieving reality than any other medium. Besides, what we count as real or realist depends on the context in which we are looking, and what we expect from it. The British cartoonist Norman Thelwell, for instance, is famous for his many drawings of ponies: no one could ever see a pony that looked like one of Thelwell's drawings, but at the same time his drawings are immediately and delightfully recognisable as ponies. They have a particular 'reality function', or 'truth-to-reality', that is based on the field (cartooning), the context (entertaining drawings), the narratives (children and their ponies) and the ideological framework (the endless competition of social life).

So truth-to-reality, transparent communication, tradition or utility are not the only ways to understand visual representation. For well over a century now, many practitioners have deliberately rejected the idea that they are producing mimetic works, or realistic images of the world out there. Think of advertisers with their jingles, dancing chickens and whiter-than-white laundry; think of school children learning to manipulate photographs so they no longer represent their image; think too of film-makers, and their rejection of the early twentieth-century conventions of plot and narrative. A movie like *Three Kings*, for instance, unabashedly shows the impossible in the form of the 'bullet cam' shot where, when George Clooney, who plays Special Forces Captain Archie Gates, is explaining to his subordinates why one should endeavour not to be shot, the camera follows an imaginary bullet through the air and into the abdomen of one of his fellow soldiers, and then back out again. Like Impressionist paintings which weren't so much concerned with the thing represented as with the form of representation—how light was rendered, how to explore feelings in paint—or Cubist works, which attempted to show all dimensions of an object at one moment, contemporary forms of visual representation take issue with the notion that there is just one right way of seeing and being.

Many, in fact, have gone even further away from resemblance, and from ways of alluding to the 'real' world. Think of the abstraction of American minimalism in the middle of the twentieth century when a work might be only white paint on a white canvas—Robert Rauschenberg's 'White Painting' series (1951), for instance—and in fact constitute a refusal to represent the world at all. From a different approach, but with a similar attitude, much contemporary art is almost purely self-referential (referring only to the art world). One example is the work of installation artist Ben Vautier who produced a work titled 'J'ai pas peur de Marcel' ('I'm not afraid of Marcel', 1994–96). It is a large knife grinder, exhibited with the title and a panel incorporating a quote from Marcel Duchamp. The work has virtually no 'artistic' signs apart from the fact that it is produced by a known artist, is exhibited in a recognised art museum, and of course refers to Marcel Duchamp's famous installation of a urinal, 'Fountain' (1917). Whether artists are refusing to represent reality—as in the case of abstract minimalism—or representing something that is reality only to a tiny audience—as with Vautier's work—what we have is, like Rene Magritte's famous 'This is Not a Pipe' (www.uwrf.edu/history/prints/magritte-pipe.html), artists refusing to affirm or communicate anything at all.

Given this context, and the fact that we can't rely on the evidence or the authority of our eyes to tell us the truth of what we are seeing, it can be argued that what reality means in visual culture is simply a means of communication ('it's real, or like reality, because it's telling us something true'). Whether a visual image really looks like the original or not, it has a sort of ritual function in telling its viewers something about itself, and about society in relation to itself. Look, for example, at the photograph in Figure 3.8a, an arrangement of kiln goddesses modelled on the very famous statue of the Venus of Willendorf (Figure 3.8b), believed to be 25,000 years old.

That Venus, with her vast breasts and belly, and her heavy thighs, does not in any respect call up contemporary ideals of female beauty. The statue does, however represent the notion of fertility, and for contemporary audiences it also summons up the powerful ideas of magic and religion. In the arrangement shown here, the potter is not simply reiterating the ideas communicated by the ancient craftspeople. (After all, we can't know for certain what they were communicating in their work—the past, as novelist L.P. Hartley pointed out, is a foreign country: 'they do things differently there'.) But,

Figure 3.8a Kiln goddesses

3.8b The Venus of Willendorf

because she is making such a deliberate reference to the early forms, it is worth paying attention to what is being communicated. At the basic level, we could argue, she is simply following a common practice in her field: potters often make small objects out of scraps of clay to tuck in with a firing. But many women potters, especially in the 1970s and 1980s, deliberately made them in the form of those ancient goddesses, in response firstly to their own culture (reflecting second-wave feminism and a particular perspective on women's power) and then to an idea of history, or a matriarchal prehistory. As copies of an ancient visual text, the kiln goddesses privilege fecundity and matriarchy; as late twentieth-century texts, they interrogate contemporary ideals of female beauty and the body fascism of fashion; and as objects associated with the craft of pottery, they respond to internal craft traditions, and remind practitioners of the ancient magic of the kiln.

The potter in this example is communicating something that is quite easily interpreted, because we have shared understandings of the culture and context in which she was making the objects. But even in cultures where no written records have been left to explain the significance of particular cultural forms, we can make educated guesses about what is being communicated. Most art historians seem to agree with John Berger that 'Images were first made to conjure up the appearances of something that was absent' (1972: 10), which suggests that a claim is being made to an idea of truth-to-reality as a communicative gesture. Certainly we can recognise the shapes of animals, the hunt, people, spirits and gods in visual works from prehistory, and whether these were made as forms of art (as we now understand the term) or record-keeping or religious acts, they do present an image of something not present. And whatever they might or might not indicate about what those hunter–gatherer communities understood by reality, we can see them as functional works, produced to communicate something of an event, a tradition or a belief system.

Something similar can be identified in the works of contemporary Australian Aboriginal artists who frequently—particularly in the case of rural/tribal mark-makers—produce their works not just, and not even primarily, as aesthetic objects, but for communication and record-keeping, for traditional functions and to maintain their relationship with their 'country' (land). The storyboards and bark paintings of the Papunya or Yirrkala practitioners, for instance, describe cultural practices such as clan groupings, and they both map and explain the relation of the people to the land. The artist Galarrwuy Yunupingu writes:

> When we paint—whether it is on our bodies for ceremony or on bark or canvas for the market—we are not just painting for fun or profit. We are painting, as we have always done, to demonstrate our continuing link with our country and the rights and responsibilities we have to it. We paint to show the rest of the world that we own this country and that the land owns us. Our painting is a political act. (Yunupingu 1997: 65)

No universal statements can be made about any mark-making because it is always socially, culturally and historically contingent. But the way in which various visual texts depict the thing 'not present' does tell us something about the cultural values, ideals of beauty and order, and sense of reality pertinent to that culture.

## conclusion

In this chapter we have outlined the relationship, in visual culture, between representations of reality and means of communication. But, as Stuart Hall writes:

> The symbolic power of the image to signify is in no sense restricted to the conscious level and cannot always easily be expressed in words. In fact, this may be one of the ways in which the so-called power of the image differs from that of the linguistic sign. What is often said about the 'power of the image' is indeed that its impact is immediate and powerful even when its precise meaning remains, as it were, vague, suspended—numinous. (Hall 1999: 311)

In the next chapter we will take up the question of how visual narratives may be structured, and discuss the ways in which stories can be told in this 'suspended' and 'numinous' medium, and the extent to which this medium may communicate more than unconscious or subconscious impressions.

# 4 visual narratives

## introduction

A picture, so popular culture tells us, paints a thousand words, and this is the issue we deal with in this chapter: the degree to which pictures—visual culture—can communicate or present not just forms, but stories too. We have written in earlier chapters about 'reading' visual texts, and this expression alludes to the notion that pictures, images and visual objects more generally are not just to be looked at, but contain a story, or a body of information, which we can access as we might access the content of a written text. A number of schools of visual art are identified as producers of narratives (church paintings, Pre-Raphaelites, social realism), indicating the possibility of a single image containing a story, but there is very little in the literature to indicate what is meant by 'narrative picture', or how such an object relates to what we know of narrative more generally. To explore this concept, we turn in this chapter to the question of what constitutes narrative, what its various elements are and how these elements work together. And we look at the effect that socially valued ways of organising and disseminating material have on the meaning of a visual text.

Perhaps the best way of tackling this matter is through the observation Michel de Certeau makes about the relation between stories and the everyday world:

> In modern Athens, the vehicles of mass transportation are called metaphorai. To go to work or come home, one takes a 'metaphor'—a bus or a train. Stories could also take this noble name: every day, they traverse and organize places; they select and link them together; they make sentences and itineraries out of them. They are spatial trajectories slightly . . . Narrative

structures have the status of spatial syntaxes. By means of a whole panoply of codes, ordered ways of proceeding and constraints, they regulate changes in space (or moves from one place to another) made by stories in the form of places put in linear or interlaced series . . . Every story is a travel story—a spatial practice. (Certeau 1984: 115–16)

This way of understanding the relationship between narratives and spaces applies to the visual world and its texts because, while most theorists agree that visual texts rarely provide a clear narrative, they certainly work as 'metaphorai'—providing vehicles that enable viewers to 'go somewhere else', or to craft a story. Where viewers take such a story is not entirely free, though: just as buses and trains move along particular routes, so too our reading of any visual text is limited by what is in the text, by the context in which we come across it, and by what we expect to find there based on our understanding of what kind of text it is and what kinds of stories are associated with it. In Chapter 1 we discussed these issues in terms of intertexts and genres, and we will develop these here with particular reference to how we read the narratives of visual texts.

## what is a narrative?

First, let's turn to the question of narrative which, at its simplest, means 'story'. But of course it is more complex than this: the word comes from the Latin *narrare*, 'to relate', so it denotes both what is told and the process of the telling (Toolan 1988: 1). A whole discipline exists to describe and analyse narrative, its practices, its various elements and how they come together to produce a coherent story. Narratology, or the study of narrative, begins with the ancients, and with works such as Aristotle's *Poetics*. More recently, it has been associated with structuralists like Gerard Genette and Roland Barthes' early writings, Marxists like Bertold Brecht and Georg Lukács and poststructuralists like the later Barthes or Terry Eagleton, among others. Each 'school' has a different orientation. Structuralist accounts start from the premise that people more or less reproduce the objective structures of their culture, and articulate these through all their communication—including, of course, the stories they tell, write or paint. We can find out about a society, the logic goes, by studying its social institutions and systems, and the authorised version of the way things are and how they are (or should be) done. Poststructuralists argue that this explanation is inadequate because it fails to address all the non-authorised ways in which things exist and are done, and because it can't account for the degree to which, in any society, other stories and practices challenge the authorised account. And Marxists are more concerned with the economic conditions that generate particular stories, and the power relations that mean some stories will be authorised and allowed to circulate while others will be marginalised or silenced.

But whether structuralist, poststructuralist or Marxist, most narrative theorists agree that the first, and central, issue about narrative is that stories always operate within a social context. The way we organise the content of a narrative, what elements it must have, who reads it, where it is read and what it seems to be saying are all determined by its cultural context. British comedians Peter Cook and Dudley Moore pick up on this in a sketch, set in London's National Gallery, where they try to understand the famous da Vinci cartoon that is in the gallery's collection. Pete, an out-and-out art illiterate who doesn't know a cartoon (a preparatory drawing) from a cartoon (a comic), complains about it: 'Not much of a joke as far as I'm concerned, Dud.' But Dud, who here shows an unexpected grasp of contemporary theory, explains the cartoon along the following lines: 'I bet when that da Vinci cartoon first came out, people were killing themselves laughing, Pete. It's a different culture, you see. It's Italian. We don't understand it.' Much as Pete and Dud don't find the cartoon funny because (as they understand the idea of cartoons) it's not their culture, we cannot read the stories of ancient Assyria, or the cave paintings of Lascaux, with any real assurance that we know precisely what they mean, why they were made and for whom, and what effects they had on their readers, because those cultures (we assume) are so foreign from ours in terms of organisation, identity and values. We can only be confident about the effects such works have on us now, and what those effects say about how contemporary culture is organised.

## plot and narrative

The theoretical schools or positions to which we referred also agree on the basic elements of story. Briefly, it must have a plot (what happened and why), a narrator (the point of view from which it is told), characters who participate in the story (human or otherwise), events (everything in the story that happens to or because of the characters), the time and place in which those events take place, and the causal relations which link the events together. Shlomith Rimmon-Kenan (1983) explains this by citing the following limerick:

There was a young lady from Niger
Who smiled as she rode on a tiger
They returned from the ride
With the lady inside
And the smile on the face of the tiger.

This, in her account, satisfies all the criteria of narrative. It has a plot (young woman rides tiger, is eaten); it has a narrator, or narrative viewpoint (the position from which the story is told); it has characters (the woman and the tiger), events (riding, eating), time (the duration from when she leaves, smiling, to when the tiger comes back alone) and place (within the narrator's view, and somewhere off stage); and it has causality (she smiles because she rides; the tiger smiles because it has been fed). Of course, it must be pointed out that this way of reading the limerick as a story is not entirely 'given to us': we infer it, using our cultural literacy. For instance, at no stage in the limerick is it stated that the tiger actually ate the woman. We can say, however, that since the woman is inside the tiger, and the tiger is smiling, there is a strong narrative inflection which leads us to this conclusion. In this way, it is similar to the rhetorical figure of the enthymeme, where the (absent) logical conclusion is inferred from the parts of a statement.

In order to show the difference between a strongly inflected narrative and something which merely has narrative potential, Rimmon-Kenan cites that old Valentine's Day standby:

Roses are red
Violets are blue
Sugar is sweet
And so are you.

This too has a narrator—the voice complimenting the loved one; it has a character—the sweet 'you'; but it lacks plot, time, place and causal relations. Readers can, no doubt, extract a narrative from it—maybe the traditional boy-meets-girl romance; maybe a 'forbidden love' story; maybe a lullaby for a baby; maybe a cynical parody of the romance narrative. But its story can't be secured, or pinned down—there are as many directions possible from this raw material as there are readers willing to invest the time to construct their own stories from it. For Rimmon-Kenan, then, as for most narrative theorists, any text is arguably a form of narrative in that it tells someone about something or someone, but only some will be genuine narratives—structured to tell in a relatively coherent fashion—while others are texts with narrative potential—being able only to provide springboards for stories that the readers/viewers must produce for themselves.

The photograph shown in Figure 4.1 demonstrates this: it has narrative potential and a number of narrative features, particularly character (the young man in the shot) and point of view (from which the photograph was taken, and from which we view it). It implies event, in that he seems to be dressed for a graduation ceremony. This in turn implies other causally related events—study at university before the photo, a professional life afterwards. As such, it also implies time: before, during and after the event. And, given the hairstyle, clothing, posture and facial expression of the sitter, it seems to have a historical location—we could say that it was probably late Victorian or Edwardian because of the severity and stiffness of the pose, and the formality of dress for such a young man. But, without more information in the form of an extended caption or a series of related photographs, we can't know this for sure; we can only guess at the story. It points us in a particular direction, or series of directions, but it can't 'tell' in the way a genuine narrative would, because it is a collection of signs which readers are relatively free to organise into their own story. For many theorists, this doesn't constitute genuine narrative because a story doesn't make itself or simply exist on a page or in a frame. It has to be crafted, and must comply with particular generic formulae, patterns or design 'tools'. Among these tools are the elements we have already mentioned—plot, character, time, event, and so on.

**Figure 4.1 Will Cronwright, c. 1920**

## time and narrative

Theorists of narrative argue that one of the most important design tools is time. Indeed, for Arthur Asa Berger, 'narratives, in the most simple sense, are stories that take place in time' (1997: 6)—although it is difficult to think of a story that doesn't take place in time. And Shlomith Rimmon-Kenan agrees that 'time itself is indispensable to both story and text. To eliminate it (if this were possible) would be to eliminate all narrative fiction.' (1983: 58) This makes sense when considering a verbal narrative, where the words are arranged in a linear fashion and what is being told is a sequence of events. Therefore, however the writer actually handles the issue of time, we are expected to read it in a linear fashion, to understand the time scale within which those events occur and to allow the time of the telling to map out the spatial domain of the story world.

Something similar applies to visual texts, provided they are serial or moving. Here the temporal order of events can be identified by the arrangement of icons within the frame and the juxtaposition of one frame to another. Comic strips in Western countries, for instance, are produced to be read from left to right, and from top to bottom, just as we read printed words; and the events can be organised and disclosed, much as novelist might control a narrative. But it is not so easy when we come to individual visual texts. Except for special examples, like Marcel Duchamp's 'Nude Descending a Staircase No. 2' (1912; thumbnail online at www.philamuseum.org/collections/modern_contemporary), where the figure is represented in a kind of arrested slow motion, reiterated over and over as it moves down the stairs, it is very difficult to show time unfolding within a single frame. Instead, what we get tends to be a plethora of discontinuous signs from which we must assume patterns and meanings, and not the structured organisation of signs we find in a verbal narrative. In a literary work, the events are narrated in a particular set order; in a pictorial work, by contrast, you can look in any order. W.T.J. Mitchell points out, in this regard, that 'literature is an art of time, painting is an art of space' (Mitchell 1986: 95), because book audiences are relatively static observers, reading over a period of time about the passage of time, but image audiences are active observers, walking around a static object. And, while verbal narratives are about what happened, when and to whom, in visual texts we are more likely to ask the question 'What is it?' or 'Who is it?'

We discussed the ways in which photographs have an uncertain relation to time in Chapter 3. I can look at a photograph of myself, for instance, and say both 'That's me' and 'That was me, back then'. Single-frame texts can't secure time in the way a verbal narrative does. Nor can they manipulate time as verbal narratives do, imposing on the past a certain order, flashing back and forward, narrating from the beginning to the end, or from the end to the beginning, or any combination of these. And they cannot control the order in which events are disclosed, as written texts do, because unless we are looking at a sequence of images—a graphic novel, or a film, a triptych or diptych, or the individual objects in an installation or exhibition—we can look at the various signs within the frame in pretty much any order, and for virtually any length of time.

Time, in short, cannot be 'told' in visual texts or even in narrative pictures; we can only infer it from the structure of the visual text, and the arrangement of its parts (Mitchell 1986: 100). We get some sense of the passage of time from the arrangement of bodies and objects in juxtaposition, and from the way their movement is frozen in the instance of representation, because whatever position a body is in is a fragment of a larger movement, before and after its freezing. This is heightened by the use of line: a straight line between two points, or a jagged line with acute angles, conveys the impression of movement and speed, because the eye moves quickly across the scene. Gentle, curved and easy lines convey a slower, more languid space and scene because the eye moves more lazily across them. Lines in a drawing, then, contain time and movement. The Woomera protest photograph shown in Figure 4.2 combines these two effects, including straight, hard lines and slow curves, in a way that arrests the passage of the eye. The urgency of the verticals (sticks and posts) along with the flatness of sky and ground compels rapid and jagged movement; but the lazy shadows and the regular curves of the horses' quarters slow the eye down, encouraging it to linger. Together, this contradictory effect evokes not the passage of time, but a moment of watchfulness—of waiting for the next thing to happen.

Figure 4.2 Woomera Easter protest

## content and narrative

Time is not the only issue in visual stories. Narrative can also be implied or identified in a visual text by devices such as the arrangement of the iconography or the use of perspective to provide a central focus. The use of light particularly structures the reading of the narrative: lighting draws attention to particular features in a text, and ensures we make sense of the images. Bright colours and a whimsical drawing style, for instance, create a light, possibly fantastical sense; dark images convey melancholy or threat; black-and-white immediately signals a particular aesthetic. The image shown in Figure 4.3a conveys a distinct story possibility by its use of light. The two women have their

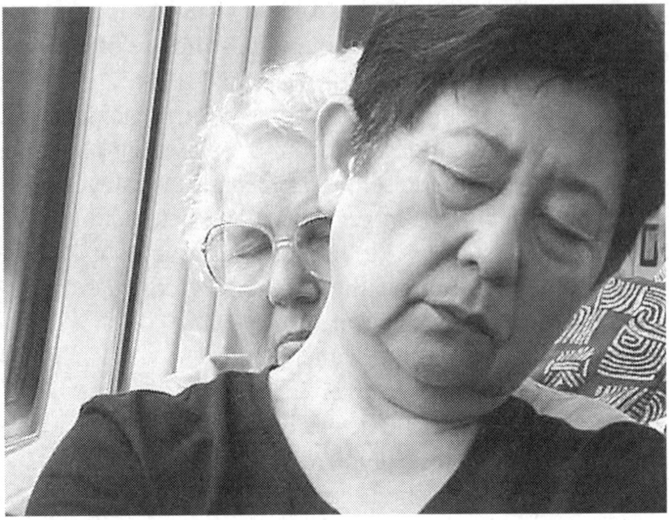

Figure 4.3 (a) 'Commuters 2' and (b) 'Commuters 1'

eyes closed, but seem to be sitting upright in a very brightly lit place; this, along with the title, insists that we see them not as being at rest, but as frozen in motion. They are commuters, and therefore are neither dead nor in prayer (which closed eyes and bowed heads in a lighted place might imply), but probably sleeping—and most likely on a relatively long trip and using public transport. They are, in short, in the kind of holding pattern demanded by public transport where there is nothing to do, little to look at and no reason to stay awake: the best solution is to fall asleep. If we had first looked at the image in Figure 4.3b the location—public transport—would have been

confirmed, and the reason for sleeping—boredom—would have been implied by the very weary expression on the woman's face, and the dozing person behind her.

Another way of organising and conveying narrative in a visual image is to depict characters making expressive movements—a smile, a hand extended in friendship, a fist raised in anger. Gombrich writes about this, describing what he calls the first obvious appeal to empathy in images: Greek narrative art of about 6–5 BCE (Gombrich 1982: 84–86). He describes a number of ancient works which express physical action through the positioning of the body and limbs, and also express a mood—a smile, a look of fear or sorrow, anticipation. He argues that we can read the emotion of a work by the context and content: much as we have assumed that the woman in Figure 4.3b is bored because of the look on her face. But we cannot know this for certain without knowledge that comes from outside the image: we might equally have read the character in 'Commuters 1' as depressed or irritated or frustrated. In Figure 4.3a, we might (without the first image and the title) have validly read the two women as having bowed their heads in prayer. Unless we know the story of the image, know the people in the image or have its meaning anchored by a caption or other text, we cannot be certain that we have read the narrative accurately.

Visual texts also use figures and techniques to convey stories through conventions known by most people in a society. The use of literary (and other) allusions is one approach; we see this in, for example, the many paintings, sculptures, stained glass windows and other illustrations that draw heavily on stories from classical myths and the Bible. Because the stories illustrated in these ways were so well and so widely known until fairly recent times, the story itself could direct the reading of the visual text. For instance, an image of a man in a robe, bent beneath the weight of a plank of timber, automatically evoked the story of Christ's trial and execution. Similarly, a painting of a semi-naked young woman watching dispassionately as a pack of hounds attacked a young man immediately reminded people of the story of Diana and Actaeon. No more would need to be contained in either image, because each comprised the sort of allusion—extremely popular in Western art up to the twentieth century—which worked because people shared knowledge of the stories being represented. Now that these stories are no longer nearly so widely known, other allusions have taken their place. The story of alienated youth, for instance, is very familiar in Western culture, and can easily be represented visually by drawing on the shared knowledge of the early deaths (and ongoing posthumous success) of musicians like Jimi Hendrix, Jeff Buckley and Kurt Cobain. This idea works as an allusion just by the representation of an unhappy young man dressed in whatever counts as alternative fashion for the day, preferably with a guitar propped somewhere in shot; and it can be used to promote radical artistic independence (in posters promoting a rock concert, for instance) or to narrativise the wasted lives of those locked in chemical dependency (say, in a Salvation Army advertisement).

What is involved in each of these examples is a relationship between the known story and the produced image, which narrative theorists term respectively *fabula* and *sjuzet* (Tomashevsky 1965: 66). Fabula is the actual sequence of (perhaps imaginary) events as they occurred; sjuzet is the representation of those events in a text. It is often difficult or impossible to identify the sjuzet in a visual text with any certainty, but if the fabula, the 'prestory', is well known and sufficiently indicated in the images, then there will be an intertext to provide a framework for reading. This doesn't mean that every reader will get it right, of course; images tend to be more anecdotal or dramatic than narrative, and to evoke, rather than tell, a story. So, though anyone who knows the conventions or figures used should understand the meaning of the sign within its context, there is always the possibility that meaning will be mislaid.

## narrative, genre and intertext

Other 'tools' that are perhaps more important than time and event in pinning down narrative and directing the readers of a text are two related principles: genre and intertextuality, which we raised in earlier chapters. Visual texts, like any texts, do not constitute a pure field—that is, we don't come to them innocently, but always read them in terms of all the other things we know and have seen, and with which we are familiar. This means that no text is entirely free-floating, or entirely subject to the whim and imagination of its viewer to make meanings or tell stories. Barthes writes: 'The variation in readings is not, however, anarchic; it depends on the different kinds of knowledge—practical, national, cultural, aesthetic—invested in the image.' (Barthes 1977: 46). So even a text that doesn't obviously have an organised narrative structure will place constraints on its viewers—in Figure 4.1, for instance, we would be hard pressed to say that the young man is about to head off to war; the absence of a military uniform precludes that.

What is it that limits the number of stories even so sparse a text can produce? Firstly, of course, the possibilities are limited by the actual content—there are no guns in this photograph. But beyond that, intertextuality and genre ensure that only certain stories can be read into visual texts by readers who share a similar context, background and history. Intertextuality, as we discussed in Chapter 1, refers to the way in which we make sense of texts on the basis of other texts with which we are familiar. Because no social practice can operate in isolation from its social context, any spoken, written or visual text will either connote or cite other texts and, by recalling these known stories, they will propel our reading in a particular direction. Our knowledge of them may be tacit, a familiarity—most people in Western society have seen old portrait photographs, so we will draw on others we have seen and perhaps know about (pictures of our own grandfathers) to make a story from this instance of the text. In other cases we may only 'get it' because we already possess literacy in the form or narrative being cited. The painting 'After Magritte', shown in Figure 5.1 in Chapter 5, demands that readers be familiar with Magritte's work. The drawing 'Bonnie's Eyes' shown in Figure 5.4, also in Chapter 5, requires that we are able to make the connection to the American gangsters Bonnie and Clyde; and it would help to know that the artist was working on a series of drawings of criminals and politicians if we really wanted to understand what story it is telling. In fact, as we argued earlier, we always make sense of texts on the basis of our intertextual knowledge, and without relevant literacies we will not be able to read a text effectively. Political cartoons are an example of this: they don't make much sense 30 years later because most of us have either forgotten the people and events concerned, or never knew them.

Genre is related to this because it is a principle of classification based on already-known stories, conventions, characters and other elements. Whenever we read a text as belonging to a particular genre, we are drawing on intertextual knowledges: we are classifying it according to its likeness to other texts with which we are familiar. The image shown in Figure 4.4, for instance, can easily be categorised into a specific genre that draws on several other genres, and we can read because of the many intertextual references and hints it offers.

Firstly, we know it is an invitation because it states as much in the top caption. It is presumably a twenty-first birthday party invitation, since the *Catch 22* title has been altered to read *Catch 21*, and the simple drawing is an intertextual reference to early childhood.

YOU ARE INVITED TO EXPERIENCE...
THE SPECIAL
WIDESCREEN
EDITION OF
THE LIFE AND TIMES OF PAUL TRAVERS
CATCH 22
1
NUGGET PRODUCTIONS PRESENTS
IN ASSOCIATION WITH P.M.HARDER PICTURES
CATCH 22
THE LIFE AND TIMES OF PAUL TRAVERS
STARRING PAUL TRAVERS
PRODUCTION DESIGNER CREATIVE PAVERS MUSIC BY DJ KENWOOD CD PLAYER
SPECIAL VISUAL EFFECTS BY B.Y.O. AND PROVIDED ALCOHOL
COSTUME DESIGNER TARGET RRP PRODUCED BY STEVEN AND KIM TRAVERS
WRITTEN AND DIRECTED BY PAUL TRAVERS
MA
15+
RESTRICTIONS APPLY TO PERSONS UNDER 15 YEARS
MEDIUM LEVEL VIOLENCE AND COARSE LANGUAGE

**Figure 4.4 Invitation**

In Western culture, a twenty-first birthday is the transition point from childhood to adulthood, which doubles the signification indicated in the captions 'invited' and 'Catch 21'. The text also tells us more about the person than just the age: we get the gender from the title ('Paul'), and we get a sense of his interests in the various intertextual references to movies. One is its likeness to the movie poster genre: the 'widescreen' claim at the top and the large title overlaid on to the visual. Another is the (intertextual) *Catch 22* reference, which is an important text for film buffs; a further indication is found in the credits at the base of the text, which include the eponymous hero and—we can guess from the family name—his parents. Tacit knowledge—familiarity with the main genre and the sub-genres—conveys both humour and a sense of the person being promoted in the invitation; literacy—direct knowledge of the text and its context—will confirm the accuracy of the reading and the story that is implied in the invitation.

Genre thus works together with intertextuality to secure the meaning of a text. But this is not all it does, or means. There are several definitions for genre. Etymologically, it simply means a particular type or kind of text, from the Latin word *genus*, or 'kind'. It is used most commonly as a kind of organisational device, a way of shelving books and arranging art galleries by putting like with like. It is also a very ancient taxonomical practice: the earliest writings on narrative classify texts into poetry, prose and drama; these are again subdivided into, say, tragedy and comedy; and in contemporary hierarchies of genre further still into 'drama', 'romance', 'horror', 'art house', 'self-help' and so on, to an almost infinite number of categories. This provides a practical dimension: with a working knowledge of genre—or kind—we can navigate video hire stores and bookshops, fairly confident we'll know what sort of text we're renting or buying. It also means that the principle of genre is one not just of classification and nomination, but also of interactions. Understanding generic order means we can quickly and efficiently make sense of any text, or any communication exchange, on the basis of its particular features.

The idea of genre includes not only what type a text might be, but also the process by which it is constructed, and the process by which readers make sense of it (Brent 1994: 2). When we come to a text, we assume a certain frame of mind based on our understanding of the genre to which it belongs and the expectations associated with that genre ('now I'm ready to be scared'; 'now I expect to be moved emotionally'; 'now I'm going to be informed'), which means we are effectively required to read the work in a particular way. This is very evident in traditional art museums, where most people assume a kind of reverential silence in the presence of the works on display; even if they are silly or comic, the fact that they have been classified as capital-A Art means people approach them with respect. But similar skill and technique applied to, say, an advertising image doesn't generate respect, because it belongs to a different genre and is likely to be found in a different context.

## the family of genres

How do we distinguish one genre from another? There are several ways in which this taxonomical principle comes into play. One is based on the principle of definition: that we know the qualities and conventions of particular genres, and assign texts to them on the basis of their compliance with the features of that genre. This has what is virtually a Platonic notion invested in it—the idea that there is an ideal form of the genre, which a particular text resembles to a greater or lesser extent. It has a commonsense appeal, too; most viewers would be able to recognise a western film or novel, for instance, on the basis of the number of horses relative to the number of cars, the number of men relative to the number of women, the number of guns relative to the number of flowers, and the amount of open country relative to the number of inner city scenes. Other genres might share many of its qualities: a historical drama, for instance, would also be likely to have horses rather than cars; it might have similar characters (the hero, the child, the love interest); and might have similar actions (the demand for physical and moral courage). But we would still be likely to identify one as a western and the other as historical drama without missing a beat because of the relative prominence of particular features and the way in which they are combined in the text.

A second approach is to classify texts into particular genres on the basis of their 'family resemblances' (Chandler 1997)—the texts in a specific genre will all 'look like' each other, in the way that all film posters have a distinct look, regardless of what type of film they are promoting and even, to a lesser extent, the origin of the film. Posters of Hollywood blockbusters are not so very different from posters produced by the Indian popular cinema industry, Bollywood, or even (to a lesser extent) French art house movies. Much like the birthday party invitation in Figure 4.4, all will have some variation on the title of the film, the name of the director and stars, photographic stills or staged shots that represent a key moment in the narrative, cinematographic credits and national classification information.

A further way of defining genres and assigning texts to categories is to make use of the concept of *prototypicality*. This is similar to the Platonic approach in that there is an original text which founds the genre, and some subsequent texts will be considered more typical of that genre than others. So we might look at the paintings on Greek urns and consider these the original texts which founded the prototypical genre of figurative paintings; subsequently, all figurative work belongs in the genre thus formed. This, of course, begs the question of how the original work was first identified as having generic qualities. When the very first painted urn was displayed, on what conventions was it based? How was it identified as founding a genre? It is very possible that it was considered only a poor version of another kind of figurative work—perhaps the poor cousin of statuary, for instance. But over time, and as enough works using similar conventions are produced, a genre as such is designated. Still, it is a flawed notion; after all, a central thread in writings about genre is that they can be identified because of the frequency with which their specific conventions and structures appear in texts. If there is initially only one, how can it be a prototype: what is it about this object that serves to inspire all its followers, and how does it inaugurate a new genre? In fact, it can only be understood to have been a prototype after enough other works are circulating—a post-hoc effect (Hoorn 2000).

Many people, when they hear the word 'genre', infer 'inferior', 'formulaic', 'unoriginal'. And certainly there is an evaluative context for the term. This comes out of a tradition in European culture of terming any picture that represented everyday life a 'genre picture'—ordinary and inferior in comparison with the grand paintings of mythological stories, classical imagery and high society life. This is a specious distinction because, as Jacques Derrida writes, 'a text cannot belong to no genre, it cannot be without . . . a genre. Every text participates in one or several genres, there is no genreless text.' (Derrida 1981: 61) But, of course, genres have no 'real' status. They are more like grammar than gravity: the effect of social convention, dynamic rather than stable, and abstractions rather than actualities (Feuer 1992: 144). Their boundaries are pretty permeable too, and there is consequently considerable overlap between genres. To make it even more confusing, many texts mix up their genres, as did the invitation above, which combines party invitation, movie poster and early childhood drawing.

## the organisation of everyday life

Given the multitude of genres, their dynamic form and the many overlaps within texts, it could be worth asking why the principle is so persistent—why is it that we still think in terms of, and make use of, genres? One answer is that they do help us get things done—to make sense of a context and know how to behave in response to that context. But, perhaps more significantly, genres are very good for marketing purposes. We mentioned above that a knowledge of genre helps us make our way through a video library; in the same way, it helps shopkeepers organise their shelves, and it helps advertisers organise campaigns and products. Indeed, it could be said that genres are intimately intertwined with capitalism. Advertising exploits the principle of genre, with pragmatic products—household cleaners, breakfast cereal, nappies—often shown in a kind of domestic genre: cheerful family members finding that the products make their lives easier. Luxury goods, on the other hand, are often promoted through photographs that resemble oil paintings, or in television advertisements backed by classical music—all designed to convey 'the good life', the world of the well-to-do.

This has a parallel form in the art world: consider the Impressionist art of the 1860s to 1880s which so often represents the bourgeoisie enjoying life, consuming luxury goods, confidently inhabiting the urban environment and enjoying its beauties and delights (Clark 1992: 40). John Berger, too, identifies this connection between visual art and commerce, writing that: 'Oil painting, before it was anything else, was a celebration of private property. As an art-form it derived from the principle that you are what you have' (Berger 1972: 139). Jeremy Tambling states: 'To investigate controlling narratives means investigating the everyday life beliefs that operate through a culture.' (1991: 3) This is very evident if we examine images within their genres—how they are variously valued, and the stories they convey about everyday life. Identifying which genres are privileged and which are debased, and then examining their content and context, tells us a great deal about what is valued in a society. Just as the medieval world considered everyday people to be worth much less than nobles (as signalled by the derogatory term 'genre pictures' for the former), the fact that advertising uses the images of wealth and leisure to promote luxury goods, with the connotation 'If you don't have money, this is not directed at you', also provides a clear statement that everyday practices—cleaning, cooking and child care—are not worth much in our society.

Genres also organise our lives within contemporary commodity culture. One important organiser of everyday life through genre and narrative is the news media, which don't just tell us what's going on, but what we need to know, what we ought to think about and what is important within the culture. The protest photograph shown in Figure 4.2 depicts a story very familiar to most of us from the late twentieth century: the story of civic disobedience, or protest. We can see this by the content: there are two opposing teams—the police with their protective helmets and uniforms and horses, the less orderly and uniform crowd of protesters on the right. The public space of protest, in which most of us live and have our work and activities organised, is signalled by the paved area on which they stand, and the steel fence on the left. But it is manifestly not a press photograph, because there is a concern with composition rather than action: the balance between barren sky and barren concrete; the asymmetry between the police and the protesters; the line of shadows falling from the police balanced by the regular vertical lines of posts, staffs and arms combine to create a sense of stasis. Time seems to be frozen; everyone is waiting for something to happen. This provides a very different sense of meaning and value than we might expect from a press photograph, where a conventional (conservative) paper might focus on individuals with dreadlocks and torn jeans, or protesters engaged in violence; or a left-wing paper would be more likely to focus on a police charge, or random violence against unarmed youths. But in any case, something is being told, and a point of view is being 'sold' to viewers.

## everyday life as narrative

We noted above that every text belongs within a genre—there cannot be a text without genre. In a similar vein, we can say that narrative pervades all of life—there cannot be life without narrative. This is not because everyone's life is necessarily structured like a narrative, as we defined it above (narrator, character, plot, event, time, place, causality). Indeed, for many of us, no plot is ever evident: causal connections between events may be very fuzzy, and there will rarely be the clarity and organisation we expect of narrative. Arthur Asa Berger (1997) goes even further, insisting that life is nothing like narrative because it is all middle, generally diffuse and basically eventless. But, as Michel de Certeau points out, life is like narrative because the principle of narrative shapes our world:

> Captured by the radio as soon as he awakens, the listener walks all day long through the forest of narrativities from journalism, advertising and television, narrativities that still find time, as he is getting ready for bed, to slip a few final messages under the portal of sleep . . . these stories have a providential and predestinating function: they organize in advance our work, our celebrations and even our dreams. (Certeau 1984: 84)

That is to say, narrative is there not because it is inherent in life, but because it envelops us and structures our practice, or our experience of practice. As social creatures, we think in story—in time, character, event and causality—and we make sense of our own lives, as well as our connections to other people and to institutions, in terms of the narratives we craft. Narrative is a site of interaction (an active verb) rather than a static object (noun), and thus social values will always be inscribed in narratives.

But to what extent is it true to say that narratives will always be present and clear in visual texts? After all, as we have noted, there are quite strict criteria for narrative, as opposed to general narrative potential, or the social narrativity that Certeau describes. Roland Barthes (1977) writes that images do and don't have a relationship to linguistic texts; imagery is a language, but it doesn't work like linguistic language. Similarly, visual texts do and don't work according to the principles of narrative. But, on the other hand, any sort of language is about performance and the construction of images because it addresses an audience, uses devices of framing, pointing and showing, and relies on metaphors and figures—so much so that the language in a text can be termed iconic rather than transparently communicative (Maclean 1988: 16). And, as any student of creative writing knows, 'good writing' is mimetic (it 'shows') and not diegetic (that is, it doesn't 'tell'). So we can say that there is a visual or iconic quality to spoken and written language, much as there is the potential for communication and narrative within any visual text.

However, many theorists argue that, in the absence of words or other interpretative signs, it is very difficult to pin down a story; strictly speaking, narratives are not built into, or accessible within, visual texts as they are in verbal texts. Mark Twain, for instance, wrote after looking at the Guido Reni painting of Beatrice Cenci, shown in Figure 4.5:

> A good legible label is usually worth, for information, a ton of significant attitude and expression in a historical painting. In Rome, people with fine sympathetic natures stand up and weep in front of the celebrated 'Beatrice Cenci the Day Before Her Execution'. It shows what a label can do. If they did not know the picture, they would inspect it unmoved, and say, 'Young Girl with Hay Fever; Young Girl with Her Head in a Bag'. (cited Mitchell 1986: 40)

**Figure 4.5 A portrait by Guido Reni reputed to be of the sixteenth-century Roman noblewoman Beatrice Cenci. The provenance of the painting has always been disputed.**

An image may indeed 'tell', but it tells without the clarity provided by words, and without the principles of narrative organisation that are readily possible in verbal language. If a picture paints a thousand words, it is also true to say that it may be read in a thousand ways, and tell myriad stories, because pictures are always open to personal interpretation, and relatively inaccessible to any who lack very specific literacies.

James Elkins writes of visual texts that their excessive ambiguity is based on the fact that they are made up of what he terms 'nonsemiotic marks—that is, they aren't comprised of linguistic or otherwise systematic or oppositional signs' (Elkins 2002). Consequently, he writes, they 'resist interpretation'. Gombrich takes a similar position, writing: 'Interpretation on the part of the image maker must always be matched by the interpretation of the viewer. No image tells its own story' (Gombrich 1996: 48). And Roland Barthes, the interpreter of visual texts, insists that 'all images are polysemous; they imply, under their signifiers, a "floating chain" of signifieds, the reader able to choose some and ignore others' (Barthes 1977: 39).

## reading images

Perhaps in consequence, the producers of visual texts through the millennia have gone to considerable effort to anchor that 'floating chain', usually by the addition of written material—even works as early as those of ancient Egypt and Greece are marked by captions and other writing that make the meaning of the visual material more clear. Medieval paintings, too, were characterised by the addition of interpretations or cues to their reading—familiar icons, tituli, scrolls, or performers who stood by the works (much as education officers do in contemporary art museums) to explain what it was all about. Silent movies of the early twentieth century relied not just on genres of performance—the villain, the vamp, the innocent—but on the pianist who musically interpreted the affect, and the captions and subtitles that propelled the action. News photographs are interpreted by their captions as much as their content; art museums put enormous effort into producing wall text to locate and explain the paintings and sculptures on display; and comic strips and graphic novels rely on the textual information as much as on the genres of drawing and reading. Given the tendency to add words, Barthes writes: 'It is not very accurate to talk of a civilization of the image—we are still, and more than ever, a civilization of writing' (1977: 38). The function of words in reference to visual texts, he writes, are firstly to anchor the meaning, and then to relay it—to direct readers in which meanings are privileged, and which are to be ignored.

This does not mean that images are readable only by the addition of text. Japanese *manga* comics, for instance, are remarkably caption-free, compared with Western comics and graphic novels. Reading *manga* means reading images—and this is the convention because of the general literacies among its audiences of cinematographic techniques, juxtaposition of features, representation of movement, and so on. Gombrich explains it in this way: 'The chance of a correct reading of the image is governed by three variables: the code, the caption and the context' (1996: 45). We need to be able to access all three, and be literate with respect to all three, if we are to make sense of it—and, clearly, *manga* readers have these literacies and can access all three anchors. Any one of them on its own would limit the narrative possibility of the image. Think of a picture which shows a snarling dog—for instance, the famous mosaic found in the ruins of Pompeii. The code is object representational, or a realistic symbol (Wallschlaeger and Busic-Snyder 1992: 381), because it looks like a dog. It might simply be a visual icon, or represent the idea of a dog or the notion of canine threat in the context of, say, household decoration. But the addition of the caption '*cave canem*' (beware of the dog) ensures that we know it is not simply a picture of the generalised notion of canine threat, but a warning against the specific family guard dog.

This is a bit disingenuous, because an image of a snarling dog at the door or gate of a home should be fairly easy to read as a warning. But if the image is more abstract—more pictographic, say—it will not necessarily communicate the story of threat quite as directly. Think of the signs on public toilets which signify male and female rooms; older style (object representational) signs, with their silhouette of a man in a top hat and a woman in crinolines, are fairly readable if we know about the cultural context—the fact that in Anglophone cultures urination is a private, secret act, to be undertaken only in designated and gender-defined areas: the 'law', as Lacan put it, of 'urinary segregation' that requires a gender distinction in these designated areas. But the contemporary signs of bipedal human forms, one in a skirt and the other not, only abstractly symbolise the idea of women and men, and are only recognisable to us because of our previous literacies. To read an iconic text correctly, we need to know the code (bipedal figure without skirt = man) and the context (sign of human form in public space = public restroom). The caption—'Men', 'Women'—is a redundancy that ensures the meaning cannot be lost. If we know the culture, the context and the code, we do not need the addition of captions to read the narrative of the sign—though, in effect, our previous knowledge acts as a kind of caption to the icon, and ensures we 'get it right'.

## image into text

The visual texts that most obviously rely on verbal language—outside of films and videos, that is—are comic strips and graphic novels, which can be defined as 'open-ended dramatic narrative about a recurring set of characters, told in a series of drawings, often including dialogue in balloons and a narrative text' (Inge 1990: xi). They are very old forms: we could identify among their antecedents the heavily annotated ancient Egyptian art works; those medieval art works that incorporated speech balloons; and of course the early twentieth-century cartoons and comics. The codes and conventions of the form were finally formalised by the twentieth century, with many of their features standardised: the arrangement of panels to govern the pattern of reading; different shaped balloons for speech and thought; conventions of movement; narratorial comment; descriptive captions; facial expressions; and onomatapoeia (Kannenberg 1996/2001).

The graphic story shown in Figure 4.6 illustrates most of these conventions. It begins with a cinematographic long shot—an establishing shot—from above the city, then immediately zooms in to street level where someone—given the cape, mask and muscles, presumably a superhero—is speeding into the frame. The title 'Blood in the Gutter' picks up on the 'mean streets' notion associated with the detective genre (so we assume he is trying to solve a problem and restore order), and the subtitle 'The case of the missing information' substantiates the detective genre, but in a parodic sense. Juxtaposing a down-and-dirty American detective sub-genre with a Miss Marple or Nancy Drew 'the case of . . .' can only be intending to make fun of the whole genre. And the empty speech bubbles and narratorial boxes reiterate this—little or nothing is being said, perhaps because it has all been said before, so often, in one formulaic text after another (and hence, perhaps, we see Sara and Butch, 'their minds rotted away by static consumption of cultural texts').

Let's look at the connection between the words and pictures in this strip to identify how its effects are produced. The drawing is very much in genre for a superhero/thriller/action narrative. Each frame replicates the zooms, jump cuts and racking shots of film, and propels the narrative by moving us, the viewers, through the space and events. Every line seems committed to action and constant movement: the hero races, leaps, dives or stands in alert readiness; even when the door is open, he can't just walk in, because that's not what heroes do. The urgency of the story is signalled partly by the hero's rapid movement and taut posture, and also by the sharp perspective in many frames—for instance, the floor boards, and the tiles that run quickly to the vanishing point, force our eyes to move quickly as well. Other conventions are obeyed too: lines indicating the direction of movement show in each frame where he has come from, where he is headed, and how rapidly. Frustration is shown in lines darting from his forehead, and the irritated onomopoetic tap ('CLICK!') of his foot on the floor. And when he dives through the doorway, the energy of his movement is signalled by the 'KA-BLAM!' that accompanies the sketch, as a narrative sound effect. The story being told, though, as the title and subtitle suggest, is parodic—making fun of both the genre of detective/superhero graphic forms, and of academic doublespeak.

It is, as are visual narratives generally, very economical in its gestures and icons; with a few lines, it conjures up a whole set, and condenses—and thus intensifies—information and action. It is also, as any still image must be, committed to representing only fragments of movement or characterisation, rather than the more nuanced forms possible in verbal texts. But it is still able to point to quite sophisticated issues of story and character. In this story, the hero is the academic who is skilled in textual analysis; his friends, Adorno-esque cultural dupes, have been vampirised by the texts they consume. It suggests that pens are indeed mightier than swords, and that a

Figure 4.6 Blood in the Gutter

SARA ... BUTCHI, THEIR MINDS, ROTTED AWAY BY STATIC CONSUMPTION OF CULTURAL TEXTS.
CLICK
SUDDENLY I REALISED HOW STUPID WE'VE BEEN
KA-BLAM
WHEN WILL PEOPLE LEARN THAT THE SECRET IS ...
... NOT WHAT THE TEXT SHOWS BUT ...
... WHA IT DOSN SHOW
TO BE CONTINU

Barthesian active reader, trained to decode and control texts, is the only one safe enough (muscled, caped and masked enough) to read them.

## conclusion

Ernst Gombrich writes that: 'There must be a great difference between a painting that illustrates a known story and another that wishes to tell a story' (1982: 101). This suggests that reading a visual narrative often effectively involves writing it. Pictures, for the most part, depict things or illustrate known stories, but don't necessarily narrativise them. In fact, with the passage of time in the Western tradition, narrative has increasingly retreated from the visual text, starting with the Renaissance when the development of linear perspective shifted the focus of the viewer from the story being depicted to the illusion of reality of three-dimensional space. And now, in the modern era, narrative has pretty much retreated from art, though it is present in graphic novels, films, television programs and other visual genres that are still committed to story.

The change, Martin Jay suggests (1993: 51), is based on more general changes in social understandings and values. In the medieval period, for instance, the world was seen as 'the book of nature'—there as an intelligible object, available to be read and containing God's order; by the Enlightenment it was an object of ('scientific') observation, without a narrative or meaning outside its functionality. By the twentieth century, with the decline in certainty about any meaning or possibility of order, visual art had turned to complete abstraction: a story-less image.

While there is, as we have seen, considerable doubt as to the capability of images to convey narrative in its strict sense, visual images have regularly had a narrative component (as seen in cave paintings, bas-reliefs, mosaics, Stations of the Cross, diptych and triptych artworks). Though, as Rosalind Krauss (1992) points out, visual texts are highly multiple and layered, and rarely transparent stories, there is always some structural principle, some structuring order, to reduce the anarchy of polysemy. Visual works may not easily tell stories, but they have huge narrative potential and great expressive power: the ability to convey emotions, ideas and attitudes; and to direct readers to particular narratives. In the next few chapters we develop this discussion by moving to discuss three of the main 'narratives' of our time: visual art, the normalising of the visual domain, and the relationship between seeing and capitalism.

# 5 visual art, visual culture

## introduction

Paintings, sculptures, drawings and art photography, though obviously part of the general field of visual culture, are often seen as somehow outside or beyond the everyday world of advertisements, television shows, magazines and family snapshots. The stories art claims to tell, and the stories that are told about it, set it apart historically and discursively from other forms of visual culture. In this chapter we take up the question of visual art, particularly the ways in which visual texts have been understood and deployed, in the Western tradition, as capital-A Art. We look specifically at the ways in which art has been transformed in modern and postmodern societies, particularly through the developments that have occurred in visual communication technologies.

Art is generally an extremely visual field, or set of practices, even if we look outside the obvious candidates of painting, drawing and sculpture. Poetry and painting, as Horace pointed out in his *Art of Poetry* (c.35 BCE), are very closely connected (*ut pictura poesis*/as is painting, so is poetry), because poets and other creative writers use figures—metaphors, tropes and similes—to conjure up mental pictures. Dance, film and theatre are highly visual, and even music—the most abstract of the arts—is frequently associated with visual imagery. And to keep our attention on the strictly visual arts, not only are the works themselves committed to visual values, so too is the field in which they exist. Think of the architecture of art museums; the design of individual exhibitions; the selection of colour for walls (changed regularly to satisfy exhibition needs); the colour and texture of the floor; the quality of frames and plinths; the bright banners promoting new exhibitions that flutter from posts up and down the highways. All of these contribute to the visual experience of the art museum, and frame the viewing of the individual works.

## the identity of art

But what is art, and what sets it apart in terms of approaches to seeing/reading visual culture? It is important to note initially that individual artworks are not necessarily qualitatively different from other objects of visual culture. If an artwork and, say, an advertisement were placed side by side, there would not necessarily be any obvious difference in their content, their value or even the media used in their production. Nor, if an artist and an advertising designer were interviewed about their ideas, would the things they say necessarily be markedly different. All the same, as a society, we generally understand the two forms and the two professions as having very different identities. Consequently we treat them differently, and typically look at their products differently. Art is assigned a cultural value that advertisements lack, so it attracts a long, slow gaze, while adverts are there for the sweeping glance only. Art historians are trained to look closely and patiently—to absorb the work with their eyes, and make out its various elements, values and qualities. Even people without art training tend to stand quietly in front of works in a gallery and look at them with a more prolonged gaze than the flickeringly impatient or tacit looking we apply to most other visual elements in our everyday lives.

But what do we mean by 'art'? Centrally, it is something peculiar to human culture. The word itself is etymologically related to 'artificial', or produced by human beings. While a landscape may be staggeringly beautiful, or terrifying in a sublime way, it is not art—not, that is, unless it has been 'artificialised': transformed by an artist into a painting or photograph or other art form. This doesn't mean that everything humans do to transform nature is art; the definition only applies to those things and practices identified as art because of the contexts of their production or location. This is not necessarily fixed once and for all; the not-art can become art through a sleight of hand or reallocation of identity because, as Raymond Williams shows, 'the distinctions [between art and other human works] are not eternal verities, or supra-historical categories, but actual elements of a kind of social organization' (1981: 130). Consequently, the meaning of art constantly evades firm definitions. In earlier periods the word 'art' was used very promiscuously: anything people did that required skill was an 'art'. Medieval or Renaissance writers, for instance, refer to the arts of war, conversation, or smithing, and what we now call 'artists' were then just artisans—ordinary workers who applied their specialised skills within collectives or guilds (Williams 1981: 59). We are more selective now, using the term to signify those things associated with the making of creative works: plastic and visual arts and crafts, creative writing, music and the performance arts—that is, objects and practices which, as Panofsky states, 'demand to be experienced aesthetically' (1955: 11).

## art versus culture

The word 'culture' is also often applied to specifically 'artistic' practices and objects—as when someone refers to a 'cultured' person who prefers to spend time at the opera than the football, for instance. But, strictly speaking, the terms 'culture' and 'art' are not interchangeable. 'Culture' is more sociological than aesthetic; it refers to what Raymond Williams calls the 'whole life of a society', and includes everything we do as collectives of human beings: intellectual and spiritual as well as aesthetic mores, tangible and intangible expressions of a community's social life. So, while 'art' provides techniques, structures and mechanisms for the production of individual artistic statements, 'culture' provides the social and ideological conditions in which works of art can be made and disseminated. And when people use 'culture' for 'art', they are usually referring to those things otherwise called 'high art': Italian opera, atonal music, experimental theatre, modernist paintings—material that is culturally important because of its antiquity, or because it has been designated as such by a relevant authority, or because it requires a special set of literacies to make sense of it.

This does register a distinction between 'art' and other social products: contemporary artworks often seem to be obscure in their communication, but anyone should be able to make sense of, say, an advertisement. As an example, recently a flyer for a major finance company arrived in my mailbox. The company logo in the top left-hand corner of the front fold anchored everything else in the text to that organisation: the exclamatory encouragement to EARN BONUS REWARDS POINTS WITHOUT SPENDING A CENT! took up the top half of the same fold, making it very clear what the purpose of this document might be; and the bottom half contained a photograph of a credit card zooming in from the left. Very foreshortened, and with a forced linear perspective (the card disappearing towards the vanishing point), it gave the impression of speed (imagine how quickly you could earn those bonus points!) and movement (imagine how widely your card will be accepted!). And because the image of the card was so large relative to the whole flyer, it also gave the impression of stability, strength and magnitude (you can trust us!).

Advertisements like this one are easily read by pretty well anyone. Some of the more creative adverts may make intertextual references that require other literacies, but even so their central message will be very accessible. Art does not necessarily work this way. Medieval and Renaissance works may have been intended to communicate clearly and directly with their audiences, but in the twenty-first century we often lack the sorts of general understandings and knowledges that obtained back then, and so may not really 'get' the whole story without additional historical information. Moreover, the twentieth century was dominated by art that became ever more obscure and internally referential, so that in many cases without a very good knowledge of the field the works are impenetrable—or at least do not communicate easily with anyone not fluent in their codes.

## reading artworks

Look, for instance, at the reproduction of 'After Magritte' in Figure 5.1. This does not communicate in a way similar to the finance company advertisement we described, nor does it have the transparency and commitment to resemblance evident in works made prior to the twentieth century. We can still read it, however, given the appropriate literacies. One starting point would be its form—by which we mean anything to do with its production that is not immediately associated with its meaning-making capacity. So here we consider medium, compositional elements, colour, line, shape, texture, and so on. In this work, the form is paint on canvas (i.e. conventionally 'art'); it is a large work, over a metre high, so it dominates a standard (household-size) wall. The artist has layered the paint, made some use of collage, and used a combination of straight lines and irregular curves, and a balance of light and dark, to create a density of texture and variety of tone.

Figure 5.1 After Magritte

That deals with the technical aspects of its production, and allows us to begin the process of unpacking the work—classifying, categorising and critiquing it. The second step is to examine its content. This includes what the work is about, what it is saying, other issues to which it might be referring (including intertexts), its subject matter, and elements such as figure, genre and narrative. In this case, the painting is dominated by a human shape without facial features (which, because of the title, would have been anticipated by anyone familiar with Magritte's work—its eponymous intertext). It is also marked by the rejection of linear perspective through the flattening out of the forms, the absence of inner coherence or simulation of three-dimensional space. In some ways, it figures a reversal of the 'normal' order: the human (culture) has become nature, with the clouded human shape in the foreground and the tree-like leg at the back; while nature has become culture, with blocks as clouds and timber floor as ground. It can also be read as conveying a sense of anxiety: the blindness of the subject, the breaking down of its body (with a hole over the heart) and the disembodied heavy leg that dominates the right half of the visual field work give this impression. And, overall, there is a sense of decay, with the human disintegrating, the landscape consumed or over-written by a built landscape, and the bricks crumbling behind the figure.

Finally, we can read the context in which it was made and disseminated, and is now being read. This directs the reader's attention towards what is going on in relation to the work being read. We take into account the cultural and social environment in which the work was produced, what is known about its maker, and the milieu in which it is circulating and has been received. In the case of this work, we would probably begin with the title, and the gesture made by the choice of name and style to early twentieth-century work, especially cubism and expressionism. If we knew, too, that it was a student work produced as part of a research assignment into the Modernists, then we could also identify the seductive power of a major art form even some 80 years later, and the reverential attitude taken by a young artist to the 'masters'. We might check the date of production, and consider the fear of environmental disaster that was as prevalent then as now, and read this as both an allegory and a response to that cultural sensibility.

This painting is clearly 'art', as we can see by the above analysis. But in fact almost anything can be considered art in the current climate, and could be read by applying the same aspects we have used to address 'After Magritte'. John Frow writes in this regard that:

> The pile of stones formed by a minor avalanche carries equally with it the possibility of being otherwise recognized; it can, for

> example, be taken for a cairn or taken to be beautiful. The condition of possibility is the same in each case. The stones, the pebble, exist within the realm of that possibility. Is there a difference, then, between the pile and the cairn? Yes, but it's one that, like that between humans and nonhumans, needs to be flattened, read horizontally as a juxtaposition rather than vertically as a hierarchy of being . . . the sort of world we live in makes it constantly possible for these two sets of kinds to exchange properties, for the heap of stones to be read as an arrangement, for the dead matter of the camera to be understood as an inscription of human work and will. The difference that seems to be one of kind is one of use and recognition. (Frow 2001)

In other words, something is art if a person or group of people with the authority to do so identify it as art, name it as such. The recognition of the gatekeepers who offered them entry to those places—agents and structures authorised by the field of art, such as galleries and curators, established artists, publishers, arts writers and critics, established theatre companies, arts administrators and government arts departments—makes the difference between whether something is a pile of stones or a cairn. And the criteria normally used by gatekeepers include whether what is presented was made, or otherwise associated with, a deliberate or conscious act on the part of an artist; whether it shows an engagement with a social or artistic issue; whether there is a concern with form and content; whether it demonstrates the desire to communicate something; or whether it incorporates the desire to create an impression, an effect, or some affect. When named as such, it leaves the world of food production, or nature, or industry, and enters the world of art.

## the field of artistic production

Bourdieu argues that art can be understood as comprising a cultural field, which he calls the 'field of cultural production' (1993). He uses the term 'field' quite specifically here, meaning everything that is done, and everyone involved in doing it, within a discrete area of social practice. This includes all the institutions involved (art museums, publishing houses, public relations firms, government arts bodies) and the people (artists, curators, directors, conservators, promoters). It incorporates all the rules, rituals, conventions and categories (exhibitions, the artistic sensibility or lifestyle, appropriate behaviour at a launch or opening night, what makes something good art) associated specifically with that activity. It includes the relation of hierarchy among the people, institutions and practices, and the grounds for judgement, evaluation and value (art for art's sake versus art for a patron; classical beauty versus avant-garde abstraction). And it is always concerned with conflict between the groups or individuals involved over what constitutes capital within that field, and how that capital is to be distributed.

The main forms of capital in the field of art are symbolic and cultural capital; economic capital takes a back seat according to the logic of value in this field. Symbolic capital—also termed distinction, or prestige—is valuable (exchangeable) within the field of art, because it is the marker of obvious success, and provides its possessors with the authority to say what counts as good art (Bourdieu 1993: 41). Cultural capital is related to this: Bourdieu refers to it variously as incorporated capital (Bourdieu 1991: 230), a 'feel for the game', or informational capital (Bourdieu 1987: 4); and it is related to expertise, and to the possession of competencies to perceive and appreciate certain products or practices. The British comedians Peter Cook and Dudley Moore made a comedy routine out of this insistence, within the art world, of valuing non-economic capital. They appeared in a gallery in London's National Gallery where, dressed in working clothes and munching sandwiches, they begin their conversation about art and aesthetics with a discussion about famous duck paintings. Pete explained that the sign of a good painting was when the ducks' eyes followed you around the room. He was so pleased with this evidence of his art literacy that he went on to explain to Dud the quality of Cezanne's 'Les grandes baigneuses', saying: 'The sign of a good painting, Dud, when people's backs are towards you, is if the bottoms follow you around the room.' Dud tried to figure this out, staring at the figures, but finally acknowledged that only his eyes were moving, and not the bottoms.

Figure 5.2 French postimpressionist Paul Cézanne's 'Les grandes baigneuses' ('The large bathers', 1906), the subject of Pete and Dud's erudite lunchtime conversation.

The humour in this skit is based on incongruity—the fact that they don't know how to behave in a gallery, and that—though they have a few buzz words—they don't know how to speak about art, in terms of the logic of the field of art anyway. Their example of art illiteracy not only shows up their lack of cultural and symbolic capital; it also shows their generally lowly status in the social field, which is heightened by their dress and accents. And this directs our attention to another facet of the cultural field: that if someone is going to spurn tacky economic capital in favour of cultural and symbolic capital, they need to have some other means of support that frees them up for this gesture. Dud and Pete clearly don't have cultural capital, and their 'poverty' is related to their much wider poverty or lack in the social field—education, money, prestige, 'background' are all lacking.

## art for art's sake (money for God's sake)

Cultural capital and symbolic capital are the 'coin' of the art world because one of the central rules in this field is that art is disinterested: since the early nineteenth century, art has been 'for art's sake', and not for trade or craft. This brings us to one of the most important structures of the field of art, from Bourdieu's point of view: its division into two opposing poles along a continuum of art practice. At one pole is art produced according to a logic which is heteronomous with respect to the wider social field—that is, art produced for commercial success, or for a political imperative, or for some other social need—and which has very little legitimacy in the broader art world. We might think here of advertising, or design, or Soviet Realist art—work undertaken to satisfy a commissioning client, not to please the muse, and work which is therefore unlikely to be purchased by an art gallery (except sometimes as a historical curiosity) or displayed in the biennales and triennales held across the globe each year. The carving reproduced in Figure 5.3 could be said to come into this category; it is part of an altar in a *marae* (Maori community) church and, despite the quality of its production, the balance of the various elements and the beauty of the face, its point is on the one hand a continuation of a particular tradition of Maori carving, and on the other a contribution to worship. The artist, however skilled and creative, was (we can assume) working for something other than art's sake—for culture, for tradition, for God.

At the other pole is work which is autonomous with respect to the economic field—the consecrated, or 'art for art's sake' approach—in which it is symbolic capital, or prestige, which is valued, and in which success is determined by the approval of other autonomous producers (Bourdieu 1993: 39). Here we find work done according to the logic identified above: self-consciousness, self-referentiality, a concern with form, an engagement with artistic issues, and so on. At its extremes, the debate between the opposing logics of autonomy and heteronomy is characterised on the one hand by William Blake's statement that 'Where any view of money exists, art cannot be carried on', and on the other by Samuel Johnson's comment that 'No man but a blockhead ever wrote, except for money' (cited in Hughes 1987: 388). To an extent, both positions are valid, and both are limited. Production of art has always depended on possession of, or access to, the necessary economic capital. As we suggested above, it is only those who can afford to please themselves who don't have to take into account the need to satisfy some sort of market or social demand as well as the demands of art. And the idea that art can or should be free from social necessity is comparatively recent; it was not until the eighteenth century that art began to assume the status of creativity and originality, of something separate from everyday life and from the interests of politics or economics (Staniszewski 1995: 111).

**Figure 5.3 Altar carving**

Of course, much contemporary art—even in Western cultures—crosses this barrier; artists typically engage with social politics in a way that 'should' be excluded by the logic of disinterested art. Annette Douglass and Chaco Kato's installation work 'A Way of Staying Alive' (Figure 5.4), does just this: while it is artistically sophisticated and aesthetically pleasing, it is designed to respond to their government's reluctance to accommodate refugees, and to address the questions of who we are, where we come from, and why we came.

The objects that make up the installation vary from comfortable suburban frocks (overprinted with shards of buildings and the

**Figure 5.4 A Way of Staying Alive**

machinery of war), through waxed, hooked garments (in white, the colour of mourning in parts of Asia), to smaller floor pieces: fragile bent-twig building frames, feathers heaped into hats, stuffed kitbags. Nets (layered hot pink over brown over blue, against white walls, above uneven old scarred wooden floors in a bright room) are also used to make a point. Nets capture, collate and connect; and in this exhibition they are scooped into points, like mountain peaks, or steep waves in a child's drawing of the sea, recalling the tenuous links between place and place, reminding us of the organic connections we share as humans, but also recalling the barricades and fences that trap asylum seekers in detention camps.

The idea of art as polarised along the autonomous/heteronomous continuum really only works for art made within a Western tradition. The Maori art historian Jonathan Mane-Wheoki provides a very different view of the field of art in his culture. He writes of a conference he attended on Pacific art, where a speaker said 'that he was not going to talk about spirituality or any of that nonsense with respect to one of the Indigenous Australian artworks he was discussing'. Spirituality is, of course, not part of contemporary Western art's logic: autonomous producers work for art's sake, and not for tradition or religion. But Mane-Wheoki rejects this imperative, responding: 'If that is the attitude of Western scholars to our sacred treasures, why would we wish to continue to engage with Western scholarship?' (Mane-Wheoki 1996: 35). His approach to art and art history incorporates, and to some extent depends on, the sacred—something that is divorced from art in the Western tradition.

## 'high' art and 'popular' culture

Bourdieu's description of the field of art as bifurcated between autonomy and heteronomy, and Mane-Wheoki's criticism of Western art as that which rejects the spiritual, raise another division that haunts art: the relation—and the distance—between (high) art and popular culture. The former is associated very closely with aesthetics, and its commitment to reason, order, clarity and refined judgement; the latter, according to classical scholars of aesthetics, is associated with sentiment, emotion, 'mere' entertainment. In this, it is very close to Bourdieu's map of the field of art as polarised between art for art's sake (autonomous) and art industry (heteronomous).

Popular culture, for Bourdieu, is produced in accordance with a heteronomous logic, because it is usually made for a commercial reason, and is designed to be as accessible as possible. Consequently, it attracts a mass audience, and presents characters, images or situations with which (it is assumed) they can easily identify. And it is not a 'consecrated' form, under the strict logic of autonomous art and its theological quality. The many critical complaints about the very popular performances of Australian pianist David Helfgott or the mass crowds drawn to exhibitions of US photographer Robert Mapplethorpe's work have often been accompanied by comments that they're just 'spectacles' rather than 'real art'.

These are common responses to work that is popular rather than made in obedience to the logic of autonomous art, difficult art, or what Loiç Wacquant calls 'the realm of mystification par excellence' (Wacquant 1993: 133). Of course, 'high art' becomes such not necessarily because of its internal constitution, but because of where, when and how it was made, and how it has been regarded by the gatekeepers. A famous example of the flexibility of designation is the work of William Shakespeare, who in his day was writing the equivalent of television dramas and comedies, and who now, 400 years later, has the patina of 'high art'. Interestingly, this is beginning to fade again to the popular as more and more film-makers rework his plays for a contemporary audience. Michael Hoffman's *A Midsummer Night's Dream* is an example of this because it was not self-consciously 'arty', but used popular actors, some contemporary arrangements and mainstream filming techniques to make the experience entertaining and accessible rather than 'educational' or 'enriching'. The cross-over effect between art and pop culture is also seen in everyday contemporary productions, such as television shows which incorporate features of both popular (commercial) culture and avant garde high art. The television comedy/drama/law show *Ally McBeal* is a case in point, being relatively complex in its characterisation and plot lines; showing 'heretical' sensibilities in its refusal to obey either the 'family values' of middle America or the strict gender politics of second-wave feminism; using pastiche and other experimental film techniques and perspectives; being poly-vocal in the numbers of views and values brought to bear; and being both self-referential and self-reflexive, reflecting on and responding to itself, rather than presenting simply a 'window on to the real world'. So, as Frow argues, popular and high art are not discrete: the terms are only useful to describe ways of appropriating artistic products (Frow 1995: 25).

But, despite the logical impracticality of the divide between art and pop culture, the concept still needs critical attention because of the effects of this sort of categorisation. The artist Hans Haacke argues that art is a form of symbolic power which 'can be put to the service of domination or emancipation' (in Bourdieu and Haacke 1995: 2). Art and pop culture are not neutrally aesthetic practices, but meaning-making symbolic practices which both reflect and inflect social values—with the capacity to establish and confirm (or sometimes challenge) those values. An example of this comes from Terry Zwigoff's 2002 movie *Ghost World* (see Figure 5.5). Thora Birch, the central character, is required to undertake remedial art classes during the school vacation, which she does resentfully. The art teacher dismisses her rather cartoon-ish drawings and, until she discovers the effect of 'found art' on the teacher, she has no hope of passing. She brings to class a large poster of an African-American man, in the old black-and-white-minstrel mode associated with the Deep South: his skin darkened with black-face, his lips huge and red, his cheeks round and shiny. Just in case we missed the point, the poster is titled 'Coon Chicken'. At first the teacher is both nonplussed and offended, but then Birch's character explains that she is challenging the idea of political correctness, and the fantasy that we are no longer a racist society. Immediately the teacher announces it as an extraordinary achievement: it is thoughtful, insightful about a serious social problem, and uses a traditionally negative representation of a black person as an instance of how visual imagery solidifies racist ideas. (This backfires, inevitably, at the exhibition where the parents and other viewers see it only as a racist image, and deny its ability to do

Figure 5.5 A still from Terry Zwigoff's *Ghost World*, 2002

anything other than shore up the notion that black Americans are ignorant, vulgar and second rate.) This whole scene (or series of scenes) exemplifies what Bourdieu writes about the politics of the field: that art is more likely to represent and reproduce consensus values than to challenge the status quo—Birch's character is failed, and her application to art school rejected, because of her exhibition of that work.

## art as value

What this suggests is that art isn't entirely free from social values and uses, although (autonomous) art has, theoretically, no involvement with economic return or obvious practical utility. Theodor Adorno writes: 'The seriousness of high art is destroyed in speculation about its efficacy' (1991: 85), and Maurice Blanchot argues that art is 'useless even to itself' (Blanchot 1982: 215) because it distances itself from the general logic of the social field, and from social and economic necessity. A well-crafted mural, for instance, may make a building more attractive, but it does not make it more efficient; a well-conceived sculpture may provide pleasure or a moment of reflection, but it does not contribute to basic human and social needs. Yet, despite the fact that the contemporary world seems to have an overwhelming commitment to economic growth and financial return, art continues to be made, and displayed, and valued.

This is, of course, because art does have social uses. Indeed, until quite recently it manifestly had utility: the early works, which were sacral or cult objects, had an obvious point—that of localising and facilitating worship, cult practice or recognition of the divine. And the representational work which dominated from the courtly period right through to the late nineteenth century also had a broad social use: the representation of individuals, objects or events which reified or commented on community life. With the emergence of what Marxist writers call 'bourgeois' art, the works become self-reflexive and self-referential—and distanced from utility (Bürger 1992: 58). But even bourgeois or post-nineteenth-century art, because of its symbolic potential, is very 'useful' in creating meanings for its maker, its viewers and in some cases its community. In Janet Wolff's terms, art constitutes 'the repositories of social value and social meaning' (Wolff 1981: 14): it reflects what is important to us, and about us, and it holds our traditions and history. This is why most nations put money into 'the arts', have national endowment funds, and build and maintain national galleries that exhibit 'Canadian art', 'British art' or 'Japanese art'. It is also why most governments have a raft of policies and legislative acts that define and determine what is done with and for art, from the various Copyright Acts among the Berne Convention signatory nations, to the Acts that regulate creative industries in a nation.

## the artistic fetish

Marxists would argue that art also exists because there is a market for it; and, because of art's limited use value, its market is at least partly determined by what many writers call its 'cult' value. This takes us back to Mane-Wheoki and the idea of the sacred character of art. In the Western tradition, the 'sacredness' of art is no longer associated with cultural tradition or religion, but is based on the authenticity of artworks, the magical property of something that is unique and singular. For instance, although pretty well everyone in the West knows in fine detail what the 'Mona Lisa' looks like, from the many postcards and other reproductions of this work, nonetheless there is always a crowd about the original that hangs in the Louvre. Knowing what something looks like, maybe having a postcard of it on your fridge, is not the same as standing before the authentic, singular object.

This effect of the original work means that art has what is called a 'fetish' quality. A fetish is an object which seems 'alienated' and abstracted from the everyday material world and which therefore holds a connection to the 'mystery' of truth. Many art objects fulfil these criteria, and their value in this case is based not on their economic—or resale—value, but on belief in their intangible properties. This is widely canvassed in the literature. Art, writes Cesar Grana, enacts a kind of social magic: it is constituted through, and depends upon, the belief that it is 'capable of making visible certain ultimate meanings which are present in ordinary events but which remain hidden in them until they are, in fact, reborn in their full spirit within the work of art' (Grana 1989: 18). Similarly, Bourdieu refers to art as 'the sacred sphere of culture' (Bourdieu 1984: 7); Nietzsche writes that: 'The existence of the world is justified only as an aesthetic phenomenon' (Nietzsche 1967: 22); and even a Marxist like Marcuse can write that a work of art is lifted out of the everyday process of reality and production, and 'assumes a significance and truth of its own' (Marcuse 1978: 8). Its special connection to truth is associated with this fetish, or cult aspect, something that is 'just felt'; the anthropologist Clifford Geertz suggests that art is a 'language of grace' which seems 'to exist in a world of its own, beyond the reach of discourse. It not only is hard to talk about it; it seems unnecessary to do so. It speaks, as we say, for itself' (1983: 94). As a supra-discursive practice, art takes on a quasi-religious significance. Walter Benjamin in fact describes the autonomous attitude as 'a theology of art' in his famous essay 'The Work of Art in the Age of Mechanical Reproduction' (Benjamin 1968: 224). He refers to this attitude as something that has its roots in the earliest artistic practices—which, he writes, were associated with magical and religious rituals, and which continue to inflect the function of art in society.

This religious or magical role is, in Benjamin's work, associated with the aura that attaches itself to an original work which bears the traces of the maker's hands. We may experience this in museums of anthropology or heritage, when we are moved by something that was handled by an ancient king, say, or that shows smudges made by a human hand millennia ago. And we also, in Benjamin's theory, experience it with works of art because of the trace of the artist's presence—though only, he writes, with works that are made by hand, rather than photographic or digital art. The graphite and watercolour drawing of a pair of eyes shown in Figure 5.6 is an example of this: they are quite different in appearance and meaning from the photograph of an eye reproduced in the Introduction (Figure i.1) for a number of reasons. The photograph is taken from a relatively long distance, because the photographer is looking through a lens, and

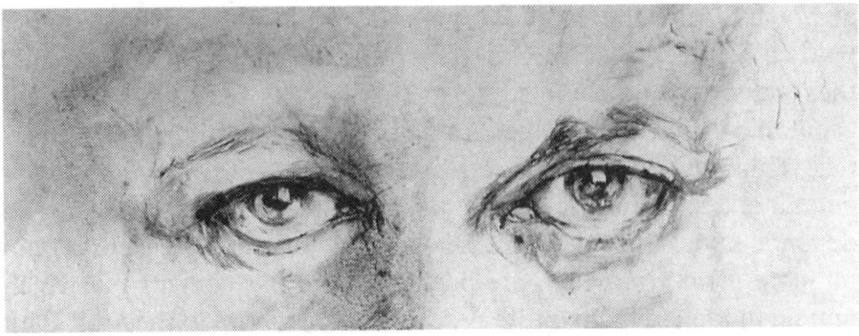

Figure 5.6 Bonnie's Eyes

allowing the camera and its film, shutter speed and f-stop to structure the reproduction. Also, in the photograph, the eye has not been fully disengaged from the face, but simply cropped back for emphasis. The photo is, strictly speaking, a synecdoche (a figure in which a part represents the whole), because the eye stands in for the whole face, the whole person, and can communicate transparently ('Here is someone, looking').

The drawing in Figure 5.6 works very differently—more along the lines of metaphor than synecdoche. This means it is transformative rather than communicatively transparent. A metaphor occurs when the thing that is the focus of attention is momentarily not itself but something new, something with properties which enhance our understanding of the original. In this drawing, the vehicle (the eyes and the hint of the face sketched about them) implies and momentarily becomes the topic (desire, demonstrated in the intensity and hunger of the gaze). It also works metaphorically because of the means of production. Line drawings exist only in the contrast between light and dark; they are born, so Lowry writes, from our need for 'a contrast between light and dark' (1967: 36). If we know that this is one of a series of drawings of the eyes of famous criminals, politicians and heads of corporations (this one, 'Bonnie's Eyes', depicts those of an archetypal female criminal), then the metaphor in this drawing works to suggest the light and dark of human ethics, of the human 'soul'. And, unlike the photograph which implies the whole person, the semi-detached eyes floating in a smudged suggestion of face call up not someone looking, but the idea of looking. The viewer's attention is drawn to sharp contrasts, so we must keep our gaze on the cleanly defined lines of the eyes themselves, and the crisp brows above, and leave in a kind of limbo the smudged and washed out nose and cheek. All the attention remains on the implacable, devouring gaze.

Drawings like this one also provide a pleasure that is different from the pleasure associated with photographs and other mechanical or digital forms of production because of the trace of human presence that remains on the work. This is associated with the fetish quality of art we mentioned above. The work shown in Figure 5.6, 'Bonnie's Eyes', has qualities we do not find in most photographs, and in particular it provides that pleasure in human contact: the association with an authentic artist in a singular work. We can identify the artist's fascination with her subject's eyes; we can note something of the process of her work, in the fact that she has selected which parts of the face to include and which to exclude or imply; and we can feel something of what Benjamin called the 'aura' associated with the marks of the movement of her hand across the page, the smudging of the graphite with her finger. Baudrillard writes:

> The fascination with artisanal objects derives from their having passed through someone's hands, and whose labour is still inscribed on them: it is the fascination with that which has been created (and which is therefore unique, since the moment of creation is irreversible). (Baudrillard 1990: 37)

There is an issue here to do with value. The more rare an object, in most cases, the greater its economic value. And certainly there is a very important process of commodification that takes place in the art world. Despite the apparent uselessness of art, it can be a very good economic investment and, ironically, the more disinterested an artist seems to be in the economic side of things—the more autonomous the artist is, and the more symbolic capital they may have acquired—the greater the economic value of their work. A commercial artist can attract only commercial rates, but a Lucien Freud can sell for millions. This again indicates the fetish quality which art can attain: fetishism relies on a belief that the 'real' content of an object—its material properties and its utility—can be abstracted to an inherent quality and a universal value (Žižek 1994: 317). An artist who is (apparently) concerned with the symbolic and 'magical' properties of work seems to be attending to the fantasy of a universal value—to be seeking out truths, rather than just fitting into the supply/demand curve of conventional economics. So their work may take on the quality of fetish and become an even more effective commodity, based on what Karl Marx terms the 'mysterious' transformation of a concrete object into something alienated from human production processes and, at least potentially, venerated.

## the withering of the aura

Contemporary technologies of artistic production and reproduction problematise this, because an effective fetish must provide a point of connection to something authentic, and to an originary moment and maker; contemporary art works' claims to authenticity are often, at best, tenuous. This, for Benjamin (1968: 215), leads to the loss—or the 'withering'—of the auratic quality of the work since, by allowing a proliferation of copies, reproduction technologies upset the notion of singularity, and present art works as conventional (albeit luxury) commodities, rather than 'authentic' pure signs, or fetishes. Certainly, electronic production and reproduction techniques diminish the value which is conventionally ascribed to an object by virtue of its connection to a 'real' artist and an originary moment of creation. Virtual objects, and objects which have been reproduced for a mass market, do not bear the marks of someone's hands, and so cannot claim this attachment to the Real. In this way, they can be considered by the standards of the arts field to lose their function of signification, and become 'mere' commodities.

But it is worth noting that Benjamin was writing in the early twentieth century; 'mechanical production' has come a long way since his day, and many (autonomous) artists are now working with digital media—and in some cases attracting economic and symbolic capital for their work. Walter Benjamin might term this 'exhibition value', which he says comes into play when the function of an art work has changed from ritual, and its artistic value/function may be 'incidental' (1968: 225). But art galleries, art writers and other gatekeepers are beginning to take it seriously, to treat it as significant work despite the absence of the trace of the hand, or the originary moment.

The work 'Future Tree' reproduced in Figure 5.7 is an example of digital production/reproduction. Its production is based on digital reproducibility: duplication and transformation that work under a logic that we can describe as autonomous. This is despite the fact that it is at least two steps away from its origins, from Benjamin's 'authentic' work: it is first a photograph rather than a drawing; and has been digitally manipulated, doubled, folded and mirrored—reduced to manufactured image and pixels. The picture field itself is sliced up into what appears to be six panels (though in reality there are only three images running vertically down the page), which denies viewers the fantasy of looking through a window on

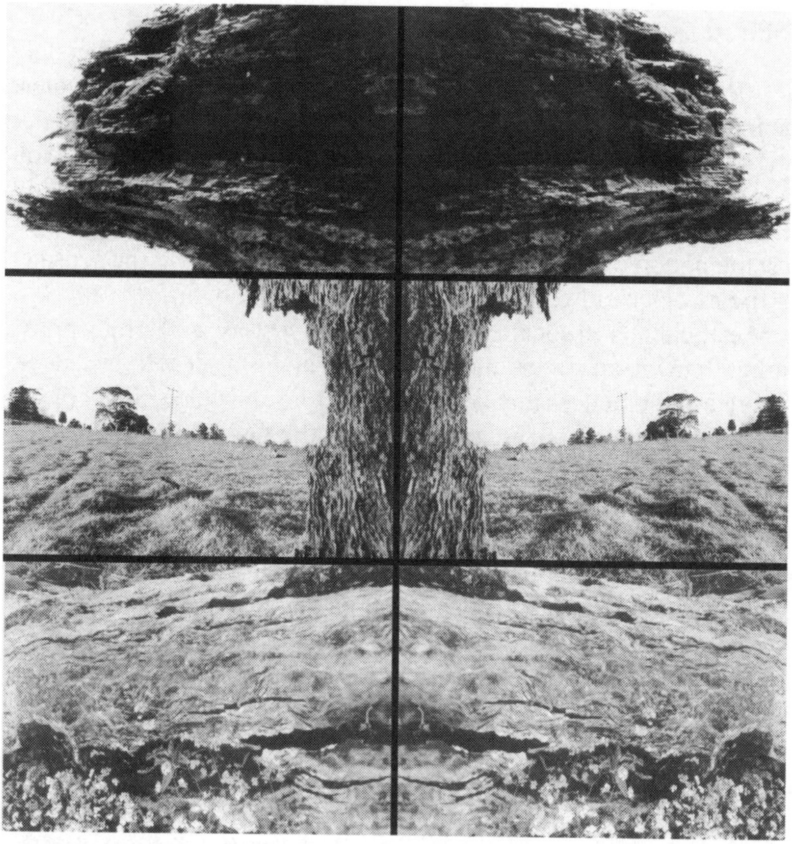

**Figure 5.7 Future tree**

to a real scene. And the word 'future' in the title projects it out of the everyday possibilities of experience. The 'tree' seems to be erupting violently out of the ground like a giant mushroom, wrenching the soil around its roots, threatening to bury the little flowers in the foreground. The word 'future' again, and the mushroom shape of the 'tree', evoke (at least for those of us who remember the Cold War) the effects of a nuclear explosion. The wasteland around the tree, the emptiness of the scene, and what appears to be the roiling of the ground across most of the visual plane support this reading, and the desolation and desecration it evokes. This seems to be a work that is didactic in some senses, in its conjuring up of human-initiated disaster, and the absence of everyday life and practice from the scene depicted here, and from the scene of its making. But it is also a work that takes up the question of aesthetics in its attention to order, form and meaning.

## aesthetic sense

We wrote earlier that the visual cultural products identified as 'art' are those objects made with a deliberately aesthetic intent. But what do we mean by aesthetics? The simplest definition, and the one most often used in everyday writings, is that it is all about beauty and taste. This is partly true, but it is not the full story. More specifically, aesthetics is called 'the sensate science', and this brings in two important issues associated with classical aesthetics: the notion of science, or knowledge and reason; and the sensate, or the involvement of the body in the experience of art.

Aesthetics is associated now with art history and philosophy, rather than visual culture more generally, and is a set of knowledges, theories and practices that address the nature and value of art objects and art experiences. Scholars working in the discipline of aesthetics are concerned with how we can evaluate the quality and value of an artwork, and with the bases of judgements of taste. It is a discipline with an ancient history, since many of the scholars of antiquity wrote about beauty, and about art and its appreciation. Plato is perhaps the earliest writer on aesthetics; his notion was that reality consists of archetypes (ideal forms), which are the models for all the objects in the social world. The logic here is that chairs, for instance, are not just chairs, but are poor simulacra of the Ideal Chair (or idea of chairness). The job of the philosopher, for Plato, was to reason, on the basis of the object, about what ideal it was imitating. The job of the artist, for Plato, was to copy that object as exactly as possible (and thus end up making a copy of a copy). Aristotle followed Plato in writing about aesthetics, but paid less attention to the ideal, and more to the order and unity of an object. He wrote about this particularly in his *Poetics (Part VII)*, and speculated (quaintly, from a contemporary viewpoint) that anything either tiny or vast couldn't be beautiful because its order could not be discerned clearly and in one moment of time. Beauty, for Aristotle, was dependent upon unity and sense of the whole. More than two millennia later, the logic of objects and the judgement of taste have changed; philosophers have lost faith in an ideal transcendental realm, and order and unity are no longer the most privileged forms within the art world.

The idea of order still had currency in the early days of aesthetics' current incarnation as a distinct discipline, with the German idealist philosophers of the eighteenth century. One of the first to write extensively about aesthetics was Alexander Baumgarten, who posited that 'the aesthetic' refers to the whole realm of human perception and sensation. Its history is thus physical rather than strictly conceptual, but nonetheless it engaged with the whole interest in reason, and was an attempt to understand and bring under the order of reason that which seemed to be outside its scope: the emotional or sensate realm. (In fact, Baumgarten termed aesthetics 'the sister of logic', or a *ratio inferior*—that is, a feminine analogue of reason, and hence inferior in terms of logic!)

## aesthetic judgement

Immanuel Kant, who is so closely identified with the discipline of aesthetics, associated sound understanding with judgement (in *The Critique of Judgement* 1790); in his estimate, the ability to judge works of art is dependent upon clarity of thought and knowledge, and not on the emotions. Beauty, in his estimate, was not simply something that might bring pleasure. In fact, Kant writes in the 'Analytic of Beauty' (1790: SS2) that: 'The delight which determines the judgement of taste is independent of all interest'. Like Plato, Kant considered the order and the form of a beautiful object to be based on universal rather than particular principles, and hence to exist outside of the subjective taste of an individual observer. This means that, for Kant, sensual gratification and personal sentiment were excluded from judgements of taste. Seeing something as beautiful meant seeing it as an image, rather than as a real object. The aesthetic object was to be regarded in terms of its formal qualities (its harmony and proportion, for instance) rather than in terms of its practical desirability (as an object to be consumed).

We can explore this by looking at the painting reproduced in Figure 5.8, Domenico Beccafumi's 'Madonna and Child with Infant John the Baptist' (c. 1542). Whatever Beccafumi and his sixteenth-century audiences may have made of this work, a nineteenth-century philosopher of aesthetics would insist that the best—indeed, the only valid—way to approach the work would be to stand back and gaze at it in a disinterested fashion. There is no room in this approach for being moved by religious awe; there is no room either for taking pleasure in the softness of the Madonna's cheek, the sensuality of her arm or the curve of the infant's body. Nor is there room for being moved by nostalgia, or personal delight—remembering, say, the pleasures of one's own early childhood, or the warmth of another's embrace. Instead, an aestheticist would be concerned to examine the formal qualities of the work: to take into account its volumetric representation—the way the work has achieved a sculptural effect with the Madonna's rich shape; the varying play of light which makes some parts recede, some move to the fore (her forehead, her right hand) so that there is a certain three-dimensionality. Our aestheticist might take into account the triangulation of the gaze of the Madonna and Child, to consider what outside the frame is attracting their attention; or analyse the strong stance of the baby, and the implication in that little frame of divine might. And the aestheticist would also identify the use of sfumato (the

**Figure 5.8 Madonna and Child with Infant John the Baptist; Domenico Beccafumi**

transition from light to dark by almost imperceptible stages) in the application of paint, and the mannerist theatricality of the work, associating it with the painter's training and environment, drawing inferences about Beccafumi's social and cultural location, his influences and the gestures these evoke. But what would not be permitted would be to associate the quality of the light with, say, romance, or the tenderness of the subjects' connection with sentiment.

## aesthetic pleasure

This shows up a curious ambivalence in classical aesthetic theory. The philosophy of aesthetics made an attempt to account for the terrain of immediate sensory experience, but ended up only valuing its formal and universal character. Michel Maffesoli writes that, where Kantian aesthetics is concerned, 'the accent [is] placed less on the artistic object as such than on the process that leads one to admire that object' (Maffesoli 1991: 9). So, though aestheticists wrote expressly about the sensate elements of aesthetic pleasure, the sphere of 'sensation' that was amenable to aesthetics was somehow above and beyond actual sensation—it was committed to process and reason. What this means in practice is that the art viewer, as a good aesthetician, could not be personally and viscerally moved by a beautiful object (or person): any pleasure taken must be pleasure in the beautiful form, for instance, rather than an actual body—something that leaves the pleasure of erotic imagery rather ungrounded. It also points out an uncomfortable relation between aesthetic analysis and the experience of art; we discussed above its cult value, its quality as fetish and as something that is not reducible to language. But of course aesthetics must reduce it to language, because this is the realm of reason and the intellect. The effort to which aesthetics seems to go to take up a disinterested position with regard to the judgement of taste does go some way towards suggesting that the very reason for considering artworks worthy of this discussion is a quasi-theology of their identity.

This theological imperative is also associated with the other side of aesthetics, the obverse of beauty, which Immanuel Kant named 'the sublime'. Kant describes it in fine detail in his 'Analytic of the Sublime' (1790: SS23). Unlike the beautiful, which is something that delights on the basis of its form, Kant writes that 'the sublime is to be found in an object even devoid of form, so far as it immediately involves, or else by its presence provokes a representation of limitlessness, yet with a superadded thought of its totality'. The sublime terrifies, rather than delights, and 'the delight in the sublime' is 'a negative pleasure' because it reminds us of our limits within a limitless world. We can experience the sublime on looking at, say, a raging storm or crashing seas—it is 'in its chaos, or in its wildest and most irregular disorder and desolation, provided it gives signs of magnitude and power, that nature chiefly excites the ideas of the sublime'. But it should be noted that the sublime is not in nature, as the beautiful may be (in, for instance, the order of the petals of a rose). Rather, nature can invoke the sublime by drawing the viewer to reflect on what is exclusively cultural:

> For the sublime, in the strict sense of the word, cannot be contained in any sensuous form, but rather concerns ideas of reason, which, although no adequate presentation of them is possible, may be excited and called into the mind by that very inadequacy itself which does admit of sensuous presentation. (Kant 1790: SS23)

The raging storm is not sublime, but because it is formless and limitless, it takes us to the sublime, evokes our terror and demands that we think about human/cultural concepts—that we apply reason to the situation. So there is, in the anguish of the sublime, a very discernable pleasure for the viewer: the pleasure in the exercise of reason that relieves the pain brought about by the terror of the sublime.

## aesthetics and the social

What we see in this discussion of Kantian aesthetics is a commitment to reason over pleasure, to cool distance over passionate engagement, to the intellect rather than the emotions. For these reasons, among others, it is often considered a highly elitist approach to visual culture, one which helps differentiate society between those with cultivated tastes (who inevitably are already privileged socially—possessing high education, social status, the leisure time to view such culture, and, often, money) and the plebeians who get weepy over a photograph of a kitten. Peter Bürger writes, in criticism of the elitism of Kantian aesthetic imperatives, that: 'With his demand that the aesthetic judgement be universal, Kant also closes his eyes to the particular interests of his class' (1992: 54). You can thus only be aesthetically disinterested if you forget interest, or pretend that the things we do in society are not always already deeply stained with personal investment.

Aesthetic judgement is not, then, a 'gift' or special skill; it is the outcome of social organisation, of class differences, of educational opportunities, though it circulates as though it is natural or pre-given.

A large body of literature shows that 'taste' is arbitrary—it changes across periods, cultures and specific contexts; and it is ideologically inflected—some things come to seem 'good taste' because it is in the interests of those in social authority to make them so. Digital culture expert Kim Veltman, for instance, points out that even styles are dependent upon ideological ordering principles. He compares the narrative structure of the art of the Middle Ages, when belief in God held everything in place, with twentieth century art where, with the death of God and the loss of any certainties of order, paintings were often reduced to 'chaos'—to 'blobs of paint and lines' (Veltman 1998). So there is nothing inherent about taste; rather, legitimate taste belongs to those who possess authorised cultural competencies because of their class, education and social status (Bourdieu, Darbel and Schnapper 1991: 39).

But although we might know about the constructedness, the arbitrariness and the ideological bases for taste, aesthetics and the art world which it analyses are still highly privileged. And the corollary to this reverential attitude to things of 'culture' is that everyday sensate experiences (such as being moved by a popular song that reminds us of our first love) are considered inferior, because they are sentimental.

## conclusion

We have seen that the field of art constitutes a special case within the whole study of visual culture because of its importance in generating symbolic and cultural capital, in organising society and in establishing criteria for taste. But in fact the ways by which we can access, or 'read', artworks are the same ones we apply to the reading of any other visual object. We can come to art, advertisements, photographs or sitcoms with a naïve eye, simply responding to the shape or content of the object; alternatively, we can use versions of the art historian's 'good eye' and examine that object closely for its production, and the iconography used to tell its story; or we can apply a more comprehensive literary and add to these readings an understanding of the iconography available to the producer in the period it was made—what sorts of stories were circulating then? How were they valued? How much freedom did a producer have to use or abuse them?—and then also take into account the present context in which the work is being read. This last approach demands a considerable literacy in the media used, in the history of that sort of work, and in understanding contemporary approaches to meaning and value, but its rewards are an ability to take a distance from the work so that we can see how and why we are touched and moved by works of visual culture, and how this particular example works on us as it does.

Across history, art has proven to be a particularly resilient and influential way of seeing—but it has always had to compete with a variety of other powerful visual regimes that predispose us to see and experience the world in ways very different to, and removed from, the worldview offered by aesthetics. In our next two chapters we turn our attention to what are arguably the most influential and pervasive visual regimes in the contemporary Western world: normalisation and capitalism.

# 6 normalising vision

## introduction

In the Marx Brothers' film *Night at the Opera*, Groucho Marx is approached and accosted by his high-society employer Margaret Dumont, who has been fruitlessly waiting for him in a restaurant while he has been dining with another woman. When Groucho denies that he was with anyone else, Margaret Dumont exclaims, 'But I saw the two of you together with my own eyes.' To which Groucho replies, 'Who are you going to believe, me or your own eyes?'

Margaret Dumont's appeal to the evidence offered by 'her own eyes' is understandable—but so, to a certain extent, is Groucho's challenge to their validity as '(eye) witnesses'. Throughout history there has been considerable debate and disagreement about which ways of seeing are more reliable or credible than others. In our previous chapter we considered how and why an artistic 'way of seeing' differs from, and is often privileged above, the perspectives offered by a related field such as advertising. In the final three chapters of this book, we will examine the ways in which particular forms of visuality—what we can call *visual regimes*—have come to be accorded an authority within Western culture, and as a consequence have exercised control and influence over how people see and understand the 'truth of the world' and, equally importantly, what they expect to see. The notion of the visual regime refers to the process whereby a particular field or group of fields (say, the sciences) manages to export its ways of seeing to most or all other fields, which in turn leads to a universalising of the authority of different forms, genres, mediums and practices of the visual to provide access to what we could call 'visual reality'. The two visual regimes that undoubtedly exercise the greatest influence over visual practices in the contemporary Western world are what we call *normalisation*, which is associated with the fields of science, bureaucracy and government, and *capitalism*, which is part of the economic field. In this chapter we will look at the defining characteristics of normalisation, and consider how it frames and influences how we see the world.

## modernity as a way of seeing

Art historian Jonathan Crary argues that the advent and development of the set of discourses, ideas, perspectives and practices that we term normalisation were tied up with the Foucauldian insight that populations were—and still are—seen (by the field of power, which includes but is not limited to the state and its various institutions) as potential resources. Institutions, bureaucratic apparatuses and their functionaries in fields such as education, health and the military looked at people not as individuals, but predominantly in terms of how they might usefully contribute to the well-being of the state. As Jonathan Crary writes in *Techniques of the Observer*, these processes, and the ways in which they produced modern subjects, were tied up with:

> the fixing of quantitative and statistical norms of behaviour. The assessment of 'normality' in medicine, psychology, and other fields became an essential part of the shaping of the individual to the requirements of institutional power in the nineteenth century, and it was through these disciplines that the subject in a sense became visible. (Crary 1990: 15–16)

So a school teacher, health worker or army officer would already know what they were looking for when they came into contact with people: signs of strong bodies, an ability to solve tasks, or a willingness to follow orders. And they would contextualise and evaluate those signs in terms of patterns and standards of normality (constituted through the use of statistical norms and behavioural templates) in much the same way that a farmer might decide which cows or sheep were suitable for breeding, and which ones should be slaughtered for meat.

In order for the state to gain the maximum benefit from its resources, people had to be subjected to techniques that regulated and orientated their thinking, seeing and general behaviour—in other words, they had to be disciplined. The best way to bring about this disciplining of the population was by training the body, which is why Foucault refers to the forms of knowledge, techniques, mechanisms and operations that were developed for analysing, defining, controlling and regulating behaviour as *biopower*. Being disciplined didn't simply mean being punished—rather, it referred to a process whereby people's bodies would be disposed to behave in a manner consistent with what the state and its various institutions considered to be normal, healthy and productive. This process was meant to train people to lead normal lives without the need to reflect on what they were doing. It started at an early stage in a person's life (a child in its family and at school learned the rules of society, the need to respect authority and the consequences of delinquency) and continued until death (manifested, for instance, through the need to consider what were the most appropriate—that is, the normal—ways to die). Just as a soldier is trained to fit into and comply with military culture instinctively, so populations were meant to accept, and be directed by, a disciplined way of behaving. When a soldier saw something that signified a superior officer (a particular uniform, stripes), he was required to behave, quite automatically, in a submissive manner. Similarly, the idea was that when the population saw signs of the state's authority (buildings, functionaries in uniforms, titles, letterheads) they would see, without questioning or hesitation, something that was greater, more powerful and more knowledgeable than themselves, and adjust their behaviour to comply with these manifest signs of the state.

Foucault identifies two major stages to this process of *disciplinarity* and *normalisation*. The first stage is best represented by Jeremy Bentham's model of the *panopticon*, which consisted of:

> a tower placed in a central position within the prison. From this tower, the guards would be able to observe every cell and the prisoners inside them, but it was designed in such a way that the prisoners would never know whether they were being observed or not. Prisoners would assume that they could be observed at any moment and would adjust their behaviour accordingly. (Danaher et al. 2000: 53–54)

The second stage of the process was *self-surveillance*, which was considered to be a more economical and effective form of regulation. Through immersion in and contact with various cultural institutions and their discourses and images, the logic went, subjects would be disposed to make themselves the objects of their own gaze, constantly monitoring and evaluating their bodies, actions and feelings. There is an old Bob Dylan song called 'Talking John Birch Society Blues', about the right-wing American political organisation of the 1950s and 1960s.

In the song, an American citizen is told (by the government, the media and by his fellow-Birchers) that communists are everywhere, and are plotting to bring America down. He checks out his fellow workers and family, and even looks under his bed, but he can't find any communists. Finally, since he knows there are communists about (the government tells him so), he turns his eyes on the last remaining suspect—himself. He starts investigating his own behaviour, adding that he hopes he doesn't find anything (presumably signs such as red clothes or folk records) that will require him to turn himself in as a communist.

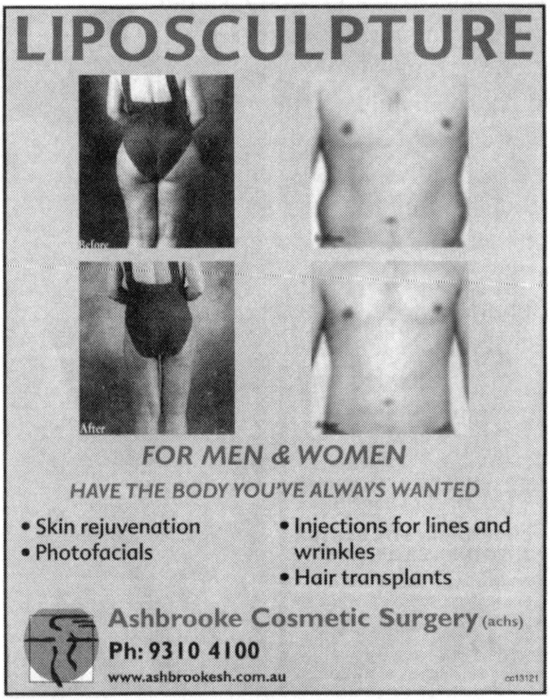
LIPOSCULPTURE
FOR MEN & WOMEN
HAVE THE BODY YOU'VE ALWAYS WANTED
• Skin rejuvenation
• Photofacials
• Injections for lines and wrinkles
• Hair transplants
Ashbrooke Cosmetic Surgery (achs)
Ph: 9310 4100
www.ashbrookesh.com.au

**Figure 6.1 More than ever before, people are resorting to invasive surgery in order to attain what they are told is a 'normal' or 'desirable' figure. Advertisements such as this are becoming increasingly common.**

On a more everyday level, people see themselves in the context of what has been designated as normal or average. So a person's height or weight, how hard they work, or how many times they have sex during the week is usually viewed and evaluated in the context of standards derived from and authorised by scientific knowledge. Communication theorist Armand Mattelart traces this specific statistical inflection back to 'the last two decades of the nineteenth century', when 'sciences based on the calculation of individual behaviour took off' (Mattelart 2003: 37). To a certain extent, this merely added to the disciplinary techniques and resources available to the state, helping 'Policemen, judges and forensic scientists . . . in their mission of social hygiene against the dangerous classes' (2003: 37). But the development of, say, 'Machines for recording the pace of work in factories, stadiums and barracks' (2003: 37) meant that knowledge, in the form of exact and specific measurements of normality, were now disseminated for the population to use against itself. It would be easy, in the light of the production of this kind of information, for workers to see themselves as lazy and unproductive, and to feel the need to work harder and longer—to be 'just like a normal person'. In the contemporary world, there is a plethora of pseudo-scientific statistics of normality, regularly articulated in newspaper articles, magazines and television shows, which both remind people of what they have to measure themselves against, and offer the means (better toothpaste, self-help books, exercise equipment, diets, cars, clothes) for achieving and surpassing such norms.

## subjective vision and the scientific gaze

This concomitant development of the reason of state and scientific knowledge not only increased what could be seen; it also changed the way in which the practices and mechanisms of seeing were understood. Jonathan Crary uses Foucault's notion of the modern discursive regime, which was predicated on the development of scientific categories, knowledge, techniques and attitudes, in order to suggest how and why new ways of understanding vision came about at the same time. He argues that, prior to the modern period, perceptual experience was considered to be largely 'given to us' by and from the external world—in other words, we more or less received the truth of the world, rather than seeing it in a subjective way. Science in the modern period, however, produced a different way of understanding perception: what Crary refers to as 'the idea of subjective vision' (1999: 12), which involved 'a severing (or liberation) of perceptual experience from a necessary relation to the external world' (1999: 12). As Crary writes:

> the rapid accumulation of knowledge about the workings of a fully embodied observer disclosed possible ways that vision was open to procedures of normalization . . . Once the empirical truth of vision was determined to lie in the body, vision (and similarly the other senses) could be annexed and controlled by external techniques of manipulation and stimulation. (Crary 1999: 12)

The insight here is both quite profound and paradoxical: the realisation that the basis of vision lay 'in the body' and was thus subjective arose at the same time as the development of science and its objective and objectifying ways of seeing, categorising and normalising people and populations. The qualities that Martin Jay identifies as leading to the supposed ocularcentricism of Greek culture—a sense of detachment and objectivity; apprehension without the need for proximity; and a 'prospective capacity for foreknowledge' (Jay 1993: 25)—were both the basis of, and developed by, Western science. These principles had been extrapolated from sixteenth- and

**Figure 6.2 Many of the great seventeenth-century Dutch painters used devices such as mirrors to explore perspective and perception. This detail from Vermeer's 'The Music Lesson' (1665) shows a young woman practising at the virginal, itself a comment on wealth and sexuality. Although she appears to be sitting straight at the instrument, in the mirror her face is turned towards her music master, possibly implying a deeper relationship between them.**

seventeenth-century scientific principles championed by practitioners such as Francis Bacon and Robert Boyle, who emphasised techniques predicated on the observable replication of phenomena in isolated, and therefore uncorrupted, contexts such as experimentation.

According to Foucault (1973), until the seventeenth century Western culture understood and saw the world in terms of the notions of resemblance and similarity: the world was a book to be read through the recognition and application of a natural order and set of categories. But this regime increasingly comes to be seen as unreliable, and as producing falsehoods and illusions. The classic example of this change of perception can be found in Miguel de Cervantes' novel *Don Quixote*, first published in 1604. The eponymous character Don Quixote is, in the words of Michel Foucault, 'the hero of the same' (1973: 46). He travels the world seeing through the categories and narratives contained in the 'extravagant romances' (1973: 46) of his age, which turn 'flocks, serving girls, and inns' into 'castles, ladies and armies' (1973: 47). When Quixote is confronted by the unreality of these resemblances, he resorts to the notion of magic as an explanation: an evil sorcerer must have intervened and cast a spell that changed things. But modern science offers a completely different explanation: there is no magic, only 'idols' (Foucault 1973: 51). The belief in idols and magic will be replaced by scientific rationalism: from the seventeenth century onwards, science will only see through and believe in analysis, evidence and trained perception (Foucault 1973: 55–6).

## knowledge, technology and the trained eye

This new (scientific) knowledge, Foucault suggests, supposedly allowed people to see 'truly'—or, at least, it claimed to be able to train and discipline the eyes to distinguish truth from illusion. Think of the example of Sherlock Holmes and Watson that we used in the introduction: both characters, but particularly Holmes, had been trained to ensure that their vision was attentive and productive. When Holmes looked at a person's face, clothes or body language, he focused his attention on the things that would enable him to call up the history and characteristics of the person which allowed him to evaluate and categorise them (as a widower, an alcoholic or poor). No matter how carefully the person tried to conceal what they really were or had done, visual clues would give them away. In other words, Holmes knew that a certain collection of visual evidence, much of which might be almost undetectable to the untrained eye (stains on a glove, a heel worn away on one side), added up to the truth about a person (the signs give you the text). The eyes could then provide a true picture of the world, but only if modern knowledge and techniques directed and looked through those eyes.

There was, of course, another side to this development of the knowledgeable, trained eye: not only did new forms of knowledge allow scientists to see more accurately, but the productivity of these trained eyes—and, importantly, the development of new technologies of seeing—went back into building even more knowledge, and producing more categories of things. The increase both in knowledge and the capacity for technology to reveal hidden detail made it easier for social scientists, bureaucrats and politicians to distinguish between and see the normal, the sane and the healthy on the one hand, and the perverted, the mad and the sick on the other.

Let's take a scientific/technological example of this process, and see how we can apply it to wider areas of seeing and categorising people and populations. Consider the photographs of snails in Figure 6.3. These photographs can be read as scientific (in terms of genre) for a number of reasons, but most obviously because the subject matter,

**Figure 6.3 Snails (a) static; (b) in motion**

along with its very minute rendering of fine detail pertaining to the snail's shape, texture, markings and distinctive features, would not normally be found within, or be of interest to, a field other than biology (though it could quite easily be taken up and aestheticised—that is, read as a piece of art or an example of the representation of something beautiful—by the (sub)field of art photography). Why, though, is this kind of visual text scientifically useful?

Quite simply, the orientation and level of detail provided by the technology not only allow scientists to compare and contrast this species with other species, but also (potentially) to make distinctions within the species itself. If we look at the photograph in Figure 6.3b we can exemplify this idea and process in more detail. Whereas the first photograph (Figure 6.3a) captures a considerable amount of detail that can be used to describe and categorise the snail, it is limited precisely in that it isolates and in a sense decontextualises that information (in that it removes, for instance, the contexts and relationships of movement). But if we have a number of consecutive stills, they can be related to one another to produce even more (contextualised) information: we don't have to extrapolate movement techniques and patterns from a single still—we can see it in action (or at least we can see the illusion of movement) over different terrains. Of course, greater numbers of (increasingly minute) stills being put together in varied contexts (eating, mating, moving over obstacles) would lead to even more (scientific) narratives—that is, knowledge—being produced.

## the human sciences and normality

The site where this scientific endeavour of discovery is most clearly played out is in the human sciences, which are constituted by those fields or disciplines such as psychology, sociology, anthropology or economics which seek out and produce knowledge of (that is, the 'truth' about) the human subject. In the first volume of *The History of Sexuality*, Foucault explains how the nineteenth century, which is conventionally represented as silent and puritanical about sexual matters, was characterised by the institutional production of vast quantities of sexual knowledge which supposedly provided access to the realities of the human subject. It did this by looking through and across accounts, testimonies, descriptions, histories, experiments, case studies, confessions and measurements which worked to bring out the truth of sexuality in the form of new scientific categories such as the homosexual, the nymphomaniac, the hysteric and the neurotic.

Today, when we look at and evaluate people—and this includes ourselves—we usually do so using these and other categories, discourses and logics (tied up with notions of normality, health, deviance, perversion and delinquency) related to, or taken directly from, the human sciences. And this tendency is accentuated as these scientific categories of truth and reality are circulated throughout popular culture, particularly in the media. This is the main reason why we have used the term 'normalising' rather than 'scientific' to designate this particular visual regime. The former picks up on and articulates the way in which particular ways of seeing associated with the field, values and practices of science produce or dispose certain types of subjectivity, viewpoints and relations (to oneself, others and society) across various scientific and non-scientific fields within a culture. While the notion of the scientific gaze refers to a set of operations that help produce the visual world, the concept of normalisation extends this operation to take into account the way the effects of that gaze are manifested socially, culturally and politically, and in both the personal and public spheres, within the logic of the reason of state.

We made the point earlier in this chapter that the notion and practices of normality were based on the presumption that if populations and bodies were trained and oriented in certain ways, they would become more productive, reliable, resilient and pliable. Moreover, this bodily orientation would be accompanied by a belief in, and acceptance of, the logic and naturalness of the normalising project itself. Or, as Pierre Bourdieu argues in this quote taken from the seventeenth-century French philosopher Blaise Pascal:

> we are as much automatic as intellectual; and hence it comes that the instrument by which conviction is attained is not demonstration alone. How few things are demonstrated! Proofs only convince the mind. Custom is the source of our strongest and most believed proofs. It inclines the automaton, which persuades the mind without its thinking about the matter. (Pascal quoted in Bourdieu 2000: 12)

Consider the photograph in Figure 6.4. It shows a group of women serving in the military, probably taken around the time of World War II. It is a genre photograph: its organisational characteristics could be replicated in a group photograph taken at a school, university, sports club or factory. This is pretty much Foucault's point: the techniques associated with normalisation were meant to be able to be extended across groups and contexts, and so pervade society. The manifestations of its logic in this photograph are numerous. Firstly, there is the imposition of order, consistency, regularity and symmetry: each person is tied in to and bound by a set of spatial relations (from left to right, top to bottom, between each other). In other words, everybody must be in line and fit into an appropriate space. Secondly, the bodies are all 'held together'—arms are at the sides or tucked behind the back, legs are roughly the same distance apart. Thirdly, all eyes are directed at the camera, which demands and receives the return of the straight and steadfast gaze.

It is almost as if the individuals captured in this shot, along with their wills and personalities, are dissolved into the identity of the group. And the only other thing that the camera requires from these individuals-as-group is that they carry out this process with a smile on their faces—or at least without any sign of dissent or discontent. Of course, to do anything else—to slouch, to look awry, to ignore spatial boundaries—is to produce a marker of non-compliance, which in turn leads to the 'what is wrong with you?' question/accusation. Signs of

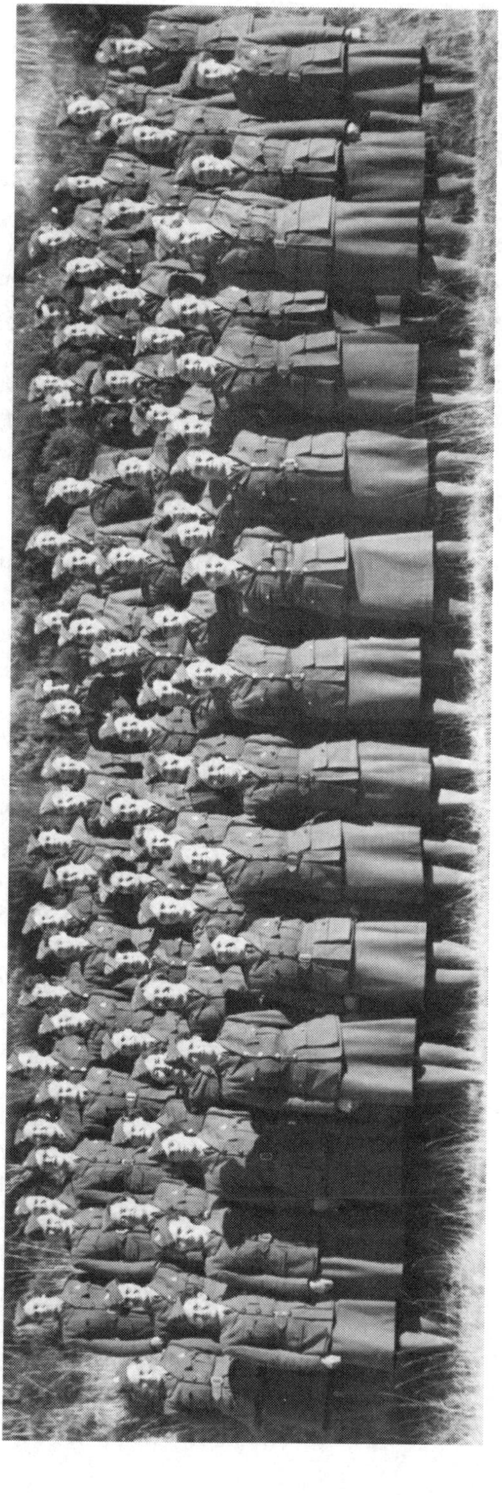

**Figure 6.4** Service women; found photograph, Wellington, New Zealand, 2000

any reluctance to conform can be read as symptoms of abnormality—that is, such behaviour can be interpreted pathologically. There is a very insistent and regulatory circularity to this logic: if you don't perform in accordance with the imperatives and bodily dispositions associated with a normal and healthy subjectivity, you are unhealthy, you will be treated accordingly, and the detection of the abnormality will be extended to explain your behaviour.

**Figure 6.5 Foucault's theory of normalisation is exemplified in Soviet realist art, which routinely showed its subjects in triumphant group poses.**

## categories and sites of normality

Similar processes help us make sense of people in terms of gender, age, race and ethnicity—categories that often refer negatively to certain groups in society. There are, for instance, various supposedly deficient and excessive performances with regard to female sexuality (frigidity, nymphomania), but nothing analogous for male sexuality; male sexual problems are typically considered purely physical (erectile dysfunction), which carries no connotations of psychic or moral failure. This does not just reflect patriarchy, it reproduces and extends it. These categories (and the many others that are employed in institutional sites such as clinics or hospitals, or which have passed into the general social field and are employed, say, in the media) more or less determine both what we see and, concomitantly, how we evaluate it. That is, female sexuality is recognisable in terms of a notion of normality, and anything that differs from the norm is considered pathological.

So adolescent girls who don't take an interest in boys, whether young men in their social circles or celebrities, might be seen by their parents as requiring psychological help of some kind, simply because they are showing signs of an 'unhealthy' interest in the company of other girls. But in all likelihood such girls will intervene against themselves before their parents or peers begin to express concern. An example of this situation occurs in the film *Ghostworld*, where two young women share a close relationship that verges on being sexualised. However, when they decide, on leaving school, to move into a flat together, a tension is introduced into their relationship that eventually pushes them apart. This tension takes the form of one girl seeming to take a sexual interest in an older, slightly 'geeky' male.

There is no real logic to the attraction, which is doomed to failure from the start, but it is functional precisely because it effects a separation of the girls, and thus ensures that they won't be drawn into an 'abnormal' sexual relationship (one goes off, perhaps to become an artist; the other gets a 'normal job'). What is interesting is that the two women can never articulate the attraction they have for each other, or the problems this (potentially) raises. The guiding hand and eyes of normalisation ensure that, even as they act out a kind of anti-social stance (making fun of their conformist friends, for example), they reject in advance the possibility of a sexual attraction and relationship which would effectively categorise them as abnormal, without their apparently knowing what they are doing, or why they are doing it.

How is this situation played out as a set of visual(ising) practices? The most obvious symptom of this situation can be found in the way the two women look at one another when they are talking. In the early part of the film the looks that accompany their dialogue are certain, unwavering, comfortable—precisely because they are in a sense 'authorised' visual exchanges: they are friends with shared histories, tastes and predilections. They clearly have an intimate relationship, but it is an intimacy that is not marked or informed, in any overt sense, by sexual desire.

The fact that they are supposed to be moving into a flat together changes this situation. In school they were thrown together, but now that they are choosing to live together (and they aren't dating any men), their relationship is transformed into something else—it is becoming (potentially) sexualised. As the move draws close, they more or less stop looking directly at one another. Why? Because looking is different now—it isn't authorised in the same way ('we're just friends'). The failed relationship with the geeky male doesn't resolve the problem—if anything, it works to foreground the possibility that when they're together, they might be looking at each other as 'more than friends'. In other words, when they visually frame and read each other's bodies now (lips, breasts, legs), they are looking from, and making meanings concomitant with, the position of a desiring subject.

Ways of seeing in the Western world are strongly informed, then, by both the pervasiveness of the scientific gaze itself, and the categories that are produced by and through that gaze—even in the most everyday of practices. An obvious example of this kind of science-influenced contextualising and visualising of the everyday—from the perspective of both the scientist and the non-scientist—occurs whenever a patient visits a medical practitioner. The latter can perform activities that, in most other sites, would be overtly sexual, such as asking the patient to remove her or his clothes, staring at them while they are partly undressed or naked, asking them questions about their bodies and personal activities, and touching or positioning them in ways normally associated with sexual intimacy. Yet these practices are (viewed as being) desexualised because of a number of factors: what the practitioner is wearing (fully dressed, in formal clothes or a medical-style coat); the discourse and mode of address (references to disease or symptoms, questions delivered in a disinterested manner); and the tenor of the relationship (the practitioner will at least appear to be unexcited, in control, sympathetic but distanced, and will treat the patient as a kind of text to be read for pathological signs).

What countenances the practitioner to be able to carry out activities of an intimate nature on other people is the notion and authority of the pure and disinterested nature of the gaze, and its accompanying movements, gestures, touches and comments. Most importantly, the site and its activities are theoretically neutral and detached, and above all else devoid of any kind of pleasure or enjoyment. The clinic or the medical practice is a public site of intimacy and control that is (supposed to be) without regard to notions of private desire that normally apply to the way we see physically intimate behaviour.

The gaze associated with the normalising visual regime is not only meant to discover the truth of the world through the processes of observation, analysis, diagnosis and prescription; it also works, at least theoretically, to shape it. For instance, the adoption of the scientific gaze is meant to ward off desire. A medical practitioner is not supposed to enjoy watching a patient undress, and the training practitioners receive is meant to allow them to see differently those things that would excite them in everyday life—like naked or physically accessible bodies. In other words, the body looks different when located in, and treated by, the sites and techniques of science.

This process does not just apply to the field of medicine; it informs many other sites and fields in Western culture. A good example of this can be seen in the Monty Python film *The Meaning of Life*, where John Cleese plays a schoolteacher giving a lesson on sexuality. Slavoj Žižek describes the scene in the following way:

> The teacher questions the pupils on how to arouse the vagina; caught in their ignorance, the embarrassed pupils avoid his gaze and stammer half-articulate answers, while the teacher repri-

> mands them severely for not practising the subject at home. With his wife's assistance, he thereupon demonstrates to them the penetration of penis into vagina; bored by the subject, one of the schoolboys casts a furtive glance through the window, and the teacher asks him sarcastically: 'Would you be kind enough to tell us what is so attractive out there in the courtyard?' (1997: 173)

The neutrality and disinterestedness of the scientific gaze is meant to empty the object being scrutinised of any (destabilising) excitement-attraction for the viewer, except that which is associated with scientific curiosity and discovery; hence the teacher and the school students see nothing but mechanical activities devoid of human content. The same regime supposedly characterises other public sites such as courtrooms. Judges, lawyers and juries supposedly view an alleged crime in much the same way as a scientist observes a dissected corpse, and are meant to sentence, prosecute and convict a criminal as if they were addressing, solving and writing up a scientific problem. And the centrality of, and capital accorded, scientific methods in policing is played out and evinced in various ways, from the deductive logic employed by Sherlock Holmes in Conan Doyle's fictions to the authority accorded forensic medicine in securing criminal convictions where there is no eye witness, or when many years have elapsed since the crime was committed.

The centrality and authority of scientific approaches in social fields is carried over into the way categories of seeing can frame everyday reality. We referred to the ways in which pathological categories such as hysteria and nymphomania were used to reproduce and extend patriarchal ways of seeing, but such categories also frame and explain people and their activities in legal, sporting, artistic and above all educational fields. Jonathan Crary, for instance, writes that:

> Over the last few years we have been reminded of the durability of attention as a normative category of institutional power, in the form of the dubious classification of an 'attention deficit disorder' (or ADD) as a label for unmanageable schoolchildren and others . . . what stands out is how attention continues to be posed as a normative and implicitly natural function whose impairment produces a range of symptoms and behaviors that variously disrupt social cohesion . . . Even after admitting that there is absolutely no experimental or empirical confirmation of an ADD diagnosis, the authors of a best-selling book on the

> subject make the claim: 'Remember that what you have is a neurological condition. It is genetically transmitted. It is caused by biology, by how your brain is wired'. (Crary 1999: 35–6)

And this authority of the biological explanation of children's behaviour in school and at other sites continues to influence how children are seen and understood, despite researchers noting the apparent paradox that: 'Many, if not most, hyperactive children are apparently able to sustain attention for a substantial period of time in high interest situations, such as watching television shows or playing video games' (Crary 1999: 37).

## the normalised subject

The reproduction and continuation of normalised ways of seeing is in a sense a circular process: social fields, institutions, techniques and mechanisms produce subjects who are inclined to see and understand the world, and everyone in it, in terms of recognisable and authorised categories, and the templates that go with them. In school, for instance, normalisation is effected through physical discipline, peer pressure, report cards, family expectations, or the way classroom spaces are arranged. This feeds back into, and validates the authority of, the institutions and process of normalisation. We can, at this point, refer back to Chapter 1 and our discussions of how we carry around with us a (more or less unconscious) set of images and ideas which we use to simultaneously evaluate and recognise what we see. There are two questions that need to be addressed here: firstly, what are the cultural processes that help produce these sets of images; and secondly, how is the relationship between these dispositions and the act of seeing manifested as a (technically explicable) practice?

These questions can be answered by looking at the ways in which the habitus—which we defined as a durable set of dispositions derived from and across our cultural history—is reinforced and complemented by what we can refer to as pervasive cultural performances of normalisation—what the American gender theorist Judith Butler refers to as authorised, iterative performances of normalisation. Butler's argument is that there are sites in a culture (most particularly the media) where we can check that our habitus is 'on track' (that is, it remains true to itself while taking into account changes in society) in terms of our body shape, clothes, mannerisms, or ways of seeing and evaluating other people. These images, ideas and performances constitute a vast store of up-to-date templates for, or models of, a normal, healthy, attractive and desirable subject. This evaluation and categorisation of each and every subject, including the self, is 'neither a single act nor a causal process initiated by the subject . . . Construction not only takes place in time, but is itself a temporal process which operates through the reiteration of norms' (Butler 1993: 10).

Cultural texts (advertisements, television shows, films, video games) are populated by types who let us know what is attractive and desirable, healthy and normal. But they do more than offer up role-model bodies; they help us understand, negotiate and see the world. We see them in pop cultural texts such as magazines and television, but also—usually in considerably less overt manifestations—in more 'serious' texts such as newspaper articles, and scientific or government reports. So, over time, this relationship between the (normalised) ways of seeing and the audience as seeing and evaluating practitioners is played out; it returns again and again in the way we look at and evaluate partners, colleagues or other people, as the normal way of (seeing) the world.

Consider what happens in soap operas such as *Neighbours* and *Eastenders*. The types of people who appear in each episode, the frequency with which they appear, the roles and activities they take on, and the way they are integrated into narratives is strictly regulated. Indigenous groups, refugees or homosexuals, for instance—and even relatively mainstream groups such as people from migrant backgrounds—are ignored, or make infrequent appearances. As a consequence, when issues concerning institutionalised racism or the treatment of asylum seekers surface in the media, it is relatively straightforward for audiences to countenance or fail to be moved by events or practices, like unequal rates of imprisonment based on ethnicity, or the internment of asylum seekers. This is because the people affected aren't obviously human in terms of the (very influential) templates made available within media texts.

Curiously, what is most central and pervasive in all these templates of acting, thinking and seeing is the notion of individualism, and the idea that I am thinking and acting and seeing of my own volition, individually, as if I were somehow able to move through the world without being taken into, and shaped by, it. So, when a young couple in, say, *Neighbours*, fall in love, rebel against school rules, wear certain types of clothes, or become involved in 'green' issues (saving dolphins, protecting forests) they (must) feel that these paths, values, decisions and ways of seeing the world are arrived at naturally, and this is often articulated through reference to body parts, such as 'my heart tells me the truth' or 'I can see the issues clearly'.

Another, everyday, example of this process is the way 'women's magazines' often publish photographs of female celebrities accompanied by captions and stories which suggest that the person has become 'fat'. Now, even leaving aside the contentious question of what is meant by someone being designated as fat, in most of these instances the person represented is not so much fat as not painfully thin. For instance, there have been numerous photographs of different ex-members of the pop group The Spice Girls showing muscular (and presumably fit and healthy) woman headed with captions such as 'Oh my God—look what's happened to Sporty Spice', while the accompanying stories make reference to over-eating, and generally to the person not looking after herself. The captions and stories that designate her body as overweight (and, by extension, unhealthy, unattractive and undesirable) are of course basing their evaluations on two related issues—what female celebrities are meant to look like (very thin), and what someone like Sporty Spice herself, as a former pop star, used to look like. As a consequence, the people who buy these magazines are disposed to see Sporty Spice's body—and, by extension, their own—in negative terms ('Oh my God, look what's happened to me!').

Of course, it is not as if the readers are being disposed and directed to see this way for the first time. These magazines' photographs and stories are part of a much wider network of representations (found in newspapers, on television, and in films, music clips, video games and advertisements, toys) which, taken together, work to produce an idea within a culture of what is a normal, desirable and healthy female body. This idea (or, more precisely, the variations on this idea) circulates within groups and becomes what Pierre Bourdieu would call a *doxa*—that is, it is accepted, relatively unthinkingly, as an ideal, truth or normality, and influences people's practices and ways of seeing, in this case the way girls and young women see, think about and evaluate their own bodies and the bodies of other girls and women.

But how does this process—and, as a corollary, these attitudes and effects—work at the level of what we have called 'reading the visual'? Doxa function in visual texts as master signs which dominate, organise and explicate other signs in a text. We can say that a doxa of seeing has been established if a large part of a culture agrees to or accepts the idea that a particular substance-type (a version of the female body, for instance) has a natural attribute (it is healthy, sexy, normal). When we see photographs of women, we will tend to look at and focus on certain crucial parts or aspects of that type (a slender waist; small hips and buttocks; petite features). If the parts correspond to the idealised substance-type, then we will be inclined to see and read the person positively; if not, they can be seen as comic, or unhealthy, or undesirable. Even if there are other signs that we could take into account to produce our visual text and what it means (such as clothes, or how the person is posed), it is the master signs that generally count. So a picture of a large-thighed or heavy-hipped former Spice Girl frolicking in the surf surrounded by lots of adoring men, and clearly having fun, will still be reduced to: 'She can't really be happy, she's fat.'

## conclusion

In this chapter we have looked at the ways in which visual practices have been influenced by what we designated the visual regime of normalisation, which we suggested grew out of the relationship between the reason of state and the need to discipline populations on the one hand, and new forms of scientific thinking which produced and authorised new categories for evaluating and seeing populations on the other. This gave rise to templates of normality, which were produced in scientific fields, and disseminated across the cultural institutions of the state. These templates allowed state functionaries to measure people against, and discipline them in terms of, specific and measurable accounts of what it was to be a normal, average, healthy citizen, but they were also used as a means of initiating and facilitating self-surveillance.

These templates of normality came to be utilised beyond the call and logic of the reason of state: they were increasingly taken up by capitalism and the media and used as a means of promoting consumption, in the form of lifestyles and products which claimed to be able to transform the way people saw themselves, and how they were seen by others. So, while normalisation continues to influence how and what we see, it now does so with a strong capitalist inflection. In our next chapter, we consider how capitalism influences and orients our reading of the visual.

# 7 selling the visual

## introduction

In the previous chapter we referred to the Foucauldian notion that from the eighteenth century onward, the state, through the introduction of knowledge and techniques associated with the concept of biopower, intervened in an unparalleled way in the lives of its citizens by analysing, and attempting to regulate and discipline, their bodies and behaviour. But Foucault also makes it clear that the state eventually accepted the point that constant state intervention in people's lives was not necessarily the best way to produce productive citizens. The state needed to maintain its role of intervening in and regulating people's affairs in order to ensure citizens weren't leading unhealthy and unproductive lives, but at the same time there was a powerful social movement—what Foucault calls the 'attitude' of liberalism—which argued that 'the free enterprise of individuals' (1997: 73) was the best principle for producing greater wealth and prosperity.

Liberalism broke with the 'reason of state' and its interventionist policies. It took advantage of the growing importance of economics to the state, and of the state's inclination to draw back from intervention, in order to ensure the free enterprise of individuals and the (partial) withdrawal of government from society, while giving greater rein to the free market and to individualism. The capitalist, market-driven society that characterises the contemporary West is not the same as liberalism, but it is one of the paths that liberalism has taken over the last 150 or so years. In this chapter we consider, firstly, how capitalism has challenged and in a sense largely displaced the visual regime of normalisation and, secondly, the new 'ways of seeing' that it has brought in as replacements.

## capitalism, culture and the Frankfurt School

The notion of capitalism as a kind of visual regime is probably most famously theorised and articulated in the work of the Frankfurt School's Theodor Adorno (1991) and his contemporary, Walter Benjamin (1968). For Benjamin, the capitalist system and its technologies (particularly mass production) strip away the 'aura' that provides unique cultural artefacts with their supposed innate value. He saw this process as a potentially liberating development because, in undermining notions such as originality and genius, it could facilitate a break from the authority of high cultural institutions (such as universities and royal societies) that served as the arbiters of cultural value. In other words, a whole order of things and meanings dependent on the authority of exclusivity had been replaced by the democratising free flow of the market. Texts which were authorised as valuable, such as paintings or sacred writings, and which were the possessions of—and thus associated with—elite groups, were now free to circulate throughout society as copies. Everyone could now own a Rembrandt or Vermeer print, or a (small) replica of the Venus de Milo. But what was more important was the effect this change would have on the way people saw the world: works of art or sacred texts were no longer part of a chain of signs that inevitably led to, and authorised the worldviews of, the elites.

For Theodor Adorno, these processes, and the market interventions in the field of culture in general, were disastrous because they brought about the denigration of human faculties and virtues. Prior to the domination of capitalism, Bosch's paintings or Michelangelo's sculptures were recognised and pronounced as valuable by cultural elites, and served as exemplars for the wider population. Of course, another of their functions was to reproduce and naturalise regimes of power and value—think, for instance, of the manner in which Italian Renaissance art helped authorise and legitimate the power of the Catholic Church. But Adorno (1991) argues that certain works of art (usually those that have survived across history) draw attention to the limits that a society places on what and how things are seen. That is, they both reproduce the worldviews that they are produced by and within, and go beyond them. However, once questions of cultural value are taken away from authorised institutions and practitioners (schools, universities, academics, artists) and moved into the domain of the marketplace, people only end up being exposed to texts aimed at the lowest common denominator—texts that Adorno regards as simplistic and sensationalist, and which don't challenge them to think beyond a normalised worldview.

## baudrillard and simulation



In their different ways, Benjamin and Adorno anticipated what Jean Baudrillard (1990, 1993) terms the advent of contemporary culture as a form of *simulation*. Baudrillard argues that the traditional, pre-modern and pre-capitalist discourses and perspectives which categorised and evaluated the world—which were based on, and privileged, members of classes such as the aristocracy or the clergy, or those who possessed cultural capital such as education) have been replaced by a democratic and market-driven framework which has largely rendered obsolete, or at the very least transformed, distinctions and values such as high and low culture, originality, authority and taste.

These values and hierarchies (which are still influential, as we saw in our discussion of art and aesthetics in Chapter 5) constituted the grid through which people saw the world and their place in it. In other words, the dominant classes (the clergy and the aristocracy, making use of scribes and artists) produced a very limited and relatively unambiguous series of signs and texts which represented, articulated and authorised social relations, duties, and modes of behaviour. Think, for a moment, of Medieval English or French churches and castles. It is almost impossible to escape from the visual exchange they initiate; you look at them from a position of relative insignificance (you have, in every sense, to look up to them) while they look back at you from their place of grandeur, power and permanence (they always look down on you). They are the sign of a power relationship which translates into every other part and activity of the social sphere: few could doubt, or speak against, the power manifested in these buildings. Now, of course, there are plenty of imposing buildings in the contemporary world, but they don't function in exactly the same way. A medieval cathedral was unambiguously a sign of God's greatness and power, and this was passed along what we call the chain of signs associated with the cathedral—the clergy, their costumes, the texts they produced, ceremonies they presided over, and the words they spoke. As we will explain later, this process does not apply to the sign systems that characterise the contemporary Western world: the sight of the skyscraper canyons that dominate modern cities is just as likely to elicit a sense of disenchantment as one of wonder or awe, and the logic of fashion dictates that many buildings go from being considered innovative to dated in a very short time span.

**Figure 7.1 St Mary's Church Studley Royal, built in the 1870s, is a perfect example of the nineteenth-century desire to recreate the form and majesty of medieval architecture.**

The proof of the reality and genuineness of the pre-modern world order was in the *signs* that it produced. And those signs translated into narratives about who was important and who wasn't, why some groups were more powerful and deserving than others, and what responsibilities and options each person had within that system. A peasant living in a feudal world was in a sense caught up in a narrative in which their place was already given, and which directed the way in which a whole class of people more or less had to see, and live within, the world. According to Baudrillard (1993), the end of the feudal order and the advent of capitalism changed the relationship between signs, the world and how people saw things:

> The counterfeit (and simultaneously, fashion) is born with the Renaissance, with the destruction of the feudal order by the bourgeois order and the emergence of overt competition at the level of signs of distinction. There is no fashion in a caste society, nor in a society based on rank, sincc assignation is absolute and there is no class mobility. Signs are protected by a prohibition which ensures their total clarity and confers an unequivocal status on each. Counterfeit is not possible in the ceremonial, unless in the form of black magic and sacrilege, which is precisely what makes the mixing of signs punishable as a serious offence against the very order of things . . . In feudal or archaic caste societies, in cruel societies, signs are limited in number and their circulation is restricted . . . The arbitrariness of the sign begins when, instead of bonding two persons in an inescapable reciprocity, the signifier starts to refer to a disenchanted universe of the signified, the common denominator of the real world, towards which no-one any longer has the least obligation. (1993: 50)

A film which comically depicts a society caught somewhere between these two worldviews is *Monty Python and the Holy Grail*. The film is set in feudal Britain, but some characters are given modern worldviews and discourses. For instance, when King Arthur comes upon a couple of peasants, he expects them to do his bidding but they refuse to cooperate. Arthur attempts to impose his authority by reminding them that he is their king, but they reply that they 'didn't vote for him'. Of course, people didn't vote for kings—their positions were authorised by the sign systems that we referred to previously; as one character says in another scene: 'He must be a king. He hasn't got any shit on him'. When the peasants demand to know how Arthur became king, he goes into a lengthy and poetic speech about how the

Lady of the Lake extended Excalibur to him, to which the peasants reply: 'Strange women lying in ponds distributing swords is no basis for a system of government'.

What we have here is the clash of two worldviews, without the possibility of common ground being found or negotiated. For Arthur, signs are unambiguous, and the sight of the Lady of the Lake handing him Excalibur is a perfectly legitimate basis for government—or at least the assumption of power. But for the (anarcho-syndicalist) peasants, the sight of a 'strange woman in a lake' handing somebody a sword has no authority or meaning, apart from being an oddity. And it certainly doesn't translate as a legitimate procedure within the field of government. On one level, the film is pointing to the way these two political systems are incompatible, but on another level it is about the way signs have lost their mooring—or at the very least are open to contestation. The move here is one from a notion of seeing the world in terms of a preordained, authorised and largely incontestable order of things (the world is 'God's book'), to the 'subjective vision' that we discussed in our previous chapter.

This democratising process took on an even more arbitrary form with the advent of the domination and saturation of society by market-driven capitalism, and the concomitant rise of the media as cultural arbiters. Signs can be pulled in from anywhere and combined, regardless of cultures, fields, genres and historical periods. The Italian writer Umberto Eco provides an example of this mix-what-doesn't-match approach to culture in his description, in *Travels in Hyperreality*, of William Randolph Hearst's California 'castle', which is full of a diverse combination of art objects, buildings and architectural styles from across geography and history:

> Amid Roman sarcophagi, and genuine exotic plants, and remade baroque stairways, you pass Neptune's pool, a fantasy Greco-Roman temple peopled with classical statues including (as the guidebook points out with fearless candor) the famous Venus rising from the water, sculpted in 1930 by the Italian sculptor Cassou, and you reach the Great House, a Spanish-Mexican-style cathedral with two towers (equipped with a thirty-six-bell carillon), whose portal frames an iron gate brought from a sixteenth-century Spanish convent, surrounded by a Gothic tympanum with the Virgin and Child. The floor of the vestibule encloses a mosaic found in Pompeii, there are Gobelins on the walls, the door into the Meeting Hall is by Sansovino, the great hall is fake Renaissance presented as Italo-French. A series of choir stalls comes

> from an Italian convent . . . the tapestries are seventeenth-century Flemish . . . The billiard room has a Gothic tapestry, the projection room . . . is all fake Egyptian. (Eco 1986b: 22–3)

Hearst's 'pleasure dome' is symptomatic of the relationship between capitalism and visuality in two main ways. Firstly, there is now only one context that makes sense of, values and determines how things are viewed: the market. Egyptian, Italian Renaissance or Greco-Roman cultural objects can be mixed and seen together because the 'old contexts' in which they were located (history, art, geography), and which constituted the frames through which we saw them, have been dismantled. Something is now viewed as valuable not predominantly because of how or by whom it was crafted, its age or its historical significance, but in terms of how those factors translate into commodity cost. Secondly, and as a corollary, the notion that art, say, provides an insight into, and a critique of, culture and society is irrelevant, since the link between what the work is and where it came from is now effectively severed.

## commoditising the world

There is another important aspect to the spread of capitalism which has had an effect on how people see the world, and which is tied up with the issue of what we can call the inalienable dimension of society and culture. Western societies have always treated certain areas as not being reducible to the market—in other words, as not being for sale. This has not always been applied consistently: for instance, human beings are (theoretically) not for sale in the contemporary world, but they were in many places throughout history—in the United States in the first half of the nineteenth century, for example. Capitalism works to remove, as far as possible, the dimension of the inalienable, starting with land and property, and theoretically stopping at nothing. John Frow writes that the commodification of real property in Great Britain in the nineteenth century:

> is the model for the extension of exclusive property rights to other forms of value, and as the legal historian George Armstrong argues, 'the expansion of commodification to include even more forms of value fosters an ideology supportive of this process so that stable ownership, the right to exclude and to alienate, are no longer characteristics of some forms of value, they are social expectations for all forms of value'. The history of the capitalist mode of production is, on this account, a history of the progres-

sive extension of the commodity form to new spheres. The most succinct formulation I know of this historical logic is Wallerstein's statement that capitalism's endless drive to accumulate capital 'pushes towards the commodification of everything'. (Frow 1997: 134)

A version of this idea of the colonisation of everyday life by capitalism can be seen in Jean-Pierre Jeunet and Marc Caro's 1995 film *The City of Lost Children*, which tells a story of the attempt of an ageing, evil character called Krank and his gang of clones to steal the dreams of children. The capitalist thread of the movie pervades this world in one form or another precisely because almost everybody in the film is marked out and treated, first and foremost, in terms of what Arjun Appadurai (1988) calls the *process of commoditisation*. This, for Appadurai, refers to the situation where a thing or person is viewed predominantly in terms of its or their exchange value. The children are the primary examples of this in the film. They are either kidnapped in order to be sold to Krank (that is, first their persons are commoditised and then their dreams), or else they are used by criminal elements as thieves and pickpockets (their small size, agility and unthreatening demeanour making them invaluable in this regard).

Childhood is highly marketable in Western societies: wide-eyed children are used by advertisers to 'sell' banks, family cars and new government policies, and by social groups to promote their issues—family values, universal education, regulation of paedophilia. *The City of Lost Children* plays with these notions and uses of childhood, showing a modern world where adults are exploitative, dreams become full of sinister intent, and innocence exists only to be corrupted. The opening sequence is, in this regard, a coda for the whole film. The camera frames a realistic image of a traditional, charming Christmas scene, where a small child, pyjama-ed and in bed in a room filled with toys, watches wide-eyed as Santa emerges from the chimney to offer him a wind-up toy. The child initially seems taken with this, and the impression is of the sanctity of childhood and children's dreams of Christmas. But this illusion quickly breaks down as one Santa after another emerges from the chimney in a relentless reiteration that turns the enchantment of Christmas into something threatening. The walls and ceiling and furniture sway and melt; the Santas crowd the bedroom space, sipping from hipflasks, touching everything in the room while the noise builds to cacophony. The child bursts into tears, scrambles out of his crib and, keeping a fearful eye on the Santas, snatches up his teddy bear from the shelf. His enchanted world has become a nightmare.

In this first scene, the movie's central threads are conveyed: the nightmare that masquerades as children's dreams; the commodisation and corruption of innocence in the service of self-interest; and, above all, the disenchantment of the world of childhood. The bleakness of the world is mirrored in the setting: an unnamed and perpetually dark and fog-bound French port. The buildings, technologies and elements all seem to be made of the same material, and to merge into a largely undifferentiated mass. The green filter over the whole—whether the laboratory, the harbour or domestic interiors—renders a sickly light that taints every scene. The dirt, the excessive size of objects, the complex interconnections of machinery, the hand-turned gramophones, the absence of the familiar clean lines of digital technology are all reminiscent of late nineteenth-century factories where children's lives were effectively bought and sold by capitalists.

## the everyday as commodity

How does the vision of this film, and the visual regime of capitalism in general, translate into and inform everyday practices? One of the most obvious examples is the burgeoning trade in body parts, and the exchangeability of babies and children. A story was reported recently of a couple in Russia who were alleged to be raising their orphaned grandson in order to sell off his body parts. Apparently the couple had already reached an agreement with different buyers over prices for his eyes, kidneys and liver. At the appropriate time the child was to have been (carefully) slaughtered, dismembered and delivered, piece by piece, to clients. And more recently there was a report of a woman in the United Kingdom who was legally deprived of her child after she entered into an agreement to sell it to one couple, and then reneged and sold the child to another couple who had offered a higher price.

In *Time and Commodity Culture*, John Frow refers to similar reports of incidents and trends; although they are narrated in a manner which locates them on 'the verge of mythology', he maintains this does not deny 'the reality of the traffic in human organs' (Frow 1997: 169), or the increased colonisation of the bodies of the poor by the rich:

> A *Times* report on a 1993 BBC documentary, *The Body Parts Business* . . . documents a number of cases not just of sale of body parts but of forcible removal as a prelude to sale. One of the cases is that of Pedro Reggi, a patient in the Montes de Orca psychiatric

clinic outside Buenos Aires, whose cornea were dug out with coffee spoons and who was then thrown into a sewer and left to die . . . The documentary identifies a number of other cases of organized theft of organs from living people. Eight hundred children are said to have been kidnapped in 1992 in Tegucigalpa (Honduras), many of them for sale of their body parts. Similarly, evidence is presented of the organized kidnapping of people in Moscow for their organs, which are sold to the West at vast profit . . . 'Although the sale of human tissue is illegal in Russia, the investigators found a company which in one year extracted 700 organs, including kidneys, hearts and lungs, over 1,400 liver sections, 18,000 thymus glands, 2,000 eyes and more than 3,000 pairs of testicles. Another company offered to sell 600 kidneys at $20,000 each.' (Frow 1997: 166–7)

A more everyday example of this issue can be found in the ways in which subjects are involved or tied into the process of what Arjun Appadurai calls *commoditisation*, or more specifically the commodity situation 'in the social life of any thing' where 'its exchangeability (past, present, or future) for some other thing is its socially relevant feature' (Appadurai 1988: 130). In some ways, the process of what we can call 'self-commoditisation' is simply an extension of the logic of self-surveillance that we discussed in our previous chapter: whereas subjects had previously directed normalising eyes on to themselves (literally seeing themselves through, and comparing themselves to, templates of normality constituted by fields of knowledge such as medicine, education, psychology and sociology), now the same process is given a capitalist inflection. What the eyes have to consider now, in addition to 'Am I normal and healthy?', are questions such as 'Am I desirable?', 'Do I look wealthy?', 'Am I fashionable?' Indeed 'looking normal' might even constitute a negative: in certain fields and milieu, capital would accrue only if the person looked strange, odd, quirky or unusual (just like everyone else in that field).

Consider Figure 7.2, which shows a photograph of two young women, who look as though they are about to go out to some function—a party perhaps, or a nightclub or concert. We can relate the notion of commoditisation to the photograph in two main ways. Firstly, they have dressed themselves in an eye-catching and presumably fashionable way. They are wearing low-cut shirts, which draws attention to their sexuality. They are also wearing an usual combination of glass beads, distinctive hats (the first is a top hat, the second a 1920s-style fur hat) and shirts made of a heavily textured fabric.

Figure 7.2 Serious Us

Moreover, they have produced themselves, allowing for some variations (the woman on the right has a nose stud, the one on the left is wearing glasses), as a (kind of) pair. What these details articulate is that they are fashion-literate—or at the very least, that they are perfectly aware that they producing themselves within, and playing with, a particular fashion genre (let's call it post-punk).

There is a second way in which the women are commoditising themselves which is both related to, and distinct from, their status as fashion(able) texts. Let's return to the military group photograph we referred to in our previous chapter (Figure 6.5). One of the things we noted was the way the camera, in that very official context, demanded some kind of acquiescence—quite simply, the women were (more or less) required to smile. With the two women in this photograph there is a very different relationship between the camera and its objects. Their gazes are anything but acquiescent; in fact, one might suggest that their responses to the camera (inquisitive/reflective and wary/defiant) fit in with the post-punk performances associated with their clothes. At the moment the camera takes the photograph, both women are putting on performances of fashion-as-subjectivity predicated on a certain kind of post-punk literacy (involving dress sense, how to look at the camera and how much flesh to expose). The payoff for these (successful) performances, of course, is the acquiring of capital—or something that can be exchanged for something else within a field—among their friends, the photographer or the people they meet at the function they are to attend.

There is a considerable difference between seeing someone as if they were an object of study and a site of symptoms (as is the case with the normalising regime, and as exemplified in the military photograph), and seeing somebody (or oneself) as if they were a commodity—as fashionable and fashion literate (as in the photograph of the two women), or again as a series of pieces and parts (eyes, liver, heart) to be sold, as is the case with capitalism. And yet, within contemporary Western societies, we often make use of both these (at times explicitly contradictory) visual regimes more or less simultaneously and successfully, in much the same way that, in human sight, binocular vision is seamlessly transformed into what seems like monocularism.

## seeing things twice

Let's consider the two images of the child that were at the centre of our discussion of *The City of Lost Children*: the healthy, normal, passive, naïve and threatened, as opposed to the child as consumer/commodity. Both these images can both be found, simultaneously, in contemporary Western media. A 1999 article written by Marion Hume and Jennifer Sexton, titled 'Exploitable Chic', exemplifies the extent to which a more or less de facto acceptance of the overt sexualising of child subjectivity exists side by side—and more or less unproblematically—with a strong moral condemnation of the way this contributes to the 'corruption and exploitation' of childhood. The article focuses on the use of teen and pre-teen females as models in fashion shows, predominantly in Italy but increasingly throughout the fashion world. It introduces the issue in the following way:

> The fashion show opens with a tiny child, her blond hair tumbling down to her thighs. 'Watch out', says the American editor seated next to me, 'here comes the next babymodel scandal'. Next day, there is talk of an anti-child exploitation law being tabled for discussion in the Italian parliament. It is about time. Every season a new crop of 'babymodels', as these children on the cusp of puberty are known, appears in Milan and one of them is always touted as the next supermodel. Every season a fledgling, her body barely developed under the couple of layers of sheer chiffon a designer thinks suits her, appears on the catwalk and the Italian

newspaper *Corriere della Sera* whips up a *scandalo*. (Hume and Sexton 1999: 13)

Two statements are being made here, and they are reiterated throughout the article. The first is that so-called 'babymodels' are appearing more frequently in fashion shows and shots. Despite the claim that this is largely an Italian phenomenon, the authors go on to list examples of this kind of practice in the United States (although models can't be signed up until they turn sixteen), France (although a special licence is required for children under sixteen) and other Western countries. The second point being made is that these practices are unambiguously scandalous, immoral and exploitative. What bridges the two perspectives is the way in which the commoditised subjectivity/sexuality of children is circulated, simultaneously, as a form of incitement to desire and a threat against morality and nature.

The article about child models clearly is informed by, and performs, a sense of moral repugnance and outrage. Yet there is a story to tell, a scandal to sell and young female bodies to be displayed for readers. In some ways, the newspaper is simply reproducing the visual discourse that has made young girls such important commodities within the fashion industry. While child models are employed because they bring a 'pencil-thinness that the international fashion business continues to require' (Hume and Sexton 1999: 13), what makes them particularly attractive to the industry is the prospect of 'a young teenager projecting adult sexuality on the catwalk' (1999: 13)—either because 'fashion is all about sexuality and playing with images, and designers will push it to the absolute limit' or, as a corollary, because the *frisson* of (more or less) forbidden sexuality also provides excellent publicity (based on the notion that the occasional 'acceptable *scandalo*' is good for business). But by combining child models and sexuality, the industry draws charges of indulging in both pornography and, more seriously, paedophilia: Ursula Hufnagl of *Chic* is quoted as saying that such a practice 'really reeks of paedophilia' and Peter Chadwick, a modelling agent, calls it 'a bit Lolita-ish'. Hence the resultant moral outrage.

The article picks up on the idea of (helpless) children being ruthlessly exploited by way of reference to the 'the breakdown of the Soviet Union and the huge influx of beautiful adolescents who arrive on Paris streets expecting them to be paved with gold'. On the question of designers stopping at thinking 'it was clever to sell clothes to women by revealing the little breasts of a child', the authors write:

> Not in Italy, where octogenerian designer Mila Scheon and her youthful design team allowed little Tatiana's body to be revealed. The company's press officer, Daniela Mazzolari, says: 'She is very confident, she was born on a catwalk. She seems for sure older than twelve . . . She speaks little English, but clearly she is not shy', Mazzolari says about Tatiana, who told reporters in broken English: 'It is just a game'. (Hume and Sexton: 13)

And it *is* a game, one which is being played, to some extent, by the same people—in this case, the authors of the article, but more generally the media—who express moral outrage at this 'exploitative sexualising' of children. The 'proof' of this can be found in the photographs that accompany the article: there are four of them, all of Tatiana modelling outfits which reveal a great deal of her body, and all of which could be read (if discovered, for instance, on a pornographic web site) as paedophilic. The important point, however, is not that the authors or the media are hypocrites; rather, it is that such images are readily available, and can be transmitted and published across and within the mainstream media.

What this testifies to is the fact that sexualised images of children, and the subjectivities associated with them, are simultaneously both scandalous and already integrated into contemporary Western cultures through the diffusive powers of capitalism and/as the media. In other words, Tatiana and others like her (and the performances and subjectivities they produce) are caught up in a more general commoditising of all aspects of culture (including supposedly inalienable sites) that is mainly carried out through the media, as advertising (depicting the latest Italian fashions), straight news stories (reporting a fashion show) or as scandals (baby-models!). And this transmission can be understood as both a symptom (the media are only representing subjectivities which have more or less passed into mainstream culture) and a cause (the more frequently such subjectivities are represented, the more quickly they pass into mainstream culture) of the commoditisation of 'inalienable childhood'. At the same time, the circulation of these images constitutes one small part of an incitement to the public, governments and institutions to beware the dangers to children posed by those people (perverts, deviants, paedophiles, child molesters—groups easily equated, in the media, with homosexuals) who would corrupt inalienable, desexualised childhood.

## conflicted vision

There are, however, moments and contexts when this process doesn't work, and when a particular way of looking (such as capitalism) can seem inappropriate, comic and even immoral, regardless of how privileged or authorised it (normally) is. In order to explore this issue, we need to return to Bourdieu's notions of habitus and cultural fields, which we first introduced in Chapter 1.

For Bourdieu, the habitus is a set of durable dispositions (values, ideas, ways of seeing, thinking and acting) which produce us as subjects, while cultural fields are constituted by institutions, discourses, rules, protocols, practices and forms of cultural capital. Now, as subjects pass through, are influenced by and take on the habitus associated with a cultural field, they will be inclined to privilege, and utilise, whichever visual regime is dominant within those fields. But as subjects from one field work in or come into contact with different fields, they may be required—at least temporarily—to change the way they see the world. And if they aren't literate enough to understand this, they suffer the consequences. An obvious point of potential 'visual conflict' can be found when everyday human social relations are viewed from an overt capitalist perspective. As Baudrillard makes clear, the logic of capitalism is about individuals and individual interests, desires and benefits. Everything else, including our friends and family, should be viewed as objects and, more specifically, as (potential) commodities. Of course, this attitude is not meant to be expressed in any open or public way; and when it is, it constitutes a scandal—which only goes to reinforce its truth 'as practice'.

An example of this occurs in an episode of the American sitcom *Frasier*. When radio psychiatrist Frasier Crane takes a call, the (male) listener asks for advice about his relationship with his partner. Crane asks about the caller's level of commitment to the woman, and is told that 'he's happy enough, but he'd like to upgrade to a better model'. Crane is horrified at what he regards as the callous treatment of a person as a thing, but in the course of the show he finds himself caught up in the same logic of practice: he is going out with one woman, but is led to believe that other women are interested in him. He reduces his personal affairs, in a covert way, to a form of calculation, based on an evaluation of the different kinds and amounts of capital each woman brings with her, and his chances of succeeding with each one. In other words, Crane literally looks at each of the women through, and compares them to, templates of desirability, predominantly with regard to bodily features such as hair, face, breasts and legs, but also in terms of other factors loosely gathered under the rubric of 'personality'. What is interesting about Crane's 'eying off' of various women in the series (one of its main motifs is his search for romance) is that while due weight and emphasis is always given to non-bodily aspects in determining whether a woman is a potential romantic partner, the only women he ever seriously considers being involved with are all conventionally beautiful—in other words, his eyes are only attracted to them if they more or less comply with that very physically oriented 'template of desirability' (which of course is mediated to some extent by the clothing the women are wearing, such as short skirts or low-cut dresses). It is ironic that Crane employs a bodily-oriented way of seeing in virtually all his (potentially) romantic dealings, but because he 'screens out' conventionally unattractive women (they never pass his more or less unconscious 'attractiveness test', and consequently are never 'seen' as potential partners) the question of his commoditising women never arises—until he (inadvertently) articulates his position in the example referred to above, which ends up with him being shunned by all the women involved, who are outraged at being treated as commodities.

## attention!

While subjects within Western societies are more or less obliged to view the world and everything in it within the frames of dominant visual regimes, and to synthesise or ignore the contradictions within them, this does not necessarily mean that they consistently provide the attention that the institutions, sites and cultural texts connected to those regimes (advertising agencies, schools, the media) require of them. Partly this is because, as we saw with our example of driving a car in Chapter 1, there is an economy of attention at work in every act of visualising—we usually pay attention only when it is needed. But to a certain extent the means that capitalism (and normalisation) employ to fix attention also function, simultaneously, as an incitement to distraction. As Jonathan Crary writes, the problem of attention:

> was elaborated within an emergent economic system that demanded attentiveness of a subject in a wide range of new productive and spectacular tasks, but whose internal movement was continually eroding the basis of any disciplinary attentiveness. Part of the cultural logic of capitalism demands that we accept as natural switching our attention rapidly from one thing to another. Capital, as an accelerated exchange and circulation, necessarily produced this kind of human perceptual adaptability

and became a regime of reciprocal attentiveness and distraction. (Crary 1999: 29–30)

It would be wrong to assume, however, that capitalism simply undermines the attentiveness required by the techniques of normalisation. As Foucault points out, rather than producing docile bodies (and eyes), the pedagogical approach associated with normalisation often brings about a lack of attention—or, even worse, attention wanders towards discourses, stories, ideas, strategies, techniques and values—that is, ways of seeing—which are opposed to, or try to resist, the operations of power. Foucault points out that prison, for instance, brings criminals together where they can exchange information, and mutually reinforce what Bourdieu calls the habitus and practical knowledge of their field of operation.

The issue of attention is also central to capitalism, but in a different way. A capitalist visual regime is characterised by the imperative to produce the subject as an individual, which involves isolating her or him from any (continuous) sense of communal identity. Like the scientific/normalising regime, it also needs to apprehend the viewer's attention—in this case, in order to produce that individual as desiring and consuming, rather than docile and compliant. But at the same time that 'grab for attention' is bound up in a more general (capitalist) imperative that compels the eyes to wander. How and why does capitalism both sequester our attention, and then make use of this situation to engender a kind of commodity-driven optical 'wanderlust'?

## the desiring eye

When we pass a shop window or an advertising display, the visual production, presentation and arrangement of the space and the commodities within are meant to fix the subject's attention and produce a kind of desiring gaze. Television and web sites are even more efficacious in this respect: as Crary (1999) suggests, their architecture of individuation works to sequester viewers from any sense of community. But they also produce a sense of privacy and intimacy which is constitutive of desire. This is facilitated, of course, through the gaze of commodities themselves, directed specifically at audiences as the only (possible) viewer. Clothes, jewellery, sporting goods and bodies function, in a sense, to address everyone as 'you and only you'; the result is an identification that is comforting, pleasurable and, above all else, inextricably bound up with desire.

The problem, however, is that capitalism can only ever really *excite* the eye—it can never *satisfy* it. The theoretical approach that we can employ to address this issue of the relationship between identity and desire/consumption is associated with the field of psychoanalysis and in particular the work of Jacques Lacan (1977). Lacan's version of the production of subjectivity has a very ocularcentric inflection. He suggests that children initially understand themselves as disconnected 'bits and pieces', until they reach what he calls the 'mirror stage'. When the child sees their reflection, there is a recognition that all the pieces belong together—in other words, sight produces the illusion of self-unity. The problem is that this unity is seen as being 'somewhere and someone'; from this point on, the child will look to an other in order to recuperate this sense of unity which is simultaneously given, and taken away, at the mirror stage.

In very basic psychoanalytical terms, then, our identity is always subject to what we can call an 'order of lack'—that is, we are called up (interpellated by fields such as the media) as lacking something that will complete us (romance, success, various possessions that function as status symbols), and which capitalism is only too happy to provide—at a price. Of course, this 'circle of desire' can never be completed because there is (literally) nothing behind those commodities. But we continue to move from one commodity to another looking for the one thing (or person as thing) that will satisfy us. In this sense, desire has no real end except in terms of the (re)creation of itself; what we desire is desire itself.

So, while my eyes may be excited and taken in by any number of commodities (clothes, a car, pornography) which promise to satisfy me and my desire, what they are really excited by is not the object 'in itself, but the promise of satisfaction that comes through the acquisition of commodities, and which is manifested in any number of ways (I think I look more attractive in these clothes; people will notice and envy me in this car; watching pornography will provide me with physical pleasure). The problem is that, even if these commodities do provide what they promise in the short term, the twin (and highly compatible) logics of capitalism and desire will ensure that all commodities eventually lose their magic (the clothes fall out of fashion, the car gets old, repeated viewing of the film makes everything that happens seem predictable and boring). But of course there is a whole world of (potential) commodities that the eyes can move on to, starting the process all over again.

## conclusion

In this and our previous chapter we have looked at the two dominant visual regimes—normalisation and capitalism—and considered the ways in which they influence and orient our perspective on, and understanding of, the world. One of the questions that we dealt with, however, was the extent to which these two contradictory (and in a sense mutually exclusive) visual regimes can coexist and (productively) frame social vision, and overcome the imperatives to distraction (which causes the schoolboy to ignore Cleese's sex lesson; or the shopper to 'wander across' the commodities of capitalism). The answer to this question is inextricably bound up with techniques and strategies largely specific to the field of the media. In our next chapter we will consider both the techniques of visualisation that characterise the media, and that field's wider function as a site that facilitates the visual regimes of normality and capitalism, firstly by helping to 'fix the attention' of populations, and secondly by resolving or covering over the contradictions that arise out of 'conflicted vision'.

# 8 the media as spectacle

## introduction

The two previous chapters looked at the ways in which the dominant contemporary ways of seeing—which we've characterised as the visual regimes of normalisation and capitalism—determine or predispose our everyday visual practices, including not just how we see the world and people around us, but also how we view and read ourselves as visual texts. The field which is most active in facilitating and naturalising these two regimes is the media. Put simply, it is impossible to make sense of how and why people think, behave and come to see the world without making reference to the media and their various roles: as an alternative public sphere; as a repository for what Judith Butler (1993) calls 'authorised performances of subjectivity', and as a set of techniques for making the world available to us in an immediate and apparently straightforward way. In this chapter, we consider how contemporary visual practices are influenced by a field whose main function is arguably to provide, in Claude Lefort's words, 'the constant staging of public discussions . . . [as] spectacle, encompassing all aspects of economic, political and cultural life' (1986: 226).

## society of the spectacle

What do we understand by this reference to the media as the site of spectacles? We normally think of spectacles as extravagant, over-the-top and larger-than-life performances, something akin to chariot races in ancient Rome or the opening ceremony at sporting events such as the Olympic Games. The way we're using the term here, however, is quite different. Jonathan Crary, in his discussion of Guy Debord's influential 1960s book *The Society of the Spectacle* (Debord 1967), writes:

> Spectacle is not primarily concerned with a looking at images but rather with the construction of conditions that individuate, immobilize, and separate subjects . . . In this way attention becomes key to the operation of noncoercive forms of power . . . Spectacle is not an optics of power but an architecture. Television and the personal computer . . . are methods for the management of attention . . . even as they simulate the illusion of choices and 'interactivity'. (Crary 1999: 74–5)

Three main issues or questions are raised here. Firstly, what is it about the status of the media that enables them to attract the attention of the public? Secondly, how precisely (in a technical sense) do the media function as what Crary calls an 'architecture' of individuation? And thirdly, what is it about the relationship between the media as spectacle, their content (stories, images, ideas, genres, discourses) and the ways in which this content is processed, that enables the media to facilitate, seamlessly, the imperatives of the two (in many ways contradictory) visual regimes of normalisation and capitalism?

## the media and imagined communities

The answer to the first question is tied up—as is the development of all fields and technologies—with social, historical and political problems and imperatives. In Chapter 6 we introduced the notion of the 'reason of state', which referred to the way the state, through its bureaucracies, institutions, policies and discourses, intervened in and attempted to manage the lives and activities of its main resource: people. In the nineteenth and particularly the twentieth centuries, this process was often central to the creation of the nation state, where various groups of people—often culturally, ethnically and geographically disparate—were interpellated into what Benedict Anderson calls an 'imagined community'.

One of the most famous examples of what we can call the visual interpellation of the individual as a member of a nation state is Roland Barthes' analysis, in *Mythologies*, of a photograph from the French magazine *Paris-Match*:

> On the cover, a young Negro in a French uniform is saluting, with his eyes uplifted, probably fixed on a fold of the tricolour . . . I see very well what it signifies to me: that France is a great Empire, that all her sons, without any colour discrimination, faithfully serve under her flag, and that there is no better answer to the detractors of an alleged colonialism than the zeal shown by this Negro in serving his so-called oppressors. (1973: 116)

Most nation states and empires have their own collections of these kinds of icons—moments captured in paintings or photographs or on film which 'stand in for' and homogenise the diffuse, dispersed set of identities that make up a wider community. It is not as if the meanings that are read into these icons are natural or homogeneous in themselves; rather, they are deployed and disseminated throughout the society and its cultural sites and texts, and

**Figure 8.1 Three of the most recognisable national icons are the USA's Statue of Liberty, the Australian Digger's slouch hat and the British Bulldog's Union Jack waistcoat.**

eventually assume a considerable—and usually non-negotiable—importance and value (Barthes (1973), for instance, refers to the *Paris-Match* photograph as a myth). In a sense they become 'the real' that the nation or community actually lacks.

This explains why certain images, substances or materiality are credited with attributes that usually only apply within their communal contexts. For the United States, these would include the American flag, pictures of Uncle Sam and the Statue of Liberty. When patriotic citizens look at, say, the American flag, they see—that is, fantasise—an embodiment of a homogeneous community sharing values (truth, justice), beliefs (in God, the capitalist market) and cultural activities (baseball, eating mom's apple pie). In other words, seeing is believing (in America, or the idea of America). And when protesters burn the American flag, they do so not because they believe in its value, but precisely because they want to demonstrate their rejection of this belief.

## the media as public sphere

The above examples testify to two important propositions. Firstly, dominant and pervasive meanings about the nations and other communities—such as what virtues constitute, or what historical moments reflect, true national character—are created, transformed and exchanged within cultural institutions and communication practices. In other words, while communities are supposedly based on, and authorised and justified by, supposedly shared and continuous cultural traditions, such traditions and their meanings are themselves often 'manufactured' within cultures—an example of this is the virtual invention of national traditions and cultural icons in the colonised territories of India, Wales and Ireland in the nineteenth century. Secondly, the advent of the mass media has sped up, and increased the reach of, this process of disseminating and naturalising meanings, ideas and traditions. This change from the old-world scenario of communication as being place-dependant and limited to the 'brave new world' of instantaneous mass communication is captured perfectly in the Coen Brothers film *O Brother Where Art Thou*. The main character in the film (Ulysses Everett McGill, played by George Clooney) leads a group of convicts in an escape from a road gang. But McGill's destiny is intimately tied to the newly emerging communication technologies, for which he is a mouthpiece. Despite the context in which he finds himself—the deeply impoverished and largely rural state of Mississippi during the Great Depression—and despite the very cumbersome forms of technology the men encounter and use—upright radios, lumbering Ford pickups and sedans, chuffing trains and operator-assisted telephones—he insists on their value, and their role in humanity's future. He understands the new devices as being coterminous with progress, reason and rationality and, in the best tradition of nineteenth century optimism, tells his companions that science and technology are going to build infrastructure and networks that will link everyone, and in the process sweep away misunderstandings, superstition, poverty and injustice.

The story takes a political turn when McGill and his companions record an old-time song ('Man of Constant Sorrow') which reaches a mass audience via the radio, and catapults them to what we would now call cult status. A foreshadowing of the connection between celebrity and politics, and the connection between journey-as-progress, technology and its political contexts, becomes most evident towards the end of the film. An election is being fought for governorship of the state, between the (corrupt) incumbent and a Huey Long-style populist who holds traditional electioneering gatherings in local settings and to a relatively small audience. The incumbent, who is facing defeat, seizes on the sudden popularity of McGill and his companions—now known as the Soggy Bottom Boys—and aligns himself with them and their technology-induced fame, and their status as celebrities. His challenger takes the opposing position, rants against the group and publicly announces their criminality, with the (not-unreasonable) assumption that this would mean the incumbent would lose the election, tarred by his association with wanted criminals. Instead, the fame of the Soggy Bottom Boys legitimises the incumbent, and the challenger is the one first tarred, and then run out of town. The technological developments that allowed the Soggy Bottom Boys to become famous are not at all connected with progress and reason, but rather with a fleeting popular mood, and with political self-interest. But, in a way that is not altogether unfamiliar in the contemporary world, they prove decisive and irrevocably alter the political landscape.

Why and how have the media assumed such a central place in contemporary Western culture? In order to address this question, we have first to consider how and why the media have come to function as a kind of global public sphere. Since the advent of the so-called globalising communication technologies in the 1970s, there has been a strong push—largely emanating from the United States—to open up the world to the 'free flow' of media corporations and technologies. The catchcry of globalisation—recycled from neoliberal doctrines that date from the eighteenth century—is that nothing should stand in the way of the circulation of information, images and ideas, because once the public sphere is available to the unregulated spread of knowledge and information, ignorance will be replaced by reason, difference by mutual understanding, barbarism and backwardness by civilisation and progress, and tyranny by democracy. What was consistently articulated in television and newspapers reports from Afghanistan during the 2002 American invasion, for instance, was that once local women were exposed to the images of Western consumer culture (television, clothes, bodies, appliances,

DVDs) they would automatically throw off their burkhas and 'become Western'.

The role of the media as a kind of public sphere was (almost inadvertently) taken on, in the West, by non-commercial and non-aligned institutions such as the UK public broadcaster the BBC, though increasingly it has come to include all the media. But the processes and technologies associated with globalisation have radically changed this relationship between the state, the media and the public sphere. Most importantly, there has been a concentration of the global media and communications market in fewer hands, coming from an increasingly smaller number of countries (predominantly the United States and Europe), a process which has been accentuated by 'symbiotic' corporate mergers or 'arrangements' which have brought together different resources, technologies and 'content' merging to form super corporations—Time-Warner, Disney, Viacom and News Corporation are examples of this. States often closely monitored or even controlled what was said by whom in the nascent media public sphere (based on different logics and rationales such as protecting public morality, educating the population, looking after national interests and promoting community values), but at the same time there was, in many national broadcasters, a tradition of independence closely aligned to the original notion of the public sphere as a site of critique. The new corporatised media-as-public-sphere, on the other hand, are largely committed not to 'criticism of the state, or to facilitating information and communication among the people' (Schirato and Webb 2003: 177), but to meeting the market imperative.

The influence that is wielded in the social field by these multinational corporations, and more generally by the institutions, values and logics of the media, has brought about a situation where the media not only stand in for the public sphere, they have colonised and now dominate virtually every aspect of the social, cultural and political fields in the contemporary West, to the extent that we can talk about 'the advent of a virtual identification between the media and the civil society' (Schirato and Webb 2003: 172). An example of this process can be seen in the development of the relationship, over the last 40 years or so, between the media and the field of sport. Sport may seem an odd example to refer to when discussing the public sphere, but we need to remember that, for many people (predominantly, but not exclusively, men) throughout the world, sport is the site where their individual or communal identity is most commonly linked and articulated. In other words, people project and envisage more or less a one-to-one relationship between themselves and, say, a football team, or between themselves and other supporters of that team. So issues that affect their team impinge upon them and their identity as social beings. This is what is behind the truism that many people turn to the sporting pages first when they pick up a newspaper: those are the issues that concern them the most.

Of course, an argument could be made that sporting identifications belong in the personal, rather than the public, sphere of society. Interestingly, however, it is the (relatively recent) domination of the field of sport by the media that has helped to make sport an unequivocally public sphere issue. All over the world, the replacement of what we could call a sports-for-itself vision of the field and its institutions, activities and values (notions of loyalty, fair play, and soon) by the visual regime of capitalism, with its emphasis on seeing everything (teams, players, traditions) as a commodity, has provoked a strong social backlash amongst fans, who feel that they are being alienated from what was a relatively inalienable part of their culture and identity (for instance, teams that have existed in one location for 50 years can suddenly be disbanded because they are unprofitable, or moved to another place to suit television markets). The media are, of course, central to this question of the increased profitability of sport: most of the revenue that goes to pay professional sportspeople or build new facilities comes from media contracts, or at the very least is dependent on the publicising of sporting events through the media. Perversely, when fans wish to object to this state of affairs where 'their game' has been taken from them, they inevitably have to communicate this dissatisfaction through the media (by writing into or appearing on sports shows, using largely institutionalised online forums, or even by arranging to have their protests covered by the media) precisely because the media are the 'only game in town' when it comes to articulating public sphere issues.

The explanation that is put forward for this development is based, predictably, on a form of technological determinism: the advent of computers, satellite broadcasting, digitalisation and real-time communications has meant that few areas and activities around the world—let alone within a nation—are inaccessible to the media. And the media have also enhanced their public sphere role by setting themselves up as the site which facilitates all the activities of community and communication, through the influence they wield over the fields of politics, culture and economics.

## techniques of individuation and isolation

How does this process of the creation and management of publics by and through the media tie in with Crary's assertion that the main function of the media-as-spectacle is to bring about the individuation and isolation of people? Michel Foucault suggests that the original function of the spectacle as a site where the Crown and governments performed their power (for instance, through public executions) was abandoned precisely because it showed that there was nothing to power but an, at times, inadequate performance. In the opening to *Discipline and Punish* (1995), we are presented with Foucault's famous description of what we could call an old-fashioned spectacle, the torture and execution of the regicide Damiens, who is taken on a cart to a scaffold where:

> the flesh will be torn from his breasts, arms, thighs and calves with red-hot pincers, his right hand, holding the knife with which he committed the said parricide, burnt with sulphur, and, on those places where the flesh will be torn away, wax and sulphur melted together and then his body drawn and quartered by four horses and his limbs consumed by fire. (Foucault 1995: 3)

What Foucault's descriptions of the appalling subsequent procedures and actions reveal is that the law is an ass that cannot even work out how many horses it takes to tear a body apart; technology finds slaughter a messy and unexpectedly complex business, even when pincers are designed for the occasion; and confessors turn up after the man's soul has already departed his body. What we have in these descriptions are egregious examples of both underkill (nobody can make Damien's body behave and comply with the wishes of the executioners) and overkill (why does it take so many people and so much power to achieve so little?). As Foucault suggests, this kind of spectacle had to go because it provided too many examples of how the law (as well as the Crown) was anything but all-powerful; and such sights of ineptitude were likely to embolden and incite crowds and mobs to acts of disobedience, rather than cow or impress them. In the modern period, however, people are rarely given the opportunity to congregate in shapeless, unruly, unpredictable and potentially threatening crowds or mobs. Power is no longer exercised as old-fashioned spectacle, but through such devices as regulatory architecture. Cities and towns, for instance, were 'recreated' with the imperative to produce manageable—that is, pacified—spaces. And even anti-government demonstrations and protests have to comply, to a certain extent, with the imperatives of bureaucracy (getting permission to hold a rally, marching down streets chosen and cordoned off by the police) as well as the media (when is the best time to attract a big crowd that will look impressive, and attract media attentions).

Old-style state or political spectacles have not entirely disappeared (think of the rallies and military parades that used to happen in Soviet Europe, and still occur in nations such as North Korea), but these events have largely been replaced by media-specific events and genres (interviews, debates, political advertising), which redefine the visual and architectural relationship between state and the people. The media still calls us up as members of a community held together by normative values and principles and an attachment to what Claude Lefort (1986) calls capitalised ideas (democracy, freedom, childhood, the market, the family), but this act of interpellation is now carried out through the media as an architecture of individuation and isolation.

There are two ways in which this occurs. Firstly and most obviously, the programs, images and speakers seem to be addressing 'only me'. When I am called up by the media, a technological *entre nous* (that is, a 'between us') is brought into being which effectively pulls me out of any social and spatial relationships I have (familial, communal, personal, domestic), and demands that I pay attention to what is being shown on the 'box' (television, computer, film screen) in front of me. In a sense, television and other media function like private booths at peep shows: we move into a simulated private space where the show, it promises, is for us and us only, with the presumption that we will reciprocate. Even when a group of people gather together to watch a media event (a sporting contest, for instance), the main interactions are usually not within the gathered audience, but between individuals and the screen (hence manifestations of abuse, elation or despair are directed to the technology—think of those cartoons that show a sports fan with a foot stuck through a television screen). And this tendency is even more accentuated with interactive video games and more generally with the advent of cyberspace, which (claims to) literally extract you from this world and take you into another one.

The second way in which the media can be understood as an architecture of isolation and individuation is through reference to Claude Lefort's notion of the relationship between the mass media and what he calls *invisible ideology* (Lefort 1986). We have referred to his notion of capitalised ideas, which can be understood as a set of empty values that we are all more or less required to believe and perform a commitment to, but which in fact mean only what the field of power wants them to mean at any time. So the value of 'freedom', for instance, might be associated with civil rights in one context (as in 'the people who destroyed the Twin Towers were attacking our freedom of speech'), and the erosion of those same civil liberties in another ('people who speak against the war on terror are threatening our freedom').

## the imperative to communicate

Lefort's point is not that the mass media simply take on the task of circulating and reinforcing these capitalised ideas. On the contrary: for Lefort the advent of the mass media ushers in a new type of politics, constituted by endless performance of communication and the imperative to communicate. Through the media, invisible ideology makes room for most groups, regardless of social standing. In fact, the less social standing the better, in one sense, because this demonstrates the openness of the system, a process of unending reciprocity that is also a process of unending communication. With invisible ideology, the performance of communication and community (the two terms are virtually synonymous here) takes the place of, and makes irrelevant, the kinds of political antagonisms that Lefort identifies as the defining characteristic of the democratic state. In other words, political activities, ideas, differences and relationships are all played out between the individual viewer and what is being staged as politics (interviews, chat shows, documentaries) on the screen.

Of course, this display of communication and 'representativeness' is always loaded or skewed in terms of who speaks, who is chosen to represent different points of view, the kinds of questions that are asked, or the background information or commentary that is provided or withheld. Moreover, there are several ways in which groups and positions are in a sense disqualified from being seen or heard—hence the importance of the media campaign to portray Islam and Muslims as barbaric, misogynistic and inhuman during the post-September 11 period, especially leading up to the invasion of Afghanistan. And even if contradictions are thrown up or become evident during discussions, they are usually resolved or lost in the performance of communication itself. In other words, the main function of the media is not to interrogate meanings or stories, but to facilitate a (very quick) looking at, and recognition of, the performances that are given.

## time and effect

This brings us to the relationship between the media as spectacle, their content (stories, images, ideas, genres, discourses) and ways in which this content is processed. How do the media dissolve politics and difference? And, more specifically, how do they function to regulate, monitor and pacify on the one hand, and excite desire on the other? In a sense we need to go back to Baudrillard's notion, introduced in the previous chapter, that signs are detached from each other and also from any historical contexts and referents. In the same way, the media only show events in isolation. Ethnic cleansing in Eastern Europe, globalisation, political instability in Africa, Islamic terrorism: all these issues are picked up by virtually every media organisation at the same time, 'done to death' and then discarded as if they ceased to exist or hold any further significance. They can always be recalled, of course, but only if enough newspapers or television programs decide they are newsworthy again. This is what we call a *politics of affect*—every image of, say, a woman dressed in a burkha or a flooded Chinese village is instantly recognisable and explicable, without regard to thought, history or any kind of contextual analysis or consideration, as 'one of the same' (the burkha equates with barbarism and oppression; destitute Chinese simply demonstrate the difficulty of life in that nation).

Pierre Bourdieu describes commercial television programs (although we can, to some extent, extrapolate and include virtually all the mainstream media in the West) as circuses dominated by the twin constraints of 'time' and 'effect' (Bourdieu 1998). He makes the point that the very limited time available to 'do' a news story, for instance, means that issues are pared back, decontextualised and explicated in terms of simple binaries (right/wrong, business/unions, men/women, citizens/foreigners). In a sense, the same is true of non-news genres, such as soaps and sit-coms. But news programs provide the best example of this process: stories which are connected to one another only in the sense that they happened at the same time (a flood in China, a celebrity divorce, a meeting of Heads of State) are thrown together in an order which is not so much arbitrary as interest-driven ('Are people tired of hearing about asylum seekers?'), without explanations of contexts or antecedents. Moreover, because each event is dealt with in a minute or so, the explanation of the story has to be punchy and evoke human interest. For instance, a flood might be articulated in terms of the plight of one destitute family, or a government policy might be reduced to the effects of the policy on a single shopkeeper. And of course, once that single family is resettled or the shopkeeper's problem solved, the issue effectively 'disappears'.

These twin imperatives of time and effect make it virtually impossible for TV or radio news programs to say anything that is not sensationalised or simplistic. In fact, it really doesn't make sense for them to say anything much at all, which is why the news is invariably dominated by visuals. A 30-second description of a massacre, famine, riot or war usually produces an immediate emotional effect—which is what the news is meant to accomplish. Film of a person being beaten to death, of emaciated babies, of crowds destroying buildings, of bombs zeroing in on bridges or enemy troops can provoke an immediate and strong response (pity, anger, fear, revulsion, elation). But this action of taking the viewer 'into the story' effectively dissolves the story, at least as far as any kind of complex understanding is concerned; viewers can only become involved if they automatically sympathise or empathise with, or fear or hate, the objects of the representation.

## the politics of affect

The organisation and deployment of various signs (visual and otherwise) within a strictly controlled economy of time and effect in order to produce a narrative without a narrative—that is, the performance of an unmediated bit of the real—is probably the defining characteristic of the contemporary field of the media. We have referred to this as 'the politics of affect'; quite simply, it involves the production and reduction of events in terms of an immediate, unconsidered emotional reaction. There were many examples of this process in the recent War on Iraq: for instance between 26 and 28 March 2003, in the middle of a series of intensive bombardments of Iraqi cities by coalition forces which killed large numbers of civilians, and desert battles in which it was variously reported that somewhere between 600 and 1000 Iraqi troops had died, just about every major Western newspaper featured a large photograph, on the front page, of coalition troops taking care of, administering medicine to or feeding Iraqis. The purpose—or at least the function—of these various photographs was to obscure and replace one potential narrative, concerning the death and destruction that was occurring on a daily base in Iraq, with a second narrative about the war as a humanitarian event.

In order to get a more detailed idea of how this process works, let's look at and consider Figure 8.2, a newspaper photograph of a group of Islamic children, published in February 2003 under the heading 'Festival Seeks Peace, and a Sausage Sandwich', in terms of the techniques of seeing that we introduced in Chapter 1 (framing; selection and omission; sign and text; intertext and context; and genre). Firstly, although the scene is a festival attended by a crowd of people, it is the four female children who take up most of the frame, and therefore become the focus of the photograph. The photo is clearly staged—the children are showing the sausage sandwiches to, and smiling at, the photographer and, by extension, the newspaper readers. The girls' faces are shown in detail, and all the signs that can be identified and read from their faces and bodily gestures—the animated smiles, the wide eyes, the gesture of offering the food directly to the photographer/readers—constitute a text-as-story about happy, innocent, friendly, unthreatening and assimilated Muslims. This photograph, quite clearly, is an attempt to 'show something different'—that is, to present a more sympathetic view of Islamic people and their culture. The children are all 'humanised' by the close-up shot of them smiling—something that was absent from the media coverage of the wars in Afghanistan and Iraq. Moreover, the signs of difference that would usually serve to disqualify them from being read as 'normal' (that is, Western), such as their skin colour and clothes, are here overcome by their action of eating Western food at a barbeque.

But although the story that accompanies the photograph is oriented towards explaining the beliefs and traditions of the festival, that articulation of the validity and value of cultural difference is in a

**Figure 8.2 Islamic children**

sense subsumed under much more powerful and ubiquitous intertextual references taken from the 'War on Terror' and the War on Iraq. Both those series of events were subject to widespread, and largely homogeneous, coverage in the media, including photographs, video footage, feature articles and radio interviews, which reiterated and largely naturalised the linking of signs of difference—everything from burkhas to Islamic-style beards—to negative concepts and values such as barbarism, irrationality or threat. When viewers saw such signs, they had already seen them through the frames of these negative media categorisations many times before. In other words, they simply recognised what they already knew. In the photograph of the children at the festival, those categorisations and readings still apply, but they are now joined by a second narrative—the rejection of difference. Although the children are marked as Islamic, the action of holding out the sausage sandwich needs to be read in terms of the same belief that American soldiers took into the War on Iraq: Muslims want to be saved by America, and want to be 'like us'.

The meanings of this photograph, and of just about every other visual text in the Western media that dealt with Arabic or Islamic people or culture, were already given in terms of the 'clash of civilisations' and the 'Crusade' narratives that dominated the media after September 11 (and which had, in fact, a long history as master-narratives for making sense of and evaluating Islam in and to the West). The quintessential example of this process, of course, was the term 'War against Terror': everything that happened in the wars in Afghanistan and Iraq (the bombing and slaughter of civilians, the destruction of infrastructure, the creation of millions of refugees, the designation and treatment of prisoners as terrorists or 'battlefield detainees') was reducible to, and thus legitimated by, this designation. The logic behind this practice was simple; since the 'War against Terror' was unambiguously and unquestioningly good (who, after all, could be against a war against terror or, by extension, in favour of terrorism?), then any acts committed in its name didn't bear or require thinking about or considering—they were merely to be applauded or supported.

## genre and the politics of affect

We have suggested, following Bourdieu, that one of the defining characteristics of the Western media is that their practices are constrained by the twin imperatives of time and effect. Consequently, the meanings they make are explicable in terms of the notion of the politics of affect: signs, texts, intertexts and contexts are brought together to produce an instantly recognisable and unambiguous text-as-story. But how does the technique of seeing we discussed in Chapter 4—genre—fit in here?

We defined genre as a type of cultural text with its own features. These generic differences are to be found right across the texts produced by the different media: television documentaries and soap operas, action films and romances, and internet porn sites and electronic fantasy sports leagues all have different content, discourses, stories and styles. The photograph of the Islamic children with the sausage sandwiches, for instance, could be categorised as a 'soft news' genre photograph. It differs in a number of ways from other hard news photos, most obviously in that there is nothing serious, threatening or dramatic about the content, as would be the case with a photograph accompanying a story, say, about the war in Iraq. Soft news stories and photographs are invariably community oriented, treat their subject in a positive light, and are meant to make the reader feel good about things. The photograph of children at the Islamic festival clearly complies with these requirements. Hard news is often international or national in orientation, deals with serious—often violent—issues and stories and, rather than make the reader feel good, the intention is usually to communicate the gravity of an issue. During the 2003 invasion of Iraq, newspapers and television news programs showed visuals of bombed cities, civilian casualties in hospitals, or aircraft attacking enemy tanks or troops—all of which fulfilled the second set of criteria.

## september 11 as soap opera

How does this notion of generic difference fit in with the proposition that the media and its visuals are all largely explicable in terms of the politics of affect? The way in which, say, the CNN network processed and visually represented the events and aftermath of September 11 constitutes a quintessential example of the media as a kind of machine for producing the politics of affect. Some analysts have referred to CNN's coverage as being akin to the genre of a soap opera; this isn't far from the truth. What we need to do is to look at the relation between the politics of affect on the one hand, and the media and its genres on the other, specifically with regard to the genre of soap opera.

In our previous chapter we referred to the psychoanalytical notion, derived from Lacan, that desire is an ongoing process that can never be settled or closed down, and that capitalism feeds off and into this process through its incitement of the eye to (continue to) wander and consume. Slavoj Žižek refers to the way in which hysterics play out or perform symptoms of illness (coughing or twitching without medical reason) as the 'hysteric conversion', and he ties this into Lacan's observation that:

> the fundamental experience of man qua being-of-language is that his desire is impeded, constitutively dissatisfied: he 'doesn't know what he really wants'. What the hysterical 'conversion' accomplishes is precisely an inversion of this impediment: by means of it, the impeded desire converts into a desire for impediment; the unsatisfied desire converts into a desire for unsatisfaction; a desire to keep our desire 'open'; the fact that we 'don't know what we really want'—what to desire—converts into a desire not to know, a desire for ignorance . . . Therein consists the basic paradox of the hysteric's desire: what he desires is above all that his desire itself should remain unsatisfied . . . alive as desire. (1977: 143–4)

How does this apply to CNN's coverage of September 11? And to what extent was this coverage informed by the genre of the soap opera? The soap opera is, in a sense, the hysteric genre *par excellence*. Although soaps are meant to run at 'real life time', what actually distinguishes them from real life is the extraordinary richness of symptoms of desire and crisis. A family gathering in a soap is not played out to the rhythms of ordinary life, in which crises or symptoms of crises (in the form of affairs, betrayals, lies, antagonisms, lust, revenge, rebellion) are seldom overtly present. Rather, these crises are crammed by the dozen into half-hour or hour-long episodes, they are expected and they are never the subject of closure: the resolution of one crisis (an affair is forgiven, the couple go back to a normal, loving relationship) is always the prelude to another crisis (the wife has contacted a hit man to arrange her husband's murder; the jilted woman plots to bring down the marriage; the husband will revisit his desire for the other woman).

CNN's coverage of September 11 did not exactly fit into this generic pattern—or rather, it did not employ the genre exclusively in its reports, narratives, images and representations. Its coverage in fact used a variety of popular culture and media genres, depending on the event or issue being covered. The first few days after September 11, for instance, were characterised by versions of reality television (point the camera at the World Trade Center or other important buildings and see what happens), drama (images of George W. Bush

**Figure 8.3 As the world was transfixed by the endless replaying of video footage of a plane crashing into the World Trade Center in New York in September 2001, many commentators remarked on the similarity of the horrific images to scenes from one of the most famous disaster movies of all time, *The Towering Inferno* (1974).**

looking determined, accompanied by voiceovers stating that the president was taking control and leading America), documentary (archival footage of the Twin Towers being built, or of bin Laden, accompanied by information about his origins), action adventure (re-enactments of the struggles on the doomed flights), rescue shows (coverage of firefighters digging through the rubble), current affairs (experts discussing the political ramifications of September 11), the Western (George W. Bush's 'wanted, dead or alive' press conference), and even sport (film of, and interviews with, members of the New York Yankees and Mets 'playing for America'). But what the employment of these different genres enacted (initially at saturation level, and continuously for some months after the events) was the genre of the soap and its affiliations with the order of hysteria. Symptoms (in the form of stories, images, archival footage, statistics and photographs) were found of the crisis, but this only led to more symptoms, which were replaced again by new symptoms. The ultimate 'object of desire' and line of closure was the capture or elimination of bin Laden, but this soon gave way to the destruction of the Taliban and the capture of Mullah Omar, which in turn was replaced by the elimination of Saddam Hussein, and the regimes in North Korea, Iran, Syria and so on *ad infinitum*.

The 'War on Terror' constituted an interesting example of how the media, as a field, adhere to the imperatives of the fields of the state and capitalism while at the same time looking after their own interests. Clearly the media were 'doing their bit for the war'—for example, by showing missiles and smart bombs zeroing in on, and destroying, so-called targets in Iraq (villages, bridges, military compounds), while accompanying these visuals with testimonies to the power, efficacy and righteousness of the actions—largely through the reproduction of military or state discourses about collateral damage, or missions being accomplished. In a sense, this took political and military events out of the 'real', so to speak, and lodged them within a visual fantasy space not altogether removed from the genre of (military or violent) computer games. The footage was produced in such a way that the dehumanising effect of a phrase like 'collateral damage' was transferred to visual text; we were shown technology in action, but usually not the scenes of dismembered bodies or hospitalised civilians that were the consequences of that technology.

At the same time as the media were reproducing this visually sanitised version of events in Afghanistan and Iraq, and the concomitant message of Western/American power and control, they were also endeavouring to commoditise the war, and to keep audiences interested and attentive. But, as interest waned, the media were more or less forced, as we suggested earlier, to find new symptoms of crisis. This explains why the media continued to produce visuals and stories of the barbarism of the Taliban (images of children and women being whipped, of limbless victims, of desecrated Buddhist images, of mysterious, threatening bearded men and downtrodden women wearing burkhas) long after the Taliban had ceased to function as a political force. This certainly helped legitimise America's foreign policy but, perhaps more importantly, it kept the story going as a media event.

## shopping for subjectivities

We can see how the media's coverage of September 11 and its aftermath thus facilitated the reproduction of the visual regimes of normalisation and capitalism, but how does this translate, more generally, into everyday viewing practices that are constitutive of subjectivity? We suggested that the media's colonisation of society (in areas such as sport and entertainment, but also in the arts, politics and economics) has enabled it to grow exponentially, which has in turn further facilitated the intrusion of the market and the field of power into every sphere of human activity. And we also we referred, in previous chapters, to Judith Butler's (1993) notion of authorised iterative performances, with which people identify and which they incorporate into themselves and their bodies, outlooks and practices.

How does this work? The basic idea is that people generally want to be (seen as) both normal and desirable. Now, of course, there are many sites within a culture (school, church, the family, university, work, the sporting field, parties) where we learn to recognise what is normal and desirable, and to behave accordingly. But the media are by far the most pervasive and influential of those sites, precisely because they offer up an almost inexhaustible supply of images of, and templates for, normality and desirability. The media provide a huge reserve of desires and performances—a kind of mass market of subjectivities from which viewers can theoretically 'pick and choose'. The reality, of course, is somewhat more complex: as Judith Butler (1993) points out, the performances of subjectivity that are made available in the media, and the provision of the role models and exemplars that do a great deal of the work of commoditising those performances, are always already the result of a specific regime of seeing. In other words, everybody has the opportunity to identify with and become the same 'type of individual' as the originals they are copying—originals which were copied, of course, from other 'originals'. In order to explain why this kind of reproduction occurs within the marketplace of subjectivities and performances that is the media, we need to bring together Butler's notion of authorised iterative performances and Bourdieu's argument that media texts are dominated by, and the product of, the twin imperatives of time and effect.

We referred a little earlier to the relatively formulaic structure and characteristics of the soap opera: soaps in Brazil, Argentina, Mexico, the United States, Australia and Britain may have their differences (an emphasis on sexual relations and infidelities in Mexico, lots of beach scenes in Australia, the bringing together of narrative strands in pub scenes in Britain, talking 'hairstyles' in the United States), but they all follow the (more or less hysterical) imperative to produce endless, ongoing crises. But another important feature that they have in common is the consistency with which they show remarkably homogeneous character-types dealing with a very carefully regulated set of issues from relatively unvarying perspectives. The reason for this is purely commercial: producers and networks exercise very tight control over what is shown because they don't want to offend significant parts of their audience, or interfere with the 'pleasure of familiarity' with which soaps are associated. Consequently, soaps tend to reproduce dominant visual regimes (normalisation, capitalism) and their subjectivities and modes of behaviour.

This ties in, of course, with Butler's point that the crucial aspect of the relationship between iterative performances and the taking on of subjectivities is the question of authorisation. Performances that aren't authorised (homosexuality, political dissent, a rejection of the values of capitalism) simply don't get much air time, whether on television or in films, music videos or computer games. And, while it could be argued that the soap genre is quite different from other media fiction genres (say, sitcom on television, or action films), they are linked through their adherence to commercial logics and principles. This is Bourdieu's main point: the imperatives of time and effect that determine how news and current affairs are treated are a product of, and define, the commercial field, which in turn dominates what he calls the (larger) field of cultural production. In other words, just as sport becomes 'something else' (a business) when it comes to rely to heavily on the media and commercial interests, so most media fictions are produced within the logics and parameters that determine what happens, and who is seen, in soap operas.

## breaks in transmission

So can we say that the media, as de facto public sphere, simply provide authorised performances of subjectivity, and in the process reproduce dominant visual regimes (normalisation, capitalism)? The answer is mostly yes, but with a couple of qualifications. Firstly, Judith Butler (1993) has pointed out that the logic of capitalism in a sense provides the key to its own (inadvertent and occasional) unlocking. We suggested in our previous chapters that capitalism always works to incite our eyes to desire again and again: the one thing that it can't abide (and can't afford) is for our eyes to stop wandering. Capitalism will offer our eyes, and sell our desires, anything—even if it means running the risk of coming into conflict with the regime of normalisation. Think of our analysis, in the previous chapter, of the newspaper article on the 'paedophilic turn' in fashion shows and magazines. That article managed to carry off the delicate balancing act of condemning paedophilia while circulating images which could be read as paedophilic; in other words, it commoditised paedophilia while condemning it. Clearly the newspaper, and capitalism in general, understands that the sexualising of childhood is potentially big business—with regard to adults, of course, but also to children themselves, in terms of creating new desires and new products for the new, sexually aware and active child.

The media, of course, need to tread a fine line between adhering to their capitalist imperatives, while not in any way seeming to forsake their responsibilities as a de facto public sphere. However, as the recent proliferation of 'reality' television shows based on little more than prostitution and voyeurism indicate, that line is always being pushed to breaking point. This ties in with another point that Butler makes about the fact that, although certain subjectivities may be unauthorised, and even considered immoral or undesirable by large sections of the population, if that group constitutes a significant market (because its members are high income earners, or make up a sizable proportion of the population) then, to paraphrase Marx, 'they must be catered for'. The American television series *Will and Grace* is an example of this phenomenon. Will, one of the central characters, is openly gay, as are many of his friends; when Will looks at another man as a potential sexual partner, for instance, we are in effect seeing male bodies being viewed as objects of desire by another male—a 'way of seeing' which in some circles is considered repugnant or 'unnatural'. But during each episode his desires for, and relationships with, other male characters are shown as if they were authorised—as if they were natural and normal—when in fact the doxa (represented and reproduced on thousands of television and other media texts which normalise heterosexuality as the only form of sexuality) is the complete opposite. Of course, this kind of challenge to, and the going beyond, authorised subjectivity can only happen in a relatively small number of sites, so while an actor might be able to play a homosexual character (in a film, say, about AIDS), for the same actor to come out and openly profess her or his homosexuality might have a negative effect on that person's career. And, even in *Will and Grace*, the person with whom Will spends most of his time, and towards whom he is most openly affectionate, is Grace—a heterosexual woman.

There is a second reason, related to the previous point, why the media need not simply reproduce dominant ways of seeing all the time. While the media clearly function as the only viable public sphere in the contemporary West, one of the requirements of this role is to show the public sphere in toto: both its legitimate and illegitimate faces. In other words, the media need to make some effort, no matter how insignificant, to produce texts and ways of seeing which are not authorised or doxic.

## conclusion

The media largely function to facilitate and stage the society of the spectacle that Guy Debord detected in the 1960s, and this spectacle works to isolate individuals from each other through the setting up of a human–technological *entre nous*, which has become the pervasive social relationship of our time. As a corollary, the media make use of a variety of techniques (such as the politics of affect) to normalise and naturalise dominant visual regimes (particularly normalisation and capitalism) and authorised performances of subjectivity. At the same time, Judith Butler (1993) suggests that the reproduction of dominant ways of seeing and subjectivity is challenged, to a certain extent, by the 'logic of fashion', and by the need for the media to perform in accordance with their public sphere role. What this means is that the process of reproduction is occasionally interrupted by the circulation of a diversity of alternative and unauthorised images, ideas, readings and ways of seeing. In other words, while (visual) reproduction is the norm in the media, there are sites and moments when things are shown, and can be seen, differently.

If we look back at the photograph of the children at the Islamic festival in Figure 8.2, for instance, we could acknowledge and even accept the argument that this clearly well-intentioned attempt to produce a (visual) story that countered the doxic, negative version of Muslims in the Western media simply falls into the trap of tying itself to those stereotypes. Look, it seems to be saying, not all Muslims are fanatics: there are some (children) who want to be like us, and therefore aren't a threat to us and our way of life. Of course the (unconscious) emphasis is precisely on the notion that Muslims are dangerous, fanatical and constitute a threat to us—these are just the exceptions to the case that prove the case.

There is another story here, and another way of looking at this picture. What occasionally attracts the attention of viewers is the incongruity of this humanised visual representation of a group of children who happen to be Muslims, and the pervasiveness in the media of images of Muslims as anything but human—as the targets for American missiles on news footage (which often looks like nothing more than a video game), or as fanatical mobs full of potential suicide bombers. What this sort of photograph has the potential to do is to seize and hold on to our visual attention, and to interrupt the process (look, recognise, move on) of the politics of affect. In other words, it has the potential to make us look beyond a mere reflex-glance, to turn us back to think about and reflect on how, like Sherlock Holmes' companion Watson who misses all the clues in front of him, we tend to look without seeing.

Our habitus, influenced by our cultural trajectory and constantly subjected to powerful visual regimes, orients and disposes us to look quickly at whatever is in front of us, categorise it, and accept this tacit recognition as the obvious and undeniable truth. But, as Bourdieu (2000) makes clear, there are times when the habitus invites us to see and recognise a world that is no longer there, that has moved on—or we can't help but notice complexity and difference when the habitus directs us to see nothing but simplicity and uniformity. In these moments we can deduce, in Michel de Certeau's words, 'a lack of co-ordination between . . . references and the functioning of socio-cultural "authorities"', to the extent that the latter 'no longer correspond to the real geography of meaning' (Certeau 1997: 9). For Certeau, the habitus, as well as the authority of regimes of seeing, 'leaves in its midst an enormous "remainder". On our map, that is what is called culture' (Certeau 1997: 134).

# glossary

**aesthetics**—that which is concerned with beauty and taste, and their evaluation; the judgement of taste. Concerned also with the relations between knowledge/reason and the sensate—that is, the involvement of the physical self in the experience of art.

**affect; politics of affect**—affect is a technical term used to designate the emotion or attitude inscribed in a text or produced in other interactions. Politics of affect is used to explain the common media practice of producing and reducing news events to elicit an immediate, unconsidered emotional reaction—that is, deploying the emotional content of a story in a way that precludes reflection or analysis of its content.

**allegory**—a story or symbol whose meaning extends beyond the literal content, and stands for something else, usually abstract ideas of value or transcendence.

**arrested image**—in all static representation (paintings, drawing, photographs), time and movement are frozen; we seem to be seeing movement (a person walking, a tree blown in the wind), but this is the product of our filling in the missing parts, rather than seeing what is actually visible.

**biopower**—a term drawn from the writings of Michel Foucault, which refers to the technologies, knowledges, discourses, politics and practices used to bring about the production and management of a state's human resources. Biopower analyses, regulates, controls, explains and defines the human subject, its body and behaviour.

**capitalised ideas**—a term drawn from the writings of Claude Lefort which shows how certain ideas and values have been accorded so much importance in Western culture that they cease to be descriptors of something, and instead appear as proper nouns—Democracy, for instance, or Family (*see* doxa).

**capitalism**—currently, the dominant system for the organisation of economies; characterised by the private ownership of the means of production, and reliance on the market to direct economic activity and distribute economic goods and rewards. Its founding principle is the pursuit of self-interest through competition (*see* Marxism)

**commoditisation**—refers to the process of producing or considering something predominantly in terms of its exchangeability.

**constancy**—the principle of vision that means what one sees is influenced by individual tastes, dispositions and the viewer's cultural framework—that is, you see what you expect to see.

**context**—the environment in which meaning is made and communication takes place.

**cultural capital**—a form of value associated with culturally authorised tastes, consumption patterns, attributes, skills and awards. Within the field of education, for example, an academic degree constitutes cultural capital.

**cultural literacy**—a general familiarity with, and an ability to use, the official and unofficial rules, values, genres, knowledge and discourses that characterise cultural fields.

**cultural theory**—an interdisciplinary field of study with close links to the humanities and social sciences. It is considered to be committed to the theorising of politics and the politicising of theory, and hence is a discipline concerned with how to understand human and institutional relations and practices.

**distinction**—a kind of habitus (*see below*), or set of acquired tastes, that is associated with the upper classes, but which has become more generally naturalised as good and noble. A taste for fine wine, classical music and great works of art are examples of markers of distinction.

**doxa**—a set of core values and discourses which a field articulates as its fundamental principles and which tend to be viewed as inherently true and necessary. For Bourdieu, the 'doxic attitude' means bodily and unconscious submission to conditions that are in fact quite arbitrary and contingent.

**eye-witness principle**—the illusion a viewer has, when looking at an image, that everything in shot or frame is what they would have seen if standing in the same place, and at the same time, as the camera or artist who recorded the image (*see* perspective).

**field, cultural**—everything that is done, and everyone involved in doing it, within a discrete area of social practice. A cultural field can be defined as a series of institutions, rules, rituals, conventions, categories, designations and appointments which constitute an objective hierarchy, and which produce and authorise certain discourses and activities. But a field is also constituted by or out of the conflict which is involved when groups or individuals attempt to determine what constitutes capital within that field and how that capital is to be distributed.

**form**—anything to do with the technical production of a text, document or artwork that is not immediately associated with its meaning-making capacity—that is, its medium, compositional elements, colour, line, shape and texture.

**frames, cultural**—a term referring to the ways in which knowledge is organised through social values and personal experience; includes the principles of selection (of what is seen and attended to) and the ways in which media material or other information is packaged.

**Frankfurt School**—a group of Marxist-oriented thinkers who were particularly interested in the relationship between mass culture and ideology.

**genre**—text types; a principle of classification of texts based on already-known stories, conventions, characters and other elements

**habitus**—a concept drawn from the writings of Pierre Bourdieu that expresses, on the one hand, the way in which individuals 'become themselves'—develop attitudes and dispositions—and, on the other hand, the ways in which those individuals behave, or engage in practices. An artistic habitus, for example, disposes the individual artist to certain activities and perspectives that express the culturallly and historically constituted values of the artistic field.

**inalienable**—things, people and practices considered, at particular points in history, to be intrinsic to the community and therefore not subject to the values of the market. Inalienable values include honour, loyalty and family allegiance.

**intertextuality**—the process of making sense of texts by reference to other texts, or to meanings that have already been made in other texts. Because no social practice can operate in isolation from its social context, any spoken, written or visual text will either connote or cite other texts, and by recalling these known stories, will propel our reading in a particular direction.

**liberalism**—an attitude and practice that monitors and works to limit the control, intrusion or intervention of the state in the social, economic and cultural activities of its citizens.

**linear perspective**—a representation in which the world disappears to a vanishing point to give the effect of three-dimensionality (see perspective); the intersection of lines at a specific vanishing point on the horizon, which creates the effect of depth and dimension.

**Marxism**—a way of understanding the world, drawn from the writings of Karl Marx, that focuses on economic relations and class conflict; includes as an objective the attainment of a communist system of economic organisation, whereby the means of production are held in public ownership (*see* capitalism).

**metaphor**—a figure of speech in which a word or phrase literally signifying one object or idea is applied to another; the primary object is (momentarily) transformed into something else, suggesting a likeness or analogy between them (e.g. 'This room is a disaster area!')

**mimesis**—a term drawn from the writings of Aristotle and other ancient Greek philosophers, meaning 'imitation', and used to describe any text or practice that is considered to reflect an external reality.

**narrative**—stories; organised sequences of events, incorporating characters, settings, plot and causality. The term denotes both what is told, and the process of the telling.

**normalisation**—the ways in which discourses, ideas and practices associated mostly with the government and other sites of power (education, health, the military) establish norms against which people are measured (and measure themselves) to determine whether they are 'normal'. Normalisation is a means of managing populations by producing only a limited number of (authorised) ways of being and behaving.

**perspective**—all about spatial relationships; refers to the accurate depiction of three-dimensional space on a two-dimensional surface—that is, the arrangement and relative size of objects in visual images is rendered in a way that makes it true to the eye-witness principle (*see above*).

**poststructuralism**—a philosophical and conceptual set of principles and methodologies that follow structuralism (*see below*) and depart from it, focusing on the contingency and variability of practice rather than the apparent stability assumed by the structuralist perspective.

**reading**—in this context, we mean an active and a creative process of engaging with what is before our eyes, paying close attention, selecting focus, analysing the material seen, and in other ways drawing on our general and specific knowledges to make sense of what we see, and how it is organised as a visual text.

**semiotics**—an analytical approach and a research methodology that examines the use of what are called signs (*see below*) to produce meanings.

**sign**—a basic unit of communication; most simply, it is just something that has some meaning for someone (*see* text).

**simile**—a comparison between two unlike things using the words 'like', 'as' or 'than'. The point of the comparison is to draw to the attention of the reader some similar or shared characteristics (e.g. 'My love is like a red red rose').

**spectacle**—a concept, drawn from the work of Guy Debord, which is central to many understandings of how society is organised, how communication takes place, and how power relations are instituted and maintained. What is understood by 'spectacle' varies somewhat, depending on the concepts being formulated or defended, but generally speaking most theorists seem to agree that in the current era the spectacle is best understood as (at least channelled through) the mass media.

**structuralism**—a body of theory and system of analysis which inform practices in academic fields such as linguistics, anthropology, cultural studies, Marxism and psychoanalysis. Structuralism is basically the view that the social world is organised according to structures—rules, systems and forms—and that these make meaning possible.

**tacit understandings**—the ability to 'get by' adequately without engaging analytically or reflexively with the field or practice concerned (*see* visual literacy).

**text**—a collection of signs (*see above*) which are organised in a particular way to make meaning.

**trope**—the figurative use of a word or expression—that is, intentionally using a word or expression in a different sense from its original significance to give emphasis or vitality. A trope is also referred to as a 'turn' or a 'rhetorical return'—this is the notion that concepts keep re-emerging in different places and times, and carry similar meanings.

**visual literacy**—understanding the rules and conditions of seeing a particular thing in a particular context; taking an analytical and reflexive attitude to this seeing (*see* tacit understandings).

**visual regimes**—term for the ways in which particular forms of visuality have been accorded an authority within Western culture, and hence have exercised control and influence over how people see and understand the 'truth of the world', and over what they expect to see—that is, a universalising of the authority of different forms, genres, mediums and practices of the visual to provide access to what we could call 'visual reality' (*see* normalisation; capitalism).

# acknowledgements

We owe a debt of gratitude to the many artists, photographers and others who provided us with the images used in this book, including:

The Art Gallery of New South Wales (Onoe Matsusuke 1 (1770) by Ippitsusai Bunchô [p. 44]; Madonna and Child with Infant John the Baptist by Domenico Beccafumi [p. 126])
The Australian War Memorial (DA09834 [p. 171])
Caleb Byrnand (The straight parts of your body [p. 68])
Helen Byrnand (Light eye [p. 8]; Everything but the ... [p. 18]; Topography of the fork [p. 47]; Glebe notices [p. 61]; Landscape [p. 63]; 'Commuters 1' and 'Commuters 2' [p. 88]; After Magritte [p. 108]; Serious Us [p. 160])
Shirley Caspari (Lassie, c. 1920 [p. 22]; Will Cronwright c. 1920 [p. 85])
Annette Douglass and Chaco Kato (A Way of Staying Alive [p. 114])
Murray Efford (Snails (a) static; (b) in motion [p. 138])
Eric Meredith (Wear art [p. 55]; Blood in the gutter [pp. 102–3]; Future tree [p. 123])
Graham Tidy and The Canberra Times (Islamic children [p. 181])
Judi Tompkins (Kiln goddesses [p. 78])
Paul Travers (Invitation [p. 92])
Nic Vuorinen (Woomera Easter protest [p. 87])
Lorraine Webb (Bonnie's Eyes [p. 120])

Our thanks too to the unknown photographers and their subjects in the found photographs; please let us know if you recognise yourselves or your work in these reproductions. Any omission of acknowledgement is inadvertent, not deliberate. Anyone wishing to register themselves as copyright holders for subsequent impressions should contact the publishers.

And our particular thanks go to our editors, Elizabeth Weiss and Emma Cotter.

# references

Adorno, Theodor 1991, *The Culture Industry: Selected Essays on Mass Culture*, edited with an introduction by J.M. Bernstein, Routledge, London

Agamben, Giorgio 1993, *Stanzas: Word and Phantasm in Western Culture*, translated by Ronald L. Martinez, University of Minnesota Press, Minneapolis

Appadurai, Arjun (ed.) 1988, *The Social Life of Things: Commodities in Cultural Perspective*, Cambridge University Press, Cambridge and New York

Aristotle, *Poetics* (350 BCE/1907), translated by S.H. Butcher, Ebook, http://classics.mit.edu/Aristotle/poetics.html, accessed 28 June 2002

Barthes, Roland 1973, *Mythologies*, translated by A. Lavers, Granada, London

—— 1975, *The Pleasure of the Text*, translated by Richard Miller, Hill & Wang, New York

—— 1977, *Image Music Text*, selected and translated by Stephen Heath, Hill & Wang, New York

Baudelaire, Charles 1972, *Selected Writings on Art and Literature*, translated by P.E. Charvet, Penguin, London

Baudrillard, Jean 1990, *Revenge of the Crystal: Selected Writings of the Modern Object and Its Destiny*, 1968–1983, edited and translated by Paul Foss and Julian Pefanis, Pluto Press, Sydney

—— 1993, *Symbolic Exchange and Death*, translated by Iain Hamilton Grant, Sage, London

Benjamin, Walter 1968, *Illuminations*, edited with an introduction by Hannah Arendt, translated by Harry Zohn, Fontana, London

Berger, Arthur Asa 1997, *Narratives in Popular Culture, Media and Everyday Life*, Sage, London

Berger, John 1972, *Ways of Seeing*, Penguin, London

Blanchot, Maurice 1982, *The Space of Literature*, translated by Ann Smock, University of Nebraska Press, Lincoln and London

Bourdieu, Pierre 1984, *Distinction: a Social Critique of the Judgement of Taste*, translated by Richard Nice, Routledge, London

——1987, 'What Makes a Social Class? On the Theoretical and Practical Existence of Groups', translated by Loïc Wacquant and David Young, *Berkeley Journal of Sociology*, pp. 1–17

——1991, *Language and Symbolic Power*, translated by Gino Raymond and Matthew Adamson, Polity Press, Cambridge

——1993, *The Field of Cultural Production: Essays on Art and Literature*, edited and introduced by Randal Johnson, Polity Press, Cambridge

——1998, *On Television and Journalism*, translated by Priscilla Pankhurst Ferguson, Pluto Press, London

——2000, *Pascalian Meditations*, translated by Richard Nice, Polity Press, Cambridge

—— 2001, *Masculine Domination*, translated by Richard Nice, Polity Press, Cambridge

Bourdieu, Pierre and Darbel, Alain with Dominique Schnapper 1991, *The Love of Art: European Art Museums and their Public*, translated by Caroline Beattie and Nick Merrimen, Polity Press, Cambridge

Bourdieu, Pierre and Haacke, Hans 1995, *Free Exchange*, Polity Press, Cambridge

Bourdieu, Pierre with Boltanksi, Luc, Castel, Robert, Chamboredon, Jean-Claude and Schnapper, Dominique 1990, *Photography: A Middle-Brow Art*, translated by Shaun Whiteside, Stanford University Press, Stanford

Brent, Doug 1994, 'Writing Classes, Writing Genres, and Writing Textbooks', *Textual Studies in Canada* no. 4, pp. 5–15

Bürger, Peter 1992, *The Decline of Modernism*, translated by Nicholas Walker, Polity Press, Cambridge

Burgin, Victor 1999, 'Art, Common Sense and Photography' in J. Evans and S. Hall (eds), *Visual Culture: The Reader*, Sage, London, pp. 41–50

Butler, Judith 1993, *Bodies that Matter: On the Discursive Limits of 'Sex'*, Routledge, New York

Certeau, Michel de 1984, *The Practice of Everyday Life*, translated by Steven Rendall, University of California Press, Berkeley

Chandler, Daniel 1997, *An Introduction to Genre Theory*, http://users.aber.ac.uk/dgc/intgenre.html, accessed 22 March 2000

Clark, Timothy 1992, 'The Painting of Modern Life' in Francis Frascina and Jonathan Harris (eds), *Art in Modern Culture: An Anthology of Critical Texts*, Phaidon/Open University Press, London, pp. 40–50

Crane, Stephen 1960, 'The Open Boat' in *The Red Badge of Courage and Other Stories*, Signet, New York, pp. 140–64

Crary, Jonathan 1990, *Techniques of the Observer: On Vision and Modernity in the Nineteenth Century*, October/MIT Press, Cambridge, Mass

—— 1999, *Suspensions of Perception: Attention, Spectacle, and Modern Culture*, MIT Press, Cambridge, Mass

Danaher, Geoff, Tony Schirato and Jen Webb 2000, *Understanding Foucault*, Allen & Unwin, Sydney

Debord, Guy 1967/1977, *The Society of the Spectacle*, Black & Red, Detroit

—— 1997, *Culture in the Plural*, translated by Tom Conley, University of Minnesota Press, Minneapolis

Deleuze, Gilles 1986, *Cinema 1: The Movement-Image*, translated by Hugh Tomlinson and Barbara Habberjam, University of Minnesota Press, Minneapolis

Derrida, Jacques 1981, 'The Law of Genre', in W.J.T. Mitchell (ed.), *On Narrative*, University of Chicago Press, Chicago

—— 1987, *The Truth in Painting*, translated by Geoff Bennington and Ian McLeod, University of Chicago Press, Chicago

Descartes, René 1998, 'Optics', in N. Mirzoeff (ed.), *The Visual Culture Reader*, Routledge, London and New York, pp. 60–65

Ebersole, Samuel 1995 'Media Determinism in Cyberspace, www.regent.edu/acad/schcom/rojc/mdic/md.html, accessed 9 May 2002

Eco, Umberto 1986a, *Art and Beauty in the Middle Ages*, translated by Hugh Bredin, Yale University Press, New Haven and London

—— 1986b, *Travels in Hyperreality: Essays*, translated by William Weaver, Picador, London

—— 1990, *The Limits of Interpretation*, Indiana University Press, Bloomington.

Elkins, James 2002, 'Preface to the Book A Skeptical Introduction to Visual Culture', Journal of Visual Culture, vol 1/1, pp. 93–99

——n.d., 'How to Avoid Narrative in Visual Art', work in progress, posted on www.jameselkins.com, accessed 28 May 2002

Evans, Jessica and Hall, Stuart (eds) 1999, *Visual Culture: The Reader*, Sage, London

Feuer, Jane 1992, 'Genre Study and Television', in Robert C. Allen (ed.), *Channels of Discourse, Reassembled: Television and Contemporary Criticism*, Routledge, London, pp. 138–59

Finkel, Leif H. 1992, 'The Construction of Perception', in Jonathan Crary and Sanford Kwinter (eds), *Incorporations*, Zone, New York, pp. 392–405

Foucault, Michel 1995, *Discipline and Punish: The Birth of the Prison*, Vintage, New York

Freud, Sigmund 1905, *Three Essays on the Theory of Sexuality*, Standard Edition, Hogarth Press, London, vol. 7

Frow, John 1995, *Cultural Studies and Cultural Value*, Clarendon Press, Oxford

—— 1997, *Time and Commodity Culture: Essays in Cultural Theory and Postmodernity*, Clarendon Press, Oxford University Press, Oxford/New York

—— 2001, 'Things', *Journal of Critical Inquiry*, Fall, vol. 28, no. 1, www.uchicago.edu/research/jnl-crit-inq/28.1/frow.html, accessed 20 February 2002

Geertz, Clifford 1983, *Local Knowledge: Further Essays in Interpretive Anthropology*, Basic Books, New York

Gombrich, E.H. 1976, *Means and Ends: Reflections on the History of Fresco Painting*, Thames and Hudson, London

—— 1982, *The Image and the Eye: Further Studies in the Psychology of Pictorial Representation*, Phaidon, London

—— 1996, *The Essential Gombrich*, edited by Richard Woodfield, Phaidon, London

Grana, Cesar 1989, *Meaning and Authenticity: Further Essays on the Sociology of Art*, Transaction Press, New Brunswick

Hall, Stuart 1999, 'Looking and Subjectivity: Introduction', in J. Evans and S. Hall (eds), *Visual culture: The Reader*, Sage, London, pp. 309–14

Heraclitus 1953, Fragment #55, translated by Kathleen Freeman, in *The Pre-Socratic Philosophers: A Companion to Diehls*, Fragmente der Vorsokratiker, 3rd edn, Basil Blackwell, Oxford

Hoffman, Donald E. 1998, *Visual Intelligence: How We Create What We See*, W.W. Norton, New York and London

Hoorn, Johan F. 2000, 'How is a Genre Created? Five Combinatory Hypotheses', in *Comparative Literature and Culture*: vol. 2, no. 2 http://clcwebjournal.lib.purdue.edu/clcweb00-2/hoorn1-00.html, accessed 28 March 2001

Horace, *The Satires, Epistles, and Art of Poetry* (c.35BCE), The Project Gutenberg EBook #5419, translated by John Conington, http://ibiblio.org/gutenberg/etext04/hrcst10.txt, accessed 20 April 2003

Hughes, Robert 1987, *Nothing if Not Critical: Selected Essays on Art and Artists*, Collins Harvill, London

Hume, Marion and Sexton, Jennifer 1999, 'Exploitable Chic', *The Australian*, 22 October, p. 13

Inge, M. Thomas 1990, *Comics as Culture*, University Press of Mississippi, Jackson and London

Jay, Martin 1993, *Downcast Eyes: On the Denigration of Vision in Twentieth-Century French Thought*, University of California Press, Berkeley, Los Angeles /London

— 1995, 'Photo-Unrealism: The Contribution of the Camera to the Crisis of Ocularcentrism', in Stephen Melville and Bill Readings (eds), *Vision and Textuality*, Macmillan, Basingstoke, pp. 344–57

Jeunet, Jean-Pierre and Caro, Marc 1995, 'Excerpts from a Conversation' (with Alain Schlockoff and Cathy Karani), in Sony Pictures Classics, http://www.spe.sony.com/classics/city/misc/interview.html, accessed 21 November 2000

Kannenberg, Gene Jr 1996/2001, 'Form, Function, Fiction: Text, Image, and Design in the Comics Narratives of Winsor McCay, Art Spiegelman, and Chris Ware', Dissertation Proposal, University of Connecticut English Department

Kant, Immanuel 1790/1952, *The Critique of Judgement*, translated by James Creed Meredith, Clarendon Press, Oxford

Krauss, Rosalind 1992, 'In the Name of Picasso', in Francis Frascina and Jonathan Harris (eds), *Art in Modern Culture: An Anthology of Critical Texts*, Phaidon/Open University Press, London, pp. 210–21

Kuhn, Thomas 1970, *The Structure of Scientific Revolutions*, 2nd edn, University of Chicago Press, Chicago

Lacan, Jacques 1977, *Ecrits: A Selection*, translated by Alan Sheridan, Tavistock/Routledge, London

Lefort, Claude 1986, *The Political Forms of Modern Society: Bureaucracy, Democracy, Totalitarianism*, edited by John B. Thompson, MIT Press, Cambridge, Mass

Levin, David Michael (ed.) 1993, *Modernity and the Hegemony of Vision*, University of California Press, Berkeley, Los Angeles and London

Lowry, Bates 1967, *The Visual Experience: An Introduction to Art*, Prentice-Hall, Englewood Cliffs, NJ and Harry N. Abrams, New York

Maclean, Marie 1988, *Narrative as Performance: The Baudelairean Experiment*, Routledge, London

Maffesoli, Michel 1991, 'The Ethic of Aesthetics', *Theory, Culture and Society*, vol. 8, pp. 7–20

Mane-Wheoki, Jonathan 1996, 'Indigenism and Globalism: "First Nation" Perspectives in the Contemporary Art of Aotearoa/New Zealand and Te Moananui-a-Kiwa/the Pacific', in Caroline Turner and Rhana Davenport (eds), *Present Encounters: Papers from the*

*Conference of the Second Asia-Pacific Triennial of Contemporary Art*, Queensland Art Gallery and Griffith University, Brisbane, p. 35

Marcuse, Herbert 1978, *The Aesthetic Dimension: Towards a Critique of Marxist Aesthetics*, translated and revised by Herbert Marcuse and Erica Sherover, Macmillan, London

Melville, Stephen and Readings, Bill (eds) 1995, *Vision and Textuality*, Macmillan, Basingstoke

Merleau-Ponty, Maurice 1962, *Phenomenology of Perception*, translated by Colin Smith, Routledge & Kegan Paul, London

Mirzoeff, Nicholas (ed) 1998, *The Visual Culture Reader*, Routledge, London and New York

—— 1999, *An Introduction to Visual Culture*, Routledge, London and New York

—— 2000, Cultural Studies discussion list, http://www.cas.wf.edu/communication/rodman/cultstudies.index.html

Mitchell, W.T.J. 1986, *Iconology: Image, Text, Ideology*, University of Chicago Press, Chicago and London

—— 1994, 'The Pictorial Turn', in *Picture Theory*, University of Chicago Press, Chicago and London

Newton, Isaac 1730/1952, *Opticks, or a Treatise of the Reflections, Refractions, Inflections and Colours of Light*, Dover, New York

Nietzsche, Friedrich 1967, *The Birth of Tragedy*, translated by Walter Kaufmann, Vintage, New York

—— 1986, *Human, All Too Human*, translated by R.J. Hollingdale, Cambridge University Press, New York

Panofsky, Erwin 1955, *Meaning in the Visual Arts: Papers in and on Art History*, Overlook Press, Woodstock, NY

—— 1991, *Perspective as Symbolic Form*, translated by Christopher Wood, Zone, New York

—— 1995, *Three Essays on Style*, MIT Press, Cambridge, Mass

Plato 1953, 'Timaeus', in *Dialogues* vol. 3, 4th edn, translated by B. Jowett, Clarendon Press, Oxford

Plato 1994 (360BCE), *The Republic*, translated by Benjamin Jowett,

Ebook, http://classics.mit.edu//Plato/republic.html, accessed 28 November 2001

Polanyi, Michael and Prosch, Harry 1975, *Meaning*, University of Chicago Press, Chicago

Poster, Mark 2002, 'Visual Studies as Media Studies', *Journal of Visual Culture*, vol. 1, no. 1, pp. 67–70

Rimmon-Kenan, Shlomith 1983, *Narrative Fiction: Contemporary Poetics*, Methuen, London

Rybczynski, Witold 1983, *Taming the Tiger: The Struggle to Control Technology*, Viking Press, New York

Saussure, Ferdinand de 1907/1966, *Course in General Linguistics*, translated by Wade Baskin, McGraw-Hill, New York

Schirato, Tony and Webb, Jen 2003, *Understanding Globalization*, Sage, London

Schirato, Tony and Yell, Susan 2000, *Communication and Cultural Literacy*, rev. edn, Allen & Unwin, Sydney and Sage, London

Snyder, Joel 1980, 'Picturing Vision', *Critical Inquiry*, vol. 6, no. 3, Spring, pp. 499–526

Sobchack, Vivian 1995, 'Phenomenology and the Film Experience' in Linda Williams (ed.), *Viewing Positions: Ways of Seeing Film*, Rutgers University Press, New Brunswick, NJ, pp. 36–58

Staniszewski, Mary Anne 1995, *Believing is Seeing: Creating the Culture of Art*, Penguin, Harmondsworth

Tambling, Jeremy 1991, *Narrative and Ideology*, Open University Press, Milton Keynes

Tomashevsky, Boris 1965, 'Thematics' in L.T. Lemon and M.J. Reis (eds), *Russian Formalist Criticism: Four Essays*, University of Nebraska Press, Lincoln/London, pp. 61–95

Toolan, Michael J. 1988, *Narrative: A Critical Linguistic Introduction*, Routledge, London

Veltman, Kim H. 1998, *The Literature on Perspective*, www.sumscorp.com/perspective/Vol3/ch2.htm, accessed 15 June 2002

Virilio, Paul 1994, *The Vision Machine*, Indiana University Press, Bloomington and Indianapolis

Wacquant, Loïc 1993, 'From Ideology to Symbolic Violence: Culture, Class and Consciousness in Marx and Bourdieu', *International Journal of Contemporary Sociology*, vol. 30, no. 2, October, pp. 125–42

Wallschlaeger, Charles and Busic-Snyder, Cynthia 1992, *Basic Visual Concepts and Principles*, Wm Brown, Dubuque

Warnke, Georgia 1993, 'Ocularcentrism and Social Criticism' in D.M. Levin (ed.), *Modernity and the Hegemony of Vision*, University of California Press, Berkeley, Los Angeles and London, pp. 287–308

Webb, Jen, Schirato, Tony and Danaher, Geoff 2002, *Understanding Bourdieu*, Allen & Unwin, Sydney and Sage, London

Williams, Raymond 1981, *Culture*, Fontana, Glasgow

Winterson, Jeanette 1995, *Art Objects: Essays on Ecstasy and Effrontery*, Cape, London

Wolff, Janet 1981, *The Social Production of Art*, Macmillan, London

Yunupingu, Galarrwuy 1997, 'Indigenous art in the Olympic Age', *Art and Australia*, vol. 35, no. 1

Žižek, 1991, *For They Know Not What They Do: Enjoyment as a Political Factor*, Verso, London and New York

—— Slavoj (ed.) 1994, *Mapping Ideology*, Verso, London

—— 1996, *The Indivisible Remainder: An Essay on Schelling and Related Matters*, Verso, London and New York

—— 1997, *The Plague of Fantasies*, Verso, London and New York

# index